MW01171296

THE BOOKS OF ENOCH

Complete Collection - Featuring 1 Enoch, 2 Enoch, 3 Enoch, Original Illustrations, and Bonus Apocryphal Texts

DIVINE PRESS

CONTENTS

FOREWORD

Dear reader,

When we decided to publish *The Books of Enoch - Complete Collection*, we knew it had to be more than just a standard reprint. We wanted to create something special—something that would resonate with readers on a deeper level.

What makes this collection different? For one, we've included bonus apocryphal texts that are often overlooked in other editions. These additional writings provide richer context and offer new perspectives that complement the primary texts. And then there are the original illustrations, crafted specifically for this edition. These images aren't just there to decorate the pages; they're meant to draw you in, to help you visualize and feel the profound stories within.

We've approached this project with care, making sure that the text, the apocrypha, and the illustrations all work together to create a truly immersive experience.

As you start reading, we encourage you to take your time, to let the words and images sink in. The stories in these pages have been passed down through the ages for a reason—they hold truths that are still relevant today. We hope that as you explore *The Books of Enoch - Complete Collection*, you'll find insights and inspiration that stay with you long after you've turned the last page.

Welcome to this journey and enjoy the read.

-Divine Press

1 ENOCH

THE BOOK OF ENOCH (ETHIOPIAN ENOCH)

TRANSLATION: R.H. CHARLES

THE BOOK OF THE WATCHERS

CHAPTER 1

The words of the blessing of Enoch, wherewith he blessed the elect and righteous, who will be living in the day of tribulation, when all the wicked and godless are to be removed. And he took up his parable and said -Enoch a righteous man, whose eyes were opened by God, saw the vision of the Holy One in the heavens, which the angels showed me, and from them I heard everything, and from them I understood as I saw, but not for this generation, but for a remote one which is for to come. Concerning the elect I said, and took up my parable concerning them:

The Holy Great One will come forth from His dwelling, And the eternal God will tread upon the earth, (even) on Mount Sinai, [And appear from His camp] And appear in the strength of His might from the heaven of heavens.

And all shall be smitten with fear And the Watchers shall quake, And great fear and trembling shall seize them unto the ends of the earth.

And the high mountains shall be shaken, And the high hills shall be made low, And shall melt like wax before the flame

And the earth shall be wholly rent in sunder, And all that is upon the earth shall perish, And there shall be a judgement upon all (men).

But with the righteous He will make peace.

And will protect the elect, And mercy shall be upon them.

And they shall all belong to God, And they shall be prospered, And they shall all be blessed.

And He will help them all, And light shall appear unto them, And He will make peace with them'.

And behold! He cometh with ten thousands of His holy ones To execute judgement upon all, And to destroy all the ungodly:

And to convict all flesh Of all the works of their ungodliness which they have ungodly committed, And of all the hard things which ungodly sinners have spoken against Him.

CHAPTER 2

Observe ye everything that takes place in the heaven, how they do not change their orbits, and the luminaries which are in the heaven, how they all rise and set in order each in its season, and transgress not against their appointed order. Behold ye the earth, and give heed to the things which take place upon it from first to last, how steadfast they are, how none of the things upon earth change, but all the works of God appear to you. Behold the summer and the winter, how the whole earth is filled with water, and clouds and dew and rain lie upon it.

CHAPTER 3

Observe and see how (in the winter) all the trees seem as though they had withered and shed all their leaves, except fourteen trees, which do not lose their foliage but retain the old foliage from two to three years till the new comes.

CHAPTER 4

And again, observe ye the days of summer how the sun is above the earth over against it. And you seek shade and shelter by reason of the heat of the sun, and the earth also burns with growing heat, and so you cannot tread on the earth, or on a rock by reason of its heat.

CHAPTER 5

Observe ye how the trees cover themselves with green leaves and bear fruit: wherefore give ye heed and know with regard to all His works, and recognize how He that liveth for ever hath made them so. And all His works go on thus from year to year for ever, and all the tasks which they accomplish for Him, and their tasks change not, but according as God hath ordained so is it done. And behold how the sea and the rivers in like manner accomplish and change not their tasks from His commandments'.

But ye -ye have not been steadfast, nor done the commandments of the Lord, But ye have turned away and spoken proud and hard words With your impure mouths against His greatness. Oh, ye hard-hearted, ye shall find no peace.

Therefore shall ye execrate your days, And the years of your life shall perish, And the years of your destruction shall be multiplied in eternal execration, And ye shall find no mercy.

In those days ye shall make your names an eternal execration unto all the righteous, And by you shall all who curse, curse, And all the sinners and godless shall imprecate by you, And for you the godless there shall be a curse.

And all the . . . shall rejoice, And there shall be forgiveness of sins, And every mercy and peace and forbearance: There shall be salvation unto them, a goodly light.

And for all of you sinners there shall be no salvation, But on you all shall abide a curse. But for the elect there shall be light and joy and peace, And they shall inherit the earth.

And then there shall be bestowed upon the elect wisdom, And they shall all live and never again sin, Either through ungodliness or through pride: But they who are wise shall be humble.

And they shall not again transgress, Nor shall they sin all the days of their life, Nor shall they die of (the divine) anger or wrath, But they shall complete the number of the days of their life.

And their lives shall be increased in peace, And the years of their joy shall be multiplied, In eternal gladness and peace, All the days of their life

A towering, glowing figure of Enoch ascends into the heavens, surrounded by sorrowful, fallen angels with immense wings on desolate mountains under a dark, ominous sky lit by celestial light.

CHAPTER 6

And it came to pass when the children of men had multiplied that in those days were born unto them beautiful and comely daughters. And the angels, the children of the heaven, saw and lusted after them, and said to one another: 'Come, let us choose us wives from among the children of men and beget us children.' And Semjaza, who was their leader, said unto them: 'I fear ye will not indeed agree to do this deed, and I alone shall have to pay the penalty of a great sin.' And they all answered him and said: 'Let us all swear an oath, and all bind ourselves by mutual imprecations not to abandon this plan but to do this thing.' Then sware they all together and bound themselves by mutual imprecations upon it. And they were in all two hundred; who descended in the days of Jared on the summit of Mount Hermon, and they called it Mount Hermon, because they had sworn and bound themselves by mutual imprecations upon it. And these are the names of their leaders: Samlazaz, their leader, Araklba, Rameel, Kokablel, Tamlel, Ramlel, Danel, Ezeqeel, Baraqijal,Asael, Armaros, Batarel, Ananel, Zaqiel, Samsapeel, Satarel, Turel, Jomjael, Sariel. These are their chiefs of tens.

CHAPTER 7

And all the others together with them took unto themselves wives, and each chose for himself one, and they began to go in unto them and to defile themselves with them, and they taught them charms and enchantments, and the cutting of roots, and made them acquainted with plants. And they became pregnant, and they bare great giants, whose height was three thousand ells: Who consumed all the acquisitions of men. And when men could no longer sustain them, the giants turned against them and devoured mankind. And they began to sin against birds, and beasts, and reptiles, and fish, and to devour one another's flesh, and drink the blood. Then the earth laid accusation against the lawless ones.

CHAPTER 8

And Azazel taught men to make swords, and knives, and shields, and breastplates, and made known to them the metals of the earth and the art of working them, and bracelets, and ornaments, and the use of antimony, and the beautifying of the eyelids, and all kinds of costly stones, and all colouring tinctures. And there arose much godlessness, and they committed fornication, and they were led astray, and became corrupt in all their ways. Semjaza taught enchantments, and root-cuttings, 'Armaros the resolving of enchantments, Baraqijal (taught) astrology, Kokabel the constellations, Ezeqeel the knowledge of the clouds, Araqiel the signs of the earth, Shamsiel the signs of the sun, and Sariel the course of the moon. And as men perished, they cried, and their cry went up to heaven . . .

CHAPTER 9

And then Michael, Uriel, Raphael, and Gabriel looked down from heaven and saw much blood being shed upon the earth, and all lawlessness being wrought upon the earth. And they said one to another: 'The earth made without inhabitant cries the voice of their cryingst up to the gates of heaven.And now to you, the holy ones of heaven, the souls of men make their suit, saying, "Bring our cause before the Most High."' And they said to the Lord of the ages: 'Lord of lords, God of gods, King of kings, and God of the ages, the throne of Thy glory (standeth) unto all the generations of the ages, and Thy name holy and glorious and blessed unto all the ages! Thou hast made all things, and power over all things hast Thou: and all things are naked and open in Thy sight, and Thou seest all things, and nothing can hide itself from Thee. Thou seest what Azazel hath done, who hath taught all unrighteousness on earth and revealed the eternal secrets which were (preserved) in heaven, which men were striving to learn: And Semjaza, to whom Thou hast given authority to bear rule over his associates. And they have gone to the daughters of men upon the earth, and have slept with the women, and have defiled themselves, and revealed to them all kinds of sins. And the women have borne giants, and the whole earth has thereby been filled with blood and unrighteousness. And now, behold, the souls of those who have died are crying and making their suit to the gates of heaven, and their lamentations have ascended: and cannot cease because of the lawless deeds which are wrought on the earth. And Thou knowest all things before they come to pass, and Thou seest these things and Thou dost suffer them, and Thou dost not say to us what we are to do to them in regard to these.'

CHAPTER 10

Then said the Most High, the Holy and Great One spake, and sent Uriel to the son of Lamech, and said to him: 'Go to Noah and tell him in my name "Hide thyself!" and reveal to him the end that is approaching: that the whole earth will be destroyed, and a deluge is about to come upon the whole earth, and will destroy all that is on it. And now instruct him that he may escape and his seed may be preserved for all the generations of the world.' And again the Lord said to Raphael: 'Bind Azazel hand and foot, and cast him into the darkness: and make an opening in the desert, which is in Dudael, and cast him therein. And place upon him rough and jagged rocks, and cover him with darkness, and let him abide there for ever, and cover his face that he may not see light. And on the day of the great judgement he shall be cast into the fire. And heal the earth which the angels have corrupted, and proclaim the healing of the earth, that they may heal the plague, and that all the children of men may not perish through all the secret things that the Watchers have disclosed and have taught their sons. And the whole earth has been corrupted through the works that were taught by Azazel: to him ascribe all sin.' And to Gabriel said the Lord: 'Proceed against the bastards and the reprobates, and against the children of fornication: and destroy [the children of fornication and] the children of the Watchers from amongst men [and cause them to go forth]: send them one against the other that they may destroy each other in battle: for length of days shall they not have. And no request that they (i.e. their fathers) make of thee shall be granted unto their fathers on their behalf; for they hope to live an eternal life, and that each one of them will live five hundred years.' And the Lord said unto Michael: 'Go, bind Semjaza and his associates who have united themselves with women so as to have defiled themselves with them in all their uncleanness. And when their sons have slain one another, and they have seen the destruction of their beloved ones, bind them fast for seventy generations in the valleys of the earth, till the day of their judgement and of their consummation, till the judgement that is for ever and ever is consummated. In those days they shall be led off to the abyss of fire: and to the torment and the prison in which they shall be confined for ever. And whosoever shall be condemned and destroyed will from thenceforth be bound together with them to the end of all generations. And destroy all the spirits of the reprobate and the children of the Watchers, because they have wronged mankind. Destroy all wrong from the face of the earth and let every evil work come to an end: and let the plant of righteousness and truth appear: and it shall prove a blessing; the works of righteousness and truth' shall be planted in truth and joy for evermore.

And then shall all the righteous escape,

And shall live till they beget thousands of children

And all the days of their youth and their old age

Shall they complete in peace.

And then shall the whole earth be tilled in righteousness, and shall all be planted with trees and be full of blessing. And all desirable trees shall be planted on it, and they shall plant vines on it: and the vine which they plant thereon shall yield wine in abundance, and as for all the seed which is sown thereon each measure (of it) shall bear a thousand, and each measure of olives shall yield ten presses of oil. And cleanse thou the earth from all oppression, and from all unrighteousness, and from all sin, and from all godlessness: and all the uncleanness that is wrought upon the earth destroy from off the earth. And all the children of men shall become righteous, and all nations shall offer adoration and shall praise Me, and all shall worship Me. And the earth shall be cleansed from all defilement, and from all sin, and from all punishment, and from all torment, and I will never again send (them) upon it from generation to generation and for ever.

CHAPTER 11

And in those days I will open the store chambers of blessing which are in the heaven, so as to send them down upon the earth over the work and labour of the children of men. And truth and peace shall be associated together throughout all the days of the world and throughout all the generations of men.'

CHAPTER 12

Before these things Enoch was hidden, and no one of the children of men knew where he was hidden, and where he abode, and what had become of him. And his activities had to do with the Watchers, and his days were with the holy ones.And I Enoch was blessing the Lord of majesty and the King of the ages, and lo! the Watchers called me -Enoch the scribe- and said to me: 'Enoch, thou scribe of righteousness, go, declare to the Watchers of the heaven who have left the high heaven, the holy eternal place, and have defiled themselves with women, and have done as the children of earth do, and have taken unto themselves wives: "Ye have wrought great destruction on the earth: And ye shall have no peace nor forgiveness of sin: and inasmuch as they delight themselves in their children, The murder of their beloved ones shall they see, and over the destruction of their children shall they lament, and shall make supplication unto eternity, but mercy and peace shall ye not attain."'

CHAPTER 13

And Enoch went and said: 'Azazel, thou shalt have no peace: a severe sentence has gone forth against thee to put thee in bonds: And thou shalt not have toleration nor request granted to thee, because of the unright-eousness which thou hast taught, and because of all the works of godless-ness and unrighteousness and sin which thou hast shown to men.' Then I went and spoke to them all together, and they were all afraid, and fear and trembling seized them. And they besought me to draw up a petition for them that they might find forgiveness, and to read their petition in the presence of the Lord of heaven. For from thenceforward they could not speak (with Him) nor lift up their eyes to heaven for shame of their sins for which they had been condemned. Then I wrote out their petition, and the prayer in regard to their spirits and their deeds individually and in regard to their requests that they should have forgiveness and length. And I went off and sat down at the waters of Dan, in the land of Dan, to the south of the west of Hermon: I read their petition till I fell asleep. And behold a dream came to me, and visions fell down upon me, and I saw visions of chastisement, and a voice came bidding (me) I to tell it to the sons of heaven, and reprimand them.And when I awaked, I came unto them, and they were all sitting gathered together, weeping in'Abelsjail, which is between Lebanon and Seneser, with their faces covered. And I recounted before them all the visions which I had seen in sleep, and I began to speak the words of righteousness, and to reprimand the heavenly Watchers.

CHAPTER 14

The book of the words of righteousness, and of the reprimand of the eternal Watchers in accordance with the command of the Holy Great One in that vision. I saw in my sleep what I will now say with a tongue of flesh and with the breath of my mouth: which the Great One has given to men to converse therewith and understand with the heart. As He has created and given to man the power of understanding the word of wisdom, so hath He created me also and given me the power of reprimanding the Watchers, the children of heaven. I wrote out your petition, and in my vision it appeared thus, that your petition will not be granted unto you throughout all the days of eternity, and that judgement has been finally passed upon you: yea (your petition) will not be granted unto you. And from henceforth you shall not ascend into heaven unto all eternity, and in bonds of the earth the decree has gone forth to bind you for all the days of the world. And (that) previously you shall have seen the destruction of your beloved sons and ye shall have no pleasure in them, but they shall fall before you by the sword. And your petition on their behalf shall not be granted, nor yet on your own: even though you weep and pray and speak all the words contained in the writing which I havewritten. And the vision was shown to me thus: Behold, in the vision clouds invited me and a mist summoned me, and the course of the stars and the lightnings sped and hastened me, and the winds in the vision caused me to fly and lifted me upward, and bore me into heaven. And I went in till I drew nigh to a wall which is built of crystals and surrounded by tongues of fire: and it began to affright me. And I went into the tongues of fire and drew nigh to a large house which was built of crystals: and the walls of the house were like a tesselated floor (made) of crystals, and its groundwork was of crystal. Its ceiling was like the path of the stars and the lightnings, and between them were fiery cherubim, and their heaven was (clear as) water. A flaming fire surrounded the walls, and its portals blazed with fire. And I entered into that house, and it was hot as fire and cold as ice: there were no delights of life therein: fear covered me, and trembling got hold upon me. And as I quaked and trembled, I fell upon my face. And I beheld a vision, And lo! there was a second house, greater than the former, and the entire portal stood open before me, and it was built of flames of fire. And in every respect it so excelled in splendour and magnificence and extent that I cannot describe to you its splendour and its extent. And its floor was of fire, and above it were lightnings and the path of the stars, and its ceiling also was flaming fire. And I looked and saw therein a lofty throne: its appearance was as crys-tal, and the wheels thereof as the shining sun, and there was the vision of cherubim. And from underneath the throne came streams of flaming fire so that I could not look thereon. And the Great Glory sat thereon, and His raiment shone more brightly than the sun and was whiter than any snow. None of the angels could enter and could behold His face by reason of the magnificence and glory and no flesh could behold Him. The flaming fire was round about Him, and a great fire stood before Him, and none around could draw nigh Him: ten thousand times ten thousand (stood) before Him, yet He needed no counselor. And the most holy ones who were nigh to Him did not leave by night nor depart from Him. And until then I had been prostrate on my face, trembling: and the Lord called me with His own mouth, and said to me: ' Come hither,Enoch, and hear my word.' And one of the holy ones came to me and waked me, and He made me rise up and approach the door: and I bowed my face downwards.

CHAPTER 15

And He answered and said to me, and I heard His voice: 'Fear not, Enoch, thou righteous man and scribe of righteousness: approach hither and hear my voice. And go, say to the Watchers of heaven, who have sent thee to intercede for them: "You should intercede" for men, and not men for you: Wherefore have ye left the high, holy, and eternal heaven, and lain with women, and defiled yourselves with the daughters of men and taken to yourselves wives, and done like the children of earth, and begotten giants (as your) sons? And though ye were holy, spiritual, living the eternal life, you have defiled yourselves with the blood of women, and have begotten (children) with the blood of flesh, and, as the children of men, have lusted after flesh and blood as those also do who die and perish. Therefore have I given them wives also that they might impregnate them, and beget children by them, that thus nothing might be wanting to them on earth. But you were formerly spiritual, living the eternal life, and immortal for all generations of the world. And therefore I have not appointed wives for you; for as for the spiritual ones of the heaven, in heaven is their dwelling. And now, the giants, who are produced from the spirits and flesh, shall be called evil spirits upon the earth, and on the earth shall be their dwelling. Evil spirits have proceeded from their bodies; because they are born from men and from the holy Watchers is their beginning and primal origin; they shall be evil spirits on earth, and evil spirits shall they be called. [As for the spirits of heaven, in heaven shall be their dwelling, but as for the spirits of the earth which were born upon the earth, on the earth shall be their dwelling.] And the spirits of the giants afflict, oppress, destroy, attack, do battle, and work destruction on the earth, and cause trouble: they take no food, but nevertheless hunger and thirst, and cause offences. And these spirits shall rise up against the children of men and against the women, because they have proceeded from them.

CHAPTER 16

From the days of the slaughter and destruction and death of the giants, from the souls of whose flesh the spirits, having gone forth, shall destroy without incurring judgement ‑ thus shall they destroy until the day of the consummation, the great judgement in which the age shall be consummated, over the Watchers and the godless, yea, shall be wholly consummated." And now as to the watchers who have sent thee to intercede for them, who had been aforetime in heaven, (say to them): "You have been in heaven, but all the mysteries had not yet been revealed to you, and you knew worthless ones, and these in the hardness of your hearts you have made known to the women, and through these mysteries women and men work much evil on earth." Say to them therefore: "You have no peace."

CHAPTER 17

And they took and brought me to a place in which those who were there were like flaming fire, and, when they wished, they appeared as men. And they brought me to the place of darkness, and to a mountain the point of whose summit reached to heaven. And I saw the places of the luminaries and the treasuries of the stars and of the thunder and in the uttermost depths, where were a fiery bow and arrows and their quiver, and a fiery sword and all the lightnings. And they took me to the living waters, and to the fire of the west, which receives every setting of the sun. And I came to a river of fire in which the fire flows like water and discharges itself into the great sea towards the west. I saw the great rivers and came to the great river and to the great darkness, and went to the place where no flesh walks. I saw the mountains of the darkness of winter and the place whence all the waters of the deep flow. I saw the mouths of all the rivers of the earth and the mouth of the deep.

CHAPTER 18

I saw the treasuries of all the winds: I saw how He had furnished with them the whole creation and the firm foundations of the earth. And I saw the corner-stone of the earth: I saw the four winds which bear [the earth and] the firmament of the heaven. And I saw how the winds stretch out the vaults of heaven, and have their station between heaven and earth: these are the pillars of the heaven. I saw the winds of heaven which turn and bring the circumference of the sun and all the stars to their setting. I saw the winds on the earth carrying the clouds: I saw the paths of the angels. I saw at the end of the earth the firmament of the heaven above. And I proceeded and saw a place which burns day and night, where there are seven mountains of magnificent stones, three towards the east, and three towards the south. And as for those towards the east, was of coloured stone, and one of pearl, and one of jacinth, and those towards the south of red stone. But the middle one reached to heaven like the throne of God, of alabaster, and the summit of the throne was of sapphire. And I saw a flaming fire. And beyond these mountains Is a region the end of the great earth: there the heavens were completed. And I saw a deep abyss, with columns of heavenly fire, and among them I saw columns of fire fall, which were beyond measure alike towards the height and towards the depth. And beyond that abyss I saw a place which had no firmament of the heaven above, and no firmly founded earth beneath it: there was no water upon it, and no birds, but it was a waste and horrible place. I saw there seven stars like great burning mountains, and to me, when I inquired regarding them, The angel said: 'This place is the end of heaven and earth: this has become a prison for the stars and the host of heaven. And the stars which roll over the fire are they which have transgressed the commandment of the Lord in the beginning of their rising, because they did not come forth at their appointed times. And He was wroth with them, and bound them till the time when their guilt should be consummated (even) for ten thousand years.'

CHAPTER 19

And Uriel said to me: 'Here shall stand the angels who have connected themselves with women, and their spirits assuming many different forms are defiling mankind and shall lead them astray into sacrificing to demons as gods, (here shall they stand,) till the day of the great judgement in which they shall be judged till they are made an end of. And the women also of the angels who went astray shall become sirens.' And I, Enoch, alone saw the vision, the ends of all things: and no man shall see as I have seen.

CHAPTER 20

And these are the names of the holy angels who watch. Uriel, one of the holy angels, who is over the world and over Tartarus. Raphael, one of the holy angels, who is over the spirits of men. Raguel, one of the holy angels who takes vengeance on the world of the luminaries. Michael, one of the holy angels, to wit, he that is set over the best part of mankind and over chaos. Saraqael, one of the holy angels, who is set over the spirits, who sin in the spirit. Gabriel, one of the holy angels, who is over Paradise and the serpents and the Cherubim. Remiel, one of the holy angels, whom God set over those who rise.

Chapter 21

And I proceeded to where things were chaotic. And I saw there something horrible: I saw neither a heaven above nor a firmly founded earth, but a place chaotic and horrible. And there I saw seven stars of the heaven bound together in it, like great mountains and burning with fire. Then I said: 'For what sin are they bound, and on what account have they been cast in hither?' Then said Uriel, one of the holy angels, who was with me, and was chief over them, and said: 'Enoch, why dost thou ask, and why art thou eager for the truth? These are of the number of the stars of heaven, which have transgressed the commandment of the Lord, and are bound here till ten thousand years, the time entailed by their sins, are consummated.' And from thence I went to another place, which was still more horrible than the former, and I saw a horrible thing: a great fire there which burnt and blazed, and the place was cleft as far as the abyss, being full of great descending columns of fire: neither its extent or magnitude could I see, nor could I conjecture. Then I said: 'How fearful is the place and how terrible to look upon!' Then Uriel answered me, one of the holy angels who was with me, and said unto me: 'Enoch, why hast thou such fear and affright?' And I answered: 'Because of this fearful place, and because of the spectacle of the pain.' And he said unto me: 'This place is the prison of the angels, and here they will be imprisoned for ever.'

CHAPTER 22

And thence I went to another place, and he mountain [and] of hard rock. And there was in it four hollow places, deep and wide and very smooth. How smooth are the hollow places and deep and dark to look at. Then Raphael answered, one of the holy angels who was with me, and said unto me: 'These hollow places have been created for this very purpose, that the spirits of the souls of the dead should assemble therein, yea that all the souls of the children of men should assemble here. And these places have been made to receive them till the day of their judgement and till their appointed period [till the period appointed], till the great judgement (comes) upon them.' I saw (the spirit of) a dead man making suit, and his voice went forth to heaven and made suit. And I asked Raphael the angel who was with me, and I said unto him: 'This spirit which maketh suit, whose is it, whose voice goeth forth and maketh suit to heaven?' And he answered me saying: 'This is the spirit which went forth from Abel, whom his brother Cain slew, and he makes his suit against him till his seed is destroyed from the face of the earth, and his seed is annihilated from amongst the seed of men.' Then I asked regarding it, and regarding all the hollow places: 'Why is one separated from the other?' And he answered me and said unto me: 'These three have been made that the spirits of the dead might be separated. And such a division has been make (for) the spirits of the righteous, in which there is the bright spring of water. And such has been made for sinners when they die and are buried in the earth and judgement has not been executed on them in their life-time. Here their spirits shall be set apart in this great pain till the great day of judgement and punishment and torment of those who curse for ever and retribution for their spirits. There He shall bind them for ever. And such a division has been made for the spirits of those who make their suit, who make disclosures concerning their destruction, when they were slain in the days of the sinners. Such has been made for the spirits of men who were not righteous but sinners, who were complete in transgression, and of the transgressors they shall be companions: but their spirits shall not be slain in the day of judgement nor shall they be raised from thence.' Then I blessed the Lord of glory and said: 'Blessed be my Lord, the Lord of righteousness, who ruleth for ever.'

CHAPTER 23

From thence I went to another place to the west of the ends of the earth. And I saw a burning fire which ran without resting, and paused not from its course day or night but (ran) regularly. And I asked saying: 'What is this which rests not?' Then Raguel, one of the holy angels who was with me, answered me and said unto me: 'This course of fire which thou hast seen is the fire in the west which persecutes all the luminaries of heaven.'

CHAPTER 24

And from thence I went to another place of the earth, and he showed me a mountain range of fire which burnt day and night. And I went beyond it and saw seven magnificent mountains all differing each from the other, and the stones (thereof) were magnificent and beautiful, magnificent as a whole, of glorious appearance and fair exterior: three towards the east, one founded on the other, and three towards the south, one upon the other, and deep rough ravines, no one of which joined with any other. And the seventh mountain was in the midst of these, and it excelled them in height, resembling the seat of a throne: and fragrant trees encircled the throne. And amongst them was a tree such as I had never yet smelt, neither was any amongst them nor were others like it: it had a fragrance beyond all fragrance, and its leaves and blooms and wood wither not for ever: and its fruit is beautiful, and its fruit resembles the dates of a palm. Then I said: 'How beautiful is this tree, and fragrant, and its leaves are fair, and its blooms very delightful in appearance.' Then answered Michael, one of the holy and honoured angels who was with me, and was their leader.

CHAPTER 25

And he said unto me: 'Enoch, why dost thou ask me regarding the fragrance of the tree, and why dost thou wish to learn the truth?' Then I answered him saying: 'I wish to know about everything, but especially about this tree.' And he answered saying: 'This high mountain which thou hast seen, whose summit is like the throne of God, is His throne, where the Holy Great One, the Lord of Glory, the Eternal King, will sit, when He shall come down to visit the earth with goodness. And as for this fragrant tree no mortal is permitted to touch it till the great judgement, when He shall take vengeance on all and bring (everything) to its consummation for ever. It shall then be given to the righteous and holy. Its fruit shall be for food to the elect: it shall be transplanted to the holy place, to the temple of the Lord, the Eternal King.

Then shall they rejoice with joy and be glad, And into the holy place shall they enter; And its fragrance shall be in their bones, And they shall live a long life on earth, Such as thy fathers lived:

And in their days shall no sorrow or plague Or torment or calamity touch them.'

Then blessed I the God of Glory, the Eternal King, who hath prepared such things for the righteous, and hath created them and promised to give to them.

CHAPTER 26

And I went from thence to the middle of the earth, and I saw a blessed place in which there were trees with branches abiding and blooming [of a dismembered tree]. And there I saw a holy mountain, and underneath the mountain to the east there was a stream and it flowed towards the south. And I saw towards the east another mountain higher than this, and between them a deep and narrow ravine: in it also ran a stream underneath the mountain. And to the west thereof there was another mountain, lower than the former and of small elevation, and a ravine deep and dry between them: and another deep and dry ravine was at the extremities of the three mountains. And all the ravines were deep and narrow, (being formed) of hard rock, and trees were not planted upon them. And I marveled at the rocks, and I marveled at the ravine, yea, I marveled very much.

CHAPTER 27

Then said I: 'For what object is this blessed land, which is entirely filled with trees, and this accursed valley between?' Then Uriel, one of the holy angels who was with me, answered and said: 'This accursed valley is for those who are accursed for ever: Here shall all the accursed be gathered together who utter with their lips against the Lord unseemly words and of His glory speak hard things. Here shall they be gathered together, and here shall be their place of judgement. In the last days there shall be upon them the spectacle of righteous judgement in the presence of the righteous for ever: here shall the merciful bless the Lord of glory, the Eternal King. In the days of judgement over the former, they shall bless Him for the mercy in accordance with which He has assigned them (their lot).' Then I blessed the Lord of Glory and set forth His glory and lauded Him gloriously.

CHAPTER 28

And thence I went towards the east, into the midst of the mountain range of the desert, and I saw a wilderness and it was solitary, full of trees and plants. And water gushed forth from above. Rushing like a copious watercourse [which flowed] towards the north-west it caused clouds and dew to ascend on every side.

CHAPTER 29

And thence I went to another place in the desert, and approached to the east of this mountain range. And there I saw aromatic trees exhaling the fragrance of frankincense and myrrh, and the trees also were similar to the almond tree.

CHAPTER 30

And beyond these, I went afar to the east, and I saw another place, a valley (full) of water. And therein there was a tree, the colour (?) of fragrant trees such as the mastic. And on the sides of those valleys I saw fragrant cinnamon. And beyond these I proceeded to the east.

CHAPTER 31

And I saw other mountains, and amongst them were groves of trees, and there flowed forth from them nectar, which is named sarara and galbanum. And beyond these mountains I saw another mountain to the east of the ends of the earth, whereon were aloe-trees, and all the trees were full of stacte, being like almond-trees. And when one burnt it, it smelt sweeter than any fragrant odour.

CHAPTER 32

And after these fragrant odours, as I looked towards the north over the mountains I saw seven mountains full of choice nard and fragrant trees and cinnamon and pepper. And thence I went over the summits of all these mountains, far towards the east of the earth, and passed above the Erythraean sea and went far from it, and passed over the angel Zotiel. And I came to the Garden of Righteousness, and from afar off trees more numerous than I these trees and great-two trees there, very great, beautiful, and glorious, and magnificent, and the tree of knowledge, whose holy fruit they eat and know great wisdom. That tree is in height like the fir, and its leaves are like (those of) the Carob tree: and its fruit is like the clusters of the vine, very beautiful: and the fragrance of the tree penetrates afar. Then I said: 'How beautiful is the tree, and how attractive is its look!' Then Raphael the holy angel, who was with me, answered me and said: 'This is the tree of wisdom, of which thy father old (in years) and thy aged mother, who were before thee, have eaten, and they learnt wisdom and their eyes were opened, and they knew that they were naked and they were driven out of the garden.'

CHAPTER 33

And from thence I went to the ends of the earth and saw there great beasts, and each differed from the other; and (I saw) birds also differing in appearance and beauty and voice, the one differing from the other. And to the east of those beasts I saw the ends of the earth whereon the heaven rests, and the portals of the heaven open. And I saw how the stars of heaven come forth, and I counted the portals out of which they proceed, and wrote down all their outlets, of each individual star by itself, according to their number and their names, their courses and their positions, and their times and their months, as Uriel the holy angel who was with me showed me. He showed all things to me and wrote them down for me: also their names he wrote for me, and their laws and their companies.

CHAPTER 34

And from thence I went towards the north to the ends of the earth, and there I saw a great and glorious device at the ends of the whole earth. And here I saw three portals of heaven open in the heaven: through each of them proceed north winds: when they blow there is cold, hail, frost, snow, dew, and rain. And out of one portal they blow for good: but when they blow through the other two portals, it is with violence and affliction on the earth, and they blow with violence.

CHAPTER 35

And from thence I went towards the west to the ends of the earth, and saw there three portals of the heaven open such as I had seen in the east, the same number of portals, and the same number of outlets.

CHAPTER 36

And from thence I went to the south to the ends of the earth, and saw there three open portals of the heaven: and thence there come dew, rain, and wind. And from thence I went to the east to the ends of the heaven, and saw here the three eastern portals of heaven open and small portals above them. Through each of these small portals pass the stars of heaven and run their course to the west on the path which is shown to them. And as often as I saw I blessed always the Lord of Glory, and I continued to bless the Lord of Glory who has wrought great and glorious wonders, to show the greatness of His work to the angels and to spirits and to men, that they might praise His work and all His creation: that they might see the work of His might and praise the great work of His hands and bless Him for ever.

THE BOOK OF PARABLES

CHAPTER 37

The second vision which he saw, the vision of wisdom -which Enoch the son of Jared, the son of Mahalalel, the son of Cainan, the son of Enos, the son of Seth, the son of Adam, saw. And this is the beginning of the words of wisdom which I lifted up my voice to speak and say to those which dwell on earth: Hear, ye men of old time, and see, ye that come after, the words of the Holy One which I will speak before the Lord of Spirits. It were better to declare (them only) to the men of old time, but even from those that come after we will not withhold the beginning of wisdom. Till the present day such wisdom has never been given by the Lord of Spirits as I have received according to my insight, according to the good pleasure of the Lord of Spirits by whom the lot of eternal life has been given to me. Now three Parables were imparted to me, and I lifted up my voice and recounted them to those that dwell on the earth.

CHAPTER 38

The first Parable.

When the congregation of the righteous shall appear, And sinners shall be judged for their sins, And shall be driven from the face of the earth:

And when the Righteous One shall appear before the eyes of the righteous, Whose elect works hang upon the Lord of Spirits, And light shall appear to the righteous and the elect who dwell on the earth,

Where then will be the dwelling of the sinners, And where the resting-place of those who have denied the Lord of Spirits? It had been good for them if they had not been born.

When the secrets of the righteous shall be revealed and the sinners judged, And the godless driven from the presence of the righteous and elect, From that time those that possess the earth shall no longer be powerful and exalted: And they shall not be able to behold the face of the holy, For the Lord of Spirits has caused His light to appear On the face of the holy, righteous, and elect.

Then shall the kings and the mighty perish And be given into the hands of the righteous and holy. And thenceforward none shall seek for themselves mercy from the Lord of Spirits For their life is at an end.

CHAPTER 39

And it shall come to pass in those days that elect and holy children will descend from the high heaven, and their seed will become one with the children of men. And in those days Enoch received books of zeal and wrath, and books of disquiet and expulsion.

And mercy shall not be accorded to them, saith the Lord of Spirits. And in those days a whirlwind carried me off from the earth, And set me down at the end of the heavens.

And there I saw another vision, the dwelling-places of the holy, And the resting-places of the righteous.

Here mine eyes saw their dwellings with His righteous angels, And their resting-places with the holy.

And they petitioned and interceded and prayed for the children of men,
And righteousness flowed before them as water,

And mercy like dew upon the earth: Thus it is amongst them for ever
and ever.

And in that place mine eyes saw the Elect One of righteousness and of
faith, And I saw his dwelling-place under the wings of the Lord of
Spirits. And righteousness shall prevail in his days, And the righteous and
elect shall be without number before Him for ever and ever. And all the
righteous and elect before Him shall be strong as fiery lights, And their
mouth shall be full of blessing,

And their lips extol the name of the Lord of Spirits, And righteousness
before Him shall never fail, [And uprightness shall never fail before
Him.] There I wished to dwell, And my spirit longed for that dwelling-
place:

And there heretofore hath been my portion, For so has it been established concerning me before the Lord of Spirits.

In those days I praised and extolled the name of the Lord of Spirits with
blessings and praises, because He hath destined me for blessing and glory
according to the good pleasure of the Lord of Spirits. For a long time my
eyes regarded that place, and I blessed Him and praised Him, saying:
'Blessed is He, and may He be blessed from the beginning and for evermore. And before Him there is no ceasing. He knows before the world
was created what is for ever and what will be from generation unto
generation. Those who sleep not bless Thee: they stand before Thy glory
and bless, praise, and extol, saying: "Holy, holy, holy, is the Lord of
Spirits: He filleth the earth with spirits."' And here my eyes saw all those
who sleep not: they stand before Him and bless and say: 'Blessed be
Thou, and blessed be the name of the Lord for ever and ever.' And my
face was changed; for I could no longer behold.

CHAPTER 40

And after that I saw thousands of thousands and ten thousand times ten
thousand, I saw a multitude beyond number and reckoning, who stood

before the Lord of Spirits. And on the four sides of the Lord of Spirits I saw four presences, different from those that sleep not, and I learnt their names: for the angel that went with me made known to me their names, and showed me all the hidden things. And I heard the voices of those four presences as they uttered praises before the Lord of glory. The first voice blesses the Lord of Spirits for ever and ever. And the second voice I heard blessing the Elect One and the elect ones who hang upon the Lord of Spirits. And the third voice I heard pray and intercede for those who dwell on the earth and supplicate in the name of the Lord of Spirits. And I heard the fourth voice fending off the Satans and forbidding them to come before the Lord of Spirits to accuse them who dwell on the earth. After that I asked the angel of peace who went with me, who showed me everything that is hidden: 'Who are these four presences which I have seen and whose words I have heard and written down?' And he said to me: 'This first is Michael, the merciful and long-suffering: and the second, who is set over all the diseases and all the wounds of the children of men, is Raphael: and the third, who is set over all the powers, is Gabriel: and the fourth, who is set over the repentance unto hope of those who inherit eternal life, is named Phanuel.' And these are the four angels of the Lord of Spirits and the four voices I heard in those days.

CHAPTER 41

And after that I saw all the secrets of the heavens, and how the kingdom is divided, and how the actions of men are weighed in the balance. And there I saw the mansions of the elect and the mansions of the holy, and mine eyes saw there all the sinners being driven from thence which deny the name of the Lord of Spirits, and being dragged off: and they could not abide because of the punishment which proceeds from the Lord of Spirits. And there mine eyes saw the secrets of the lightning and of the thunder, and the secrets of the winds, how they are divided to blow over the earth, and the secrets of the clouds and dew, and there I saw from whence they proceed in that place and from whence they saturate the dusty earth. And there I saw closed chambers out of which the winds are divided, the chamber of the hail and winds, the chamber of the mist, and of the clouds, and the cloud thereof hovers over the earth from the beginning of the world. And I saw the chambers of the sun and moon, whence they proceed and whither they come again, and their glorious return, and how one is superior to the other, and their stately orbit, and how they do not leave their orbit, and they add nothing to their orbit and they take nothing from it, and they keep faith with each other, in accordance with the oath by which they are bound together. And first the sun goes forth and traverses his path according to the commandment of the Lord of Spirits, and mighty is His name for ever and ever. And after that I saw the hidden and the visible path of the moon, and she accomplishes the course of her path in that place by day and by night-the one holding a position opposite to the other before the Lord of Spirits.

And they give thanks and praise and rest not; For unto them is their thanksgiving rest. For the sun changes oft for a blessing or a curse, And the course of the path of the moon is light to the righteous And darkness to the sinners in the name of the Lord, Who made a separation between the light and the darkness, And divided the spirits of men, And strengthened the spirits of the righteous, In the name of His righteousness.

For no angel hinders and no power is able to hinder; for He appoints a judge for them all and He judges them all before Him.

A vast heavenly courtroom with God seated on a radiant throne, surrounded by
angelic hosts, as Enoch witnesses the judgment of the fallen angels, all set against a
backdrop of fiery clouds and celestial bodies.

CHAPTER 42

Wisdom found no place where she might dwell; Then a dwelling-place
was assigned her in the heavens.

Wisdom went forth to make her dwelling among the children of men,
And found no dwelling-place:

Wisdom returned to her place, And took her seat among the angels.

And unrighteousness went forth from her chambers: Whom she sought
not she found, And dwelt with them,

As rain in a desert And dew on a thirsty land.

CHAPTER 43

And I saw other lightnings and the stars of heaven, and I saw how He called them all by their names and they hearkened unto Him. And I saw how they are weighed in a righteous balance according to their proportions of light: (I saw) the width of their spaces and the day of their appearing, and how their revolution produces lightning: and (I saw) their revolution according to the number of the angels, and (how) they keep faith with each other. And I asked the angel who went with me who showed me what was hidden: 'What are these?' And he said to me: 'The Lord of Spirits hath showed thee their parabolic meaning (lit. 'their parable'): these are the names of the holy who dwell on the earth and believe in the name of the Lord of Spirits for ever and ever.'

CHAPTER 44

Also another phenomenon I saw in regard to the lightnings: how some of the stars arise and become lightnings and cannot part with their new form.

CHAPTER 45

And this is the second Parable concerning those who deny the name of the dwelling of the holy ones and the Lord of Spirits.

And into the heaven they shall not ascend, And on the earth they shall not come: Such shall be the lot of the sinners Who have denied the name of the Lord of Spirits, Who are thus preserved for the day of suffering and tribulation.

On that day Mine Elect One shall sit on the throne of glory And shall try their works, And their places of rest shall be innumerable.

And their souls shall grow strong within them when they see Mine Elect Ones, And those who have called upon My glorious name: Then will I cause Mine Elect One to dwell among them.

And I will transform the heaven and make it an eternal blessing and light
And I will transform the earth and make it a blessing:

And I will cause Mine elect ones to dwell upon it: But the sinners and
evil-doers shall not set foot thereon.

For I have provided and satisfied with peace My righteous ones And
have caused them to dwell before Me:

But for the sinners there is judgement impending with Me, So that I
shall destroy them from the face of the earth.

CHAPTER 46

And there I saw One who had a head of days, And His head was white like
wool, And with Him was another being whose countenance had the appearance of a man, And his face was full of graciousness, like one of the holy
angels. And I asked the angel who went with me and showed me all the
hidden things, concerning that Son of Man, who he was, and whence he was,
(and) why he went with the Head of Days? And he answered and said unto
me: This is the son of Man who hath righteousness, With whom dwelleth
righteousness, And who revealeth all the treasures of that which is hidden,

Because the Lord of Spirits hath chosen him, And whose lot hath the
pre-eminence before the Lord of Spirits in uprightness for ever.

And this Son of Man whom thou hast seen Shall raise up the kings and
the mighty from their seats, [And the strong from their thrones] And
shall loosen the reins of the strong, And break the teeth of the sinners.

[And he shall put down the kings from their thrones and kingdoms]
Because they do not extol and praise Him, Nor humbly acknowledge
whence the kingdom was bestowed upon them. And he shall put down
the countenance of the strong, And shall fill them with shame.

And darkness shall be their dwelling, And worms shall be their bed, And
they shall have no hope of rising from their beds, Because they do not
extol the name of the Lord of Spirits. [And raise their hands against the
Most High], And tread upon the earth and dwell upon it. And all their

deeds manifest unrighteousness, And their power rests upon their riches, And their faith is in the gods which they have made with their hands, And they deny the name of the Lord of Spirits,

And they persecute the houses of His congregations, And the faithful who hang upon the name of the Lord of Spirits.

CHAPTER 47

And in those days shall have ascended the prayer of the righteous, And the blood of the righteous from the earth before the Lord of Spirits.

In those days the holy ones who dwell above in the heavens Shall unite with one voice And supplicate and pray [and praise, And give thanks and bless the name of the Lord of Spirits On behalf of the blood of the righteous which has been shed, And that the prayer of the righteous may not be in vain before the Lord of Spirits, That judgement may be done unto them, And that they may not have to suffer for ever.

In those days I saw the Head of Days when He seated himself upon the throne of His glory, And the books of the living were opened before Him: And all His host which is in heaven above and His counselors stood before Him,

And the hearts of the holy were filled with joy; Because the number of the righteous had been offered, And the prayer of the righteous had been heard, And the blood of the righteous been required before the Lord of Spirits.

CHAPTER 48

And in that place I saw the fountain of righteousness Which was inexhaustible: And around it were many fountains of wisdom: And all the thirsty drank of them, And were filled with wisdom, And their dwellings were with the righteous and holy and elect. And at that hour that Son of Man was named In the presence of the Lord of Spirits, And his name before the Head of Days.

Yea, before the sun and the signs were created, Before the stars of the heaven were made, His name was named before the Lord of Spirits.

He shall be a staff to the righteous whereon to stay themselves and not fall, And he shall be the light of the Gentiles, And the hope of those who are troubled of heart.

All who dwell on earth shall fall down and worship before him, And will praise and bless and celebrate with song the Lord of Spirits.

And for this reason hath he been chosen and hidden before Him, Before the creation of the world and for evermore.

And the wisdom of the Lord of Spirits hath revealed him to the holy and righteous; For he hath preserved the lot of the righteous, Because they have hated and despised this world of unrighteousness, And have hated all its works and ways in the name of the Lord of Spirits: For in his name they are saved, And according to his good pleasure hath it been in regard to their life.

In these days downcast in countenance shall the kings of the earth have become, And the strong who possess the land because of the works of their hands, For on the day of their anguish and affliction they shall not (be able to) save themselves. And I will give them over into the hands of Mine elect:

As straw in the fire so shall they burn before the face of the holy: As lead in the water shall they sink before the face of the righteous, And no trace of them shall any more be found.

And on the day of their affliction there shall be rest on the earth, And before them they shall fall and not rise again: And there shall be no one to take them with his hands and raise them: For they have denied the Lord of Spirits and His Anointed. The name of the Lord of Spirits be blessed.

CHAPTER 49

For wisdom is poured out like water, And glory faileth not before him for evermore.

For he is mighty in all the secrets of righteousness, And unrighteousness shall disappear as a shadow, And have no continuance; Because the Elect One standeth before the Lord of Spirits, And his glory is for ever and ever, And his might unto all generations.

And in him dwells the spirit of wisdom, And the spirit which gives insight, And the spirit of understanding and of might, And the spirit of those who have fallen asleep in righteousness.

And he shall judge the secret things, And none shall be able to utter a lying word before him; For he is the Elect One before the Lord of Spirits according to His good pleasure.

CHAPTER 50

And in those days a change shall take place for the holy and elect, And the light of days shall abide upon them, And glory and honour shall turn to the holy, On the day of affliction on which evil shall have been treasured up against the sinners.

And the righteous shall be victorious in the name of the Lord of Spirits: And He will cause the others to witness (this) That they may repent And forgo the works of their hands.

They shall have no honour through the name of the Lord of Spirits, Yet through His name shall they be saved, And the Lord of Spirits will have compassion on them, For His compassion is great.

And He is righteous also in His judgement, And in the presence of His glory unrighteousness also shall not maintain itself: At His judgement the unrepentant shall perish before Him. And from henceforth I will have no mercy on them, saith the Lord of Spirits.

CHAPTER 51

And in those days shall the earth also give back that which has been entrusted to it, And Sheol also shall give back that which it has received, And hell shall give back that which it owes.

For in those days the Elect One shall arise, And he shall choose the righteous and holy from among them: For the day has drawn nigh that they should be saved.

And the Elect One shall in those days sit on My throne, And his mouth shall pour forth all the secrets of wisdom and counsel: For the Lord of Spirits hath given (them) to him and hath glorified him.

And in those days shall the mountains leap like rams, And the hills also shall skip like lambs satisfied with milk, And the faces of [all] the angels in heaven shall be lighted up with joy.

And the earth shall rejoice, And the righteous shall dwell upon it, And the elect shall walk thereon.

CHAPTER 52

And after those days in that place where I had seen all the visions of that which is hidden -for I had been carried off in a whirlwind and they had borne me towards the west-There mine eyes saw all the secret things of heaven that shall be, a mountain of iron, and a mountain of copper, and a mountain of silver, and a mountain of gold, and a mountain of soft metal, and a mountain of lead. And I asked the angel who went with me, saying, 'What things are these which I have seen in secret?' And he said unto me: 'All these things which thou hast seen shall serve the dominion of His Anointed that he may be potent and mighty on the earth.' And that angel of peace answered, saying unto me: 'Wait a little, and there shall be revealed unto thee all the secret things which surround the Lord of Spirits.

And these mountains which thine eyes have seen, The mountain of iron, and the mountain of copper, and the mountain of silver, And the mountain of gold, and the mountain of soft metal, and the mountain of lead, All these shall be in the presence of the Elect One As wax: before the fire, And like the water which streams down from above [upon those mountains], And they shall become powerless before his feet. And it shall come to pass in those days that none shall be saved, Either by gold or by silver, And none be able to escape. And there shall be no iron for war, Nor shall one clothe oneself with a breastplate. Bronze shall be of no service, And tin [shall be of no service and] shall not be esteemed, And lead shall not be desired. And all these things shall be [denied and] destroyed from the surface of the earth, When the Elect One shall appear before the face of the Lord of Spirits.'

CHAPTER 53

There mine eyes saw a deep valley with open mouths, and all who dwell on the earth and sea and islands shall bring to him gifts and presents and tokens of homage, but that deep valley shall not become full.

And their hands commit lawless deeds, And the sinners devour all whom they lawlessly oppress: Yet the sinners shall be destroyed before the face of the Lord of Spirits, And they shall be banished from off the face of His earth, And they shall perish for ever and ever.

For I saw all the angels of punishment abiding (there) and preparing all the instruments of Satan. And I asked the angel of peace who went with me: 'For whom are they preparing these Instruments?' And he said unto me: 'They prepare these for the kings and the mighty of this earth, that they may thereby be destroyed. And after this the Righteous and Elect One shall cause the house of his congregation to appear: henceforth they shall be no more hindered in the name of the Lord of Spirits.

And these mountains shall not stand as the earth before his right-eousness, But the hills shall be as a fountain of water, And the righteous shall have rest from the oppression of sinners.'

CHAPTER 54

And I looked and turned to another part of the earth, and saw there a deep valley with burning fire. And they brought the kings and the mighty, and began to cast them into this deep valley. And there mine eyes saw how they made these their instruments, iron chains of immeasurable weight. And I asked the angel of peace who went with me, saying: 'For whom are these chains being prepared?' And he said unto me: 'These are being prepared for the hosts of Azazel, so that they may take them and cast them into the abyss of complete condemnation, and they shall cover their jaws with rough stones as the Lord of Spirits commanded. And Michael, and Gabriel, and Raphael, and Phanuel shall take hold of them on that great day, and cast them on that day into the burning furnace, that the Lord of Spirits may take vengeance on them for their unrighteousness in becoming subject to Satan and leading astray those who dwell on the earth.' And in those days shall punishment come from the Lord of Spirits, and he will open all the chambers of waters which are above the heavens, and of the fountains which are beneath the earth. And all the waters shall be joined with the waters: that which is above the heavens is the masculine, and the water which is beneath the earth is the feminine. And they shall destroy all who dwell on the earth and those who dwell under the ends of the heaven. And when they have recognized their unrighteousness which they have wrought on the earth, then by these shall they perish.

CHAPTER 55

And after that the Head of Days repented and said: 'In vain have I destroyed all who dwell on the earth.' And He sware by His great name: 'Henceforth I will not do so to all who dwell on the earth, and I will set a sign in the heaven: and this shall be a pledge of good faith between Me and them for ever, so long as heaven is above the earth. And this is in accordance with My command. When I have desired to take hold of them by the hand of the angels on the day of tribulation and pain because of this, I will cause My chastisement and My wrath to abide upon them, saith God, the Lord of Spirits. Ye mighty kings who dwell on the earth, ye shall have to behold Mine Elect One, how he sits on the throne of glory and judges Azazel, and all his associates, and all his hosts in the name of the Lord of Spirits.'

CHAPTER 56

And I saw there the hosts of the angels of punishment going, and they held scourges and chains of iron and bronze. And I asked the angel of peace who went with me, saying: 'To whom are these who hold the scourges going?' And he said unto me: 'To their elect and beloved ones, that they may be cast into the chasm of the abyss of the valley.

And then that valley shall be filled with their elect and beloved, And the days of their lives shall be at an end, And the days of their leading astray shall not thenceforward be reckoned.

And in those days the angels shall return And hurl themselves to the east upon the Parthians and Medes:

They shall stir up the kings, so that a spirit of unrest shall come upon them, And they shall rouse them from their thrones,

That they may break forth as lions from their lairs, And as hungry wolves among their flocks.

And they shall go up and tread under foot the land of His elect ones [And the land of His elect ones shall be before them a threshing-floor and a highway:] But the city of my righteous shall be a hindrance to their horses.

And they shall begin to fight among themselves, And their right hand shall be strong against themselves,

And a man shall not know his brother, Nor a son his father or his mother,

Till there be no number of the corpses through their slaughter, And their punishment be not in vain.

In those days Sheol shall open its jaws, And they shall be swallowed up therein

And their destruction shall be at an end; Sheol shall devour the sinners in the presence of the elect.'

CHAPTER 57

And it came to pass after this that I saw another host of wagons, and men riding thereon, and coming on the winds from the east, and from the west to the south. And the noise of their wagons was heard, and

when this turmoil took place the holy ones from heaven remarked it, and
the pillars of the earth were moved from their place, and the sound
thereof was heard from the one end of heaven to the other, in one day.
And they shall all fall down and worship the Lord of Spirits. And this is
the end of the second Parable.

CHAPTER 58

And I began to speak the third Parable concerning the righteous and
elect.

Blessed are ye, ye righteous and elect, For glorious shall be your lot.

And the righteous shall be in the light of the sun. And the elect in the
light of eternal life: The days of their life shall be unending, And the days
of the holy without number.

And they shall seek the light and find righteousness with the Lord of
Spirits: There shall be peace to the righteous in the name of the Eternal
Lord.

And after this it shall be said to the holy in heaven That they should seek
out the secrets of righteousness, the heritage of faith: For it has become
bright as the sun upon earth, And the darkness is past.

And there shall be a light that never endeth, And to a limit (lit. 'number')
of days they shall not come, For the darkness shall first have been
destroyed, [And the light established before the Lord of Spirits] And the
light of uprightness established for ever before the Lord of Spirits.

CHAPTER 59

[In those days mine eyes saw the secrets of the lightnings, and of the
lights, and the judgements they execute (lit. 'their judgement'): and they
lighten for a blessing or a curse as the Lord of Spirits willeth. And there I
saw the secrets of the thunder, and how when it resounds above in the
heaven, the sound thereof is heard, and he caused me to see the judgements executed on the earth, whether they be for well-being and blessing, or for a curse according to the word of the Lord of Spirits. And after

that all the secrets of the lights and lightnings were shown to me, and they lighten for blessing and for satisfying.]

CHAPTER 60

A Fragment of the Book of Noah

In the year 500, in the seventh month, on the fourteenth day of the month in the life of Enoch. In that Parable I saw how a mighty quaking made the heaven of heavens to quake, and the host of the Most High, and the angels, a thousand thousands and ten thousand times ten thousand, were disquieted with a great disquiet. And the Head of Days sat on the throne of His glory, and the angels and the righteous stood around Him.

And a great trembling seized me, And fear took hold of me, And my loins gave way, And dissolved were my reins, And I fell upon my face.

And Michael sent another angel from among the holy ones and he raised me up, and when he had raised me up my spirit returned; for I had not been able to endure the look of this host, and the commotion and the quaking of the heaven. And Michael said unto me: 'Why art thou disquieted with such a vision? Until this day lasted the day of His mercy; and He hath been merciful and long-suffering towards those who dwell on the earth. And when the day, and the power, and the punishment, and the judgement come, which the Lord of Spirits hath prepared for those who worship not the righteous law, and for those who deny the righteous judgement, and for those who take His name in vain-that day is prepared, for the elect a covenant, but for sinners an inquisition. When the punishment of the Lord of Spirits shall rest upon them, it shall rest in order that the punishment of the Lord of Spirits may not come, in vain, and it shall slay the children with their mothers and the children with their fathers. Afterwards the judgement shall take place according to His mercy and His patience.' And on that day were two monsters parted, a female monster named Leviathan, to dwell in the abysses of the ocean over the fountains of the waters. But the male is named Behemoth, who occupied with his breast a waste wilderness named Duidain, on the east of the garden where the elect and righteous dwell, where my grandfather was taken up, the seventh from Adam, the first man whom the Lord of Spirits created. And I besought the other angel that he should show me the might of those monsters, how they were parted on one day and cast, the one into the abysses of the sea, and the other unto the dry land of the wilderness. And he said to me: 'Thou son of man, herein thou dost seek to know what is hidden.' And the other angel who went with me and showed me what was hidden told me what is first and last in the heaven in the height, and beneath the earth in the depth, and at the ends of the heaven, and on the foundation of the heaven. And the chambers of the winds, and how the winds are divided, and how they are weighed, and (how) the portals of the winds are reck- oned, each according to the power of the wind, and the power of the lights of the moon, and according to the power that is fitting: and the divisions of the stars according to their names, and how all the divisions are divided. And the thunders according to the places where they fall, and all the divisions that are made among the lightnings that it may lighten, and their host that they may at once obey. For the thunder has places of rest (which) are assigned (to it) while it is waiting for its peal; and the thunder and lightning are inseparable, and although not one and undivided, they both go together through the spirit and separate not. For when the lightning lightens, the thunder utters its voice, and the spirit enforces a pause during the peal, and divides equally between them; for the treasury of their peals is like the sand, and each one of them as it peals is held in with a bridle, and turned back by the power of the spirit, and pushed forward according to the many quarters of the earth. And the spirit of the sea is masculine and strong, and according to the might of his strength he draws it back with a rein, and in like manner it is driven forward and disperses amid all the mountains of the earth. And the spirit of the hoar-frost is his own angel, and the spirit of the hail is a good angel. And the spirit of the snow has forsaken his chambers on account of his strength -There is a special spirit therein, and that which ascends from it is like smoke, and its name is frost. And the spirit of the mist is not united with them in their chambers, but it has a special chamber; for its course is glorious both in light and in darkness, and in winter and in summer, and in its chamber is an angel. And the spirit of the dew has its dwelling at the ends of the heaven, and is connected with the chambers of the rain, and its course is in winter and summer: and its clouds and the clouds of the mist are connected, and the one gives to the other. And when the spirit of the rain goes forth from its chamber, the angels come and open the chamber and lead it out, and when it is diffused over the whole earth it unites with the water on the earth. And whensoever it unites with the water on the earth. For the waters are for those who dwell on the earth; for they are nourishment for the earth from the Most High who is in heaven: therefore there is a measure for the rain, and the angels take it in charge. And these things I saw towards the Garden of the Righteous. And the angel of peace who was with me said to me: 'These two monsters, prepared conformably to the greatness of God, shall feed . . .

CHAPTER 61

And I saw in those days how long cords were given to those angels, and they took to themselves wings and flew, and they went towards the north. And I asked the angel, saying unto him: 'Why have those (angels) taken these cords and gone off?' And he said unto me: 'They have gone to measure.'

And the angel who went with me said unto me: 'These shall bring the measures of the righteous, And the ropes of the righteous to the righteous, That they may stay themselves on the name of the Lord of Spirits for ever and ever.

The elect shall begin to dwell with the elect, And those are the measures which shall be given to faith And which shall strengthen righteousness.

And these measures shall reveal all the secrets of the depths of the earth, And those who have been destroyed by the desert, And those who have been devoured by the beasts, And those who have been devoured by the fish of the sea, That they may return and stay themselves On the day of the Elect One; For none shall be destroyed before the Lord of Spirits, And none can be destroyed.

And all who dwell above in the heaven received a command and power and one voice and one light like unto fire.

And that One (with) their first words they blessed, And extolled and lauded with wisdom, And they were wise in utterance and in the spirit of life.

And the Lord of Spirits placed the Elect one on the throne of glory. And he shall judge all the works of the holy above in the heaven, And in the balance shall their deeds be weighed

And when he shall lift up his countenance To judge their secret ways according to the word of the name of the Lord of Spirits, And their path according to the way of the righteous judgement of the Lord of Spirits, Then shall they all with one voice speak and bless, And glorify and extol and sanctify the name of the Lord of Spirits.

And He will summon all the host of the heavens, and all the holy ones above, and the host of God, the Cherubic, Seraphin and Ophannin, and all the angels of power, and all the angels of principalities, and the Elect One, and the other powers on the earth (and) over the water On that day shall raise one voice, and bless and glorify and exalt in the spirit of faith, and in the spirit of wisdom, and in the spirit of patience, and in the spirit of mercy, and in the spirit of judgement and of peace, and in the spirit of goodness, and shall all say with one voice: "Blessed is He, and may the name of the Lord of Spirits be blessed for ever and ever."

All who sleep not above in heaven shall bless Him: All the holy ones who are in heaven shall bless Him, And all the elect who dwell in the garden of life:

And every spirit of light who is able to bless, and glorify, and extol, and hallow Thy blessed name, And all flesh shall beyond measure glorify and bless Thy name for ever and ever.

For great is the mercy of the Lord of Spirits, and He is long-suffering, And all His works and all that He has created He has revealed to the righteous and elect In the name of the Lord of Spirits.

CHAPTER 62

And thus the Lord commanded the kings and the mighty and the exalted, and those who dwell on the earth, and said:

'Open your eyes and lift up your horns if ye are able to recognize the Elect One.' And the Lord of Spirits seated him on the throne of His glory, And the spirit of righteousness was poured out upon him, And the word of his mouth slays all the sinners, And all the unrighteous are destroyed from before his face. And there shall stand up in that day all the kings and the mighty, And the exalted and those who hold the earth, And they shall see and recognize How he sits on the throne of his glory, And righteousness is judged before him, And no lying word is spoken before him.

Then shall pain come upon them as on a woman in travail, [And she has pain in bringing forth] When her child enters the mouth of the womb, And she has pain in bringing forth.

And one portion of them shall look on the other, And they shall be terri-fied, And they shall be downcast of countenance, And pain shall seize them, When they see that Son of Man Sitting on the throne of his glory.

And the kings and the mighty and all who possess the earth shall bless and glorify and extol him who rules over all, who was hidden.

For from the beginning the Son of Man was hidden, And the Most High preserved him in the presence of His might, And revealed him to the elect.

And the congregation of the elect and holy shall be sown, And all the elect shall stand before him on that day.

And all the kings and the mighty and the exalted and those who rule the earth Shall fall down before him on their faces, And worship and set their hope upon that Son of Man, And petition him and supplicate for mercy at his hands.

Nevertheless that Lord of Spirits will so press them That they shall hastily go forth from His presence, And their faces shall be filled with shame, And the darkness grow deeper on their faces.

And He will deliver them to the angels for punishment, To execute vengeance on them because they have oppressed His children and His elect And they shall be a spectacle for the righteous and for His elect: They shall rejoice over them, Because the wrath of the Lord of Spirits resteth upon them, And His sword is drunk with their blood.

And the righteous and elect shall be saved on that day, And they shall never thenceforward see the face of the sinners and unrighteous.

And the Lord of Spirits will abide over them, And with that Son of Man shall they eat And lie down and rise up for ever and ever.

And the righteous and elect shall have risen from the earth, And ceased to be of downcast countenance. And they shall have been clothed with garments of glory,

And these shall be the garments of life from the Lord of Spirits:

And your garments shall not grow old, Nor your glory pass away before the Lord of Spirits.

CHAPTER 63

In those days shall the mighty and the kings who possess the earth implore (Him) to grant them a little respite from His angels of punishment to whom they were delivered, that they might fall down and worship before the Lord of Spirits, and confess their sins before Him. And they shall bless and glorify the Lord of Spirits, and say:

'Blessed is the Lord of Spirits and the Lord of kings, And the Lord of the mighty and the Lord of the rich, And the Lord of glory and the Lord of wisdom,

And splendid in every secret thing is Thy power from generation to generation, And Thy glory for ever and ever:

Deep are all Thy secrets and innumerable, And Thy righteousness is beyond reckoning.

We have now learnt that we should glorify And bless the Lord of kings and Him who is king over all kings.' And they shall say: 'Would that we had rest to glorify and give thanks And confess our faith before His glory!

And now we long for a little rest but find it not: We follow hard upon and obtain (it) not:

And light has vanished from before us, And darkness is our dwelling-place for ever and ever:

For we have not believed before Him Nor glorified the name of the Lord of Spirits, nor glorified our Lord]

But our hope was in the sceptre of our kingdom, And in our glory.

And in the day of our suffering and tribulation He saves us not, And we find no respite for confession

That our Lord is true in all His works, and in His judgements and His justice, And His judgements have no respect of persons.

And we pass away from before His face on account of our works, And all our sins are reckoned up in righteousness.'

Now they shall say unto themselves: 'Our souls are full of unrighteous gain, but it does not prevent us from descending from the midst thereof into the burden of Sheol.'

And after that their faces shall be filled with darkness And shame before that Son of Man, And they shall be driven from his presence, And the sword shall abide before his face in their midst.

Thus spake the Lord of Spirits: 'This is the ordinance and judgement with respect to the mighty and the kings and the exalted and those who possess the earth before the Lord of Spirits.'

CHAPTER 64

And other forms I saw hidden in that place. I heard the voice of the angel saying: 'These are the angels who descended to the earth, and revealed what was hidden to the children of men and seduced the children of men into committing sin.'

CHAPTER 65

And in those days Noah saw the earth that it had sunk down and its destruction was nigh. And he arose from thence and went to the ends of the earth, and cried aloud to his grandfather Enoch: and Noah said three times with an embittered voice: 'Hear me, hear me, hear me.' And I said unto him: 'Tell me what it is that is falling out on the earth that the earth is in such evil plight and shaken, lest perchance I shall perish with it?' And thereupon there was a great commotion, on the earth, and a voice was heard from heaven, and I fell on my face. And Enoch my grandfather came and stood by me, and said unto me: 'Why hast thou cried unto me with a bitter cry and weeping? And a command has gone forth from the presence of the Lord concerning those who dwell on the earth that their ruin is accomplished because they have learnt all the secrets of the angels, and all the violence of the Satans, and all their powers -the most secret ones- and all the power of those who practice sorcery, and the power of witchcraft, and the power of those who make molten images for the whole earth: And how silver is produced from the dust of the earth, and how soft metal originates in the earth. For lead and tin are not produced from the earth like the first: it is a fountain that produces them, and an angel stands therein, and that angel is pre-eminent.' And after that my grandfather Enoch took hold of me by my hand and raised me up, and said unto me: 'Go, for I have asked the Lord of Spirits as touching this commotion on the earth. And He said unto me: "Because of their unrighteousness their judgement has been determined upon and shall not be withheld by Me for ever. Because of the sorceries which they have searched out and learnt, the earth and those who dwell upon it shall be destroyed." And these-they have no place of repentance for ever, because they have shown them what was hidden, and they are the damned: but as for thee, my son, the Lord of Spirits knows that thou art pure, and guiltless of this reproach concerning the secrets.

And He has destined thy name to be among the holy, And will preserve thee amongst those who dwell on the earth, And has destined thy righteous seed both for kingship and for great honours, And from thy seed shall proceed a fountain of the righteous and holy without number for ever.

CHAPTER 66

And after that he showed me the angels of punishment who are prepared to come and let loose all the powers of the waters which are beneath in the earth in order to bring judgement and destruction on all who [abide and] dwell on the earth. And the Lord of Spirits gave commandment to the angels who were going forth, that they should not cause the waters to rise but should hold them in check; for those angels were over the powers of the waters. And I went away from the presence of Enoch.

CHAPTER 67

And in those days the word of God came unto me, and He said unto me: 'Noah, thy lot has come up before Me, a lot without blame, a lot of love and uprightness. And now the angels are making a wooden (building), and when they have completed that task I will place My hand upon it and preserve it, and there shall come forth from it the seed of life, and a change shall set in so that the earth will not remain without inhabitant. And I will make fast thy seed before me for ever and ever, and I will spread abroad those who dwell with thee: it shall not be unfruitful on the face of the earth, but it shall be blessed and multiply on the earth in the name of the Lord.' And He will imprison those angels, who have shown unrighteousness, in that burning valley which my grandfather Enoch had formerly shown to me in the west among the mountains of gold and silver and iron and soft metal and tin. And I saw that valley in which there was a great convulsion and a convulsion of the waters. And when all this took place, from that fiery molten metal and from the convulsion thereof in that place, there was produced a smell of sulphur, and it was connected with those waters, and that valley of the angels who had led astray (mankind) burned beneath that land. And through its valleys proceed streams of fire, where these angels are punished who had led astray those who dwell upon the earth. But those waters shall in those

days serve for the kings and the mighty and the exalted, and those who
dwell on the earth, for the healing of the body, but for the punishment of
the spirit; now their spirit is full of lust, that they may be punished in
their body, for they have denied the Lord of Spirits and see their punishment daily, and yet believe not in His name. And in proportion as the
burning of their bodies becomes severe, a corresponding change shall
take place in their spirit for ever and ever; for before the Lord of Spirits
none shall utter an idle word. For the judgement shall come upon them,
because they believe in the lust of their body and deny the Spirit of the
Lord. And those same waters will undergo a change in those days; for
when those angels are punished in these waters, these water-springs shall
change their temperature, and when the angels ascend, this water of the
springs shall change and become cold. And I heard Michael answering
and saying: 'This judgement wherewith the angels are judged is a testimony for the kings and the mighty who possess the earth.' Because these
waters of judgement minister to the healing of the body of the kings and
the lust of their body; therefore they will not see and will not believe
that those waters will change and become a fire which burns for ever.

CHAPTER 68

And after that my grandfather Enoch gave me the teaching of all the
secrets in the book in the Parables which had been given to him, and he
put them together for me in the words of the book of the Parables. And
on that day Michael answered Raphael and said: 'The power of the spirit
transports and makes me to tremble because of the severity of the judgement of the secrets, the judgement of the angels: who can endure the
severe judgement which has been executed, and before which they melt
away?' And Michael answered again, and said to Raphael: 'Who is he
whose heart is not softened concerning it, and whose reins are not troubled by this word of judgement (that) has gone forth upon them because
of those who have thus led them out?' And it came to pass when he
stood before the Lord of Spirits, Michael said thus to Raphael: 'I will not
take their part under the eye of the Lord; for the Lord of Spirits has
been angry with them because they do as if they were the Lord.
Therefore all that is hidden shall come upon them for ever and ever; for

neither angel nor man shall have his portion (in it), but alone they have received their judgement for ever and ever.

CHAPTER 69

And after this judgement they shall terrify and make them to tremble because they have shown this to those who dwell on the earth. And behold the names of those angels [and these are their names: the first of them is Samjaza, the second Artaqifa, and the third Armen, the fourth Kokabel, the fifth Turael, the sixth Rumjal, the seventh Danjal, the eighth Neqael, the ninth Baraqel, the tenth Azazel, the eleventh Armaros, the twelfth Batarjal, the thirteenth Busasejal, the fourteenth Hananel, the fifteenth Turel, and the sixteenth Simapesiel, the seventeenth Jetrel, the eighteenth Tumael, the nineteenth Turel, the twentieth Rumael, the twenty-first Azazel. And these are the chiefs of their angels and their names, and their chief ones over hundreds and over fifties and over tens]. The name of the first Jeqon: that is, the one who led astray [all] the sons of God, and brought them down to the earth, and led them astray through the daughters of men. And the second was named Asbeel: he imparted to the holy sons of God evil counsel, and led them astray so that they defiled their bodies with the daughters of men. And the third was named Gadreel: he it is who showed the children of men all the blows of death, and he led astray Eve, and showed [the weapons of death to the sons of men] the shield and the coat of mail, and the sword for battle, and all the weapons of death to the children of men. And from his hand they have proceeded against those who dwell on the earth from that day and for evermore. And the fourth was named Penemue: he taught the children of men the bitter and the sweet, and he taught them all the secrets of their wisdom. And he instructed mankind in writing with ink and paper, and thereby many sinned from eternity to eternity and until this day. For men were not created for such a purpose, to give confirmation to their good faith with pen and ink. For men were created exactly like the angels, to the intent that they should continue pure and righteous, and death, which destroys everything, could not have taken hold of them, but through this their knowledge they are perishing, and through this power it is consuming me. And the fifth was named Kasdeja: this is he who showed the children of men all the wicked smitings of spirits and demons, and the smitings of the embryo in the womb, that it may pass away, and [the smitings of the soul] the bites of the serpent, and the smitings which befall through the noontide heat, the son of the serpent named Taba'et. And this is the task of Kasbeel, the chief of the oath which he showed to the holy ones when he dwelt high above in glory, and its name is Biqa. This (angel) requested Michael to show him the hidden name, that he might enunciate it in the oath, so that those might quake before that name and oath who revealed all that was in secret to the children of men. And this is the power of this oath, for it is powerful and strong, and he placed this oath Akae in the hand of Michael.

And these are the secrets of this oath . . . And they are strong through his oath: And the heaven was suspended before the world was created, And for ever

And through it the earth was founded upon the water, And from the secret recesses of the mountains come beautiful waters, From the creation of the world and unto eternity.

And through that oath the sea was created, And as its foundation He set for it the sand against the time of (its) anger, And it dare not pass beyond it from the creation of the world unto eternity.

And through that oath are the depths made fast, And abide and stir not from their place from eternity to eternity.

And through that oath the sun and moon complete their course, And deviate not from their ordinance from eternity to eternity.

And through that oath the stars complete their course, And He calls them by their names, And they answer Him from eternity to eternity.

[And in like manner the spirits of the water, and of the winds, and of all zephyrs, and (their) paths from all the quarters of the winds. And there are preserved the voices of the thunder and the light of the lightnings: and there are preserved the chambers of the hail and the chambers of the hoarfrost, and the chambers of the mist, and the chambers of the rain and the dew. And all these believe and give thanks before the Lord of Spirits, and glorify (Him) with all their power, and their food is in every act of thanksgiving: they thank and glorify and extol the name of the Lord of Spirits for ever and ever.]

And this oath is mighty over them And through it [they are preserved and] their paths are preserved, And their course is not destroyed.

And there was great joy amongst them, And they blessed and glorified and extolled Because the name of that Son of Man had been revealed unto them.

And he sat on the throne of his glory, And the sum of judgement was given unto the Son of Man, And he caused the sinners to pass away and be destroyed from off the face of the earth, And those who have led the world astray.

With chains shall they be bound, And in their assemblage-place of destruction shall they be imprisoned, And all their works vanish from the face of the earth.

And from henceforth there shall be nothing corruptible; For that Son of Man has appeared, And has seated himself on the throne of his glory, And all evil shall pass away before his face, And the word of that Son of Man shall go forth

And be strong before the Lord of Spirits.

CHAPTER 70

And it came to pass after this that his name during his lifetime was raised aloft to that Son of Man and to the Lord of Spirits from amongst those who dwell on the earth. And he was raised aloft on the chariots of the spirit and his name vanished among them. And from that day I was no longer numbered amongst them: and he set me between the two winds, between the North and the West, where the angels took the cords to measure for me the place for the elect and righteous. And there I saw the first fathers and the righteous who from the beginning dwell in that place.

CHAPTER 71

And it came to pass after this that my spirit was translated and it ascended into the heavens: And I saw the holy sons of God. They were stepping on flames of fire: Their garments were white [and their raiment], and their faces shone like snow.

And I saw two streams of fire, and the light of that fire shone like hyacinth, and I fell on my face before the Lord of Spirits.

And the angel Michael [one of the archangels] seized me by my right hand, and lifted me up and led me forth into all the secrets, and he showed me all the secrets of righteousness.

And he showed me all the secrets of the ends of the heaven, and all the chambers of all the stars, and all the luminaries, whence they proceed before the face of the holy ones.

And he translated my spirit into the heaven of heavens, and I saw there as it were a structure built of crystals, and between those crystals tongues of living fire.

And my spirit saw the girdle which girt that house of fire, and on its four sides were streams full of living fire, and they girt that house.

And round about were Seraphin, Cherubic, and Ophannin: And these are they who sleep not And guard the throne of His glory.

And I saw angels who could not be counted, A thousand thousands, and ten thousand times ten thousand, Encircling that house.

And Michael, and Raphael, and Gabriel, and Phanuel, And the holy angels who are above the heavens, Go in and out of that house.

And they came forth from that house, And Michael and Gabriel, Raphael and Phanuel, And many holy angels without number.

And with them the Head of Days, His head white and pure as wool, And His raiment indescribable.

And I fell on my face, And my whole body became relaxed, And my spirit was transfigured;

And I cried with a loud voice, . . . with the spirit of power, And blessed and glorified and extolled.

And these blessings which went forth out of my mouth were well pleasing before that Head of Days. And that Head of Days came with Michael and Gabriel, Raphael and Phanuel, thousands and ten thousands of angels without number. [Lost passage wherein the Son of Man was described as accompanying the Head of Days, and Enoch asked one of the angels (as in xlvi. 3) concerning the Son of Man as to who he was.]

And he (i.e. the angel) came to me and greeted me with His voice, and said unto me ' This is the Son of Man who is born unto righteousness, And righteousness abides over him, And the righteousness of the Head of Days forsakes him not.' And he said unto me: 'He proclaims unto thee peace in the name of the world to come; For from hence has proceeded peace since the creation of the world, And so shall it be unto thee for ever and for ever and ever.

And all shall walk in his ways since righteousness never forsaketh him: With him will be their dwelling-places, and with him their heritage, And they shall not be separated from him for ever and ever and ever.

And so there shall be length of days with that Son of Man, And the righteous shall have peace and an upright way In the name of the Lord of Spirits for ever and ever.'

THE ASTRONOMICAL BOOK

CHAPTER 72

The book of the courses of the luminaries of the heaven, the relations of each, according to their classes, their dominion and their seasons, according to their names and places of origin, and according to their months, which Uriel, the holy angel, who was with me, who is their guide, showed me; and he showed me all their laws exactly as they are, and how it is with regard to all the years of the world and unto eternity, till the new creation is accomplished which dureth till eternity. And this is the first law of the luminaries: the luminary the Sun has its rising in the eastern portals of the heaven, and its setting in the western portals of the heaven. And I saw six portals in which the sun rises, and six portals in which the sun sets and the moon rises and sets in these portals, and the leaders of the stars and those whom they lead: six in the east and six in the west, and all following each other in accurately corresponding order: also many windows to the right and left of these portals. And first there goes forth the great luminary, named the Sun, and his circumference is like the circumference of the heaven, and he is quite filled with illuminating and heating fire. The chariot on which he ascends, the wind drives, and the sun goes down from the heaven and returns through the north in order to reach the east, and is so guided that he comes to the appropriate portal and shines in the face of the heaven. In this way he rises in the first month in the great portal, which is the fourth. And in that fourth portal from which the sun rises in the first month are twelve window-openings, from which proceed a flame when they are opened in their season. When the sun rises in the heaven, he comes forth through that fourth portal thirty mornings in succession, and sets accurately in the fourth portal in the west of the heaven. And during this period the day becomes daily longer and the night nightly shorter to the thirtieth morning. On that day the day is longer than the night by a ninth part, and the day amounts exactly to ten parts and the night to eight parts. And the sun rises from that fourth portal, and sets in the fourth and returns to the fifth portal of the east thirty mornings, and rises from it and sets in the fifth portal. And then the day becomes longer by two parts and amounts to eleven parts, and the night becomes shorter and amounts to seven parts. And it returns to the east and enters into the sixth portal, and rises and sets in the sixth portal one-and-thirty mornings on account of its sign. On that day the day becomes longer than the night, and the day becomes double the night, and the day becomes twelve parts, and the night is shortened and becomes six parts. And the sun mounts up to make the day shorter and the night longer, and the sun returns to the east and enters into the sixth portal, and rises from it and sets thirty mornings. And when thirty mornings are accomplished, the day decreases by exactly one part, and becomes eleven parts, and the night seven. And the sun goes forth from that sixth portal in the west, and goes to the east and rises in the fifth portal for thirty mornings, and sets in the west again in the fifth western portal. On that day the day decreases by two parts, and amounts to ten parts and the night to eight parts. And the sun goes forth from that fifth portal and sets in the fifth portal of the west, and rises in the fourth portal for one-and-thirty mornings on account of its sign, and sets in the west. On that day the day is equalized with the night, and becomes of equal length, and the night amounts to nine parts and the day to nine parts. And the sun rises from that portal and sets in the west, and returns to the east and rises thirty mornings in the third portal and sets in the west in the third portal. And on that day the night becomes longer than the day, and night becomes longer than night, and day shorter than day till the thirtieth morning, and the night amounts exactly to ten parts and the day to eight parts. And the sun rises from that third portal and sets in the third portal in the west and returns to the east, and for thirty mornings rises in the second portal in the east, and in like manner sets in the second portal in the west of the heaven. And on that day the night amounts to eleven parts and the day to seven parts. And the sun rises on that day from that second portal and sets in the west in the second portal, and returns to the east into the first portal for one-and-thirty mornings, and sets in the first portal in the west of the heaven. And on that day the night becomes longer and amounts to the double of the day: and the night amounts exactly to twelve parts and the day to six. And the sun has traversed the divisions of his orbit and turns again on those divisions of his orbit, and enters that portal thirty mornings and sets also in the west opposite to it. And on that night has the night decreased in length by a ninth part, and the night has become eleven parts and the day seven parts. And the sun has returned and entered into the second portal in the east, and returns on those his divisions of his orbit for thirty mornings, rising and setting. And on that day the night decreases in length, and the night amounts to ten parts and the day to eight. And on that day the sun rises from that portal, and sets in the west, and returns to the east, and rises in the third portal for one-and-thirty mornings, and sets in the west of the heaven. On that day the night decreases and amounts to nine parts, and the day to nine parts, and the night is equal to the day and the year is exactly as to its days three hundred and sixty-four. And the length of the day and of the night, and the shortness of the day and of the night arise-through the course of the sun these distinctions are made. So it comes that its course becomes daily longer, and its course nightly shorter. And this is the law and the course of the sun, and his return as often as he returns sixty times and rises, i.e. the great luminary which is named the sun, for ever and ever. And that which rises is the great luminary, and is so named according to its appearance, according as the Lord commanded. As he rises, so he sets and decreases not, and rests not, but runs day and night, and his light is sevenfold brighter than that of the moon; but as regards size they are both equal.

CHAPTER 73

And after this law I saw another law dealing with the smaller luminary, which is named the Moon. And her circumference is like the circumference of the heaven, and her chariot in which she rides is driven by the wind, and light is given to her in definite measure. And her rising and setting change every month: and her days are like the days of the sun, and when her light is uniform (i.e. full) it amounts to the seventh part of the light of the sun. And thus she rises. And her first phase in the east comes forth on the thirtieth morning: and on that day she becomes visible, and constitutes for you the first phase of the moon on the thirtieth day together with the sun in the portal where the sun rises. And the one half of her goes forth by a seventh part, and her whole circumference is empty, without light, with the exception of one-seventh part of it, and the fourteenth part of her light. And when she receives one-seventh part of the half of her light, her light amounts to one-seventh part and the half thereof. And she sets with the sun, and when the sun rises the moon rises with him and receives the half of one part of light, and in that night in the beginning of her morning the moon sets with the sun, and is invisible that night with the fourteen parts and the half of one of them. And she rises on that day with exactly a seventh part, and comes forth and recedes from the rising of the sun, and in her remaining days she becomes bright in the remaining thirteen parts.

CHAPTER 74

And I saw another course, a law for her, and how according to that law she performs her monthly revolution. And all these Uriel, the holy angel who is the leader of them all, showed to me, and their positions, and I wrote down their positions as he showed them to me, and I wrote down their months as they were, and the appearance of their lights till fifteen days were accomplished. In single seventh parts she accomplishes all her light in the east, and in single seventh parts accomplishes all her darkness in the west. And in certain months she alters her settings, and in certain months she pursues her own peculiar course. In two months the moon sets with the sun: in those two middle portals the third and the fourth. She goes forth for seven days, and turns about and returns again through the portal where the sun rises, and accomplishes all her light: and she recedes from the sun, and in eight days enters the sixth portal from which the sun goes forth. And when the sun goes forth from the fourth portal she goes forth seven days, until she goes forth from the fifth and turns back again in seven days into the fourth portal and accomplishes all her light: and she recedes and enters into the first portal in eight days. And she returns again in seven days into the fourth portal from which the sun goes forth. Thus I saw their position -how the moons rose and the sun set in those days. And if five years are added together the sun has an overplus of thirty days, and all the days which accrue to it for one of those five years, when they are full, amount to 364 days. And the over-plus of the sun and of the stars amounts to six days: in 5 years 6 days every year come to 30 days: and the moon falls behind the sun and stars to the number of 30 days. And the sun and the stars bring in all the years exactly, so that they do not advance or delay their position by a single day unto eternity; but complete the years with perfect justice in 364 days. In 3 years there are 1,092 days, and in 5 years 1,820 days, so that in 8 years there are 2,912 days. For the moon alone the days amount in 3 years to 1,062 days, and in 5 years she falls 50 days behind: and in 5 years there are 1,770 days, so that for the moon the days in 8 years amount to 21,832 days. For in 8 years she falls behind to the amount of 80 days, all the days she falls behind in 8 years are 80. And the year is accurately completed in conformity with their world-stations and the stations of the sun, which rise from the portals through which it (the sun) rises and sets 30 days.

CHAPTER 75

And the leaders of the heads of the thousands, who are placed over the whole creation and over all the stars, have also to do with the four inter-calary days, being inseparable from their office, according to the reck-oning of the year, and these render service on the four days which are not reckoned in the reckoning of the year. And owing to them men go wrong therein, for those luminaries truly render service on the world-stations, one in the first portal, one in the third portal of the heaven, one in the fourth portal, and one in the sixth portal, and the exactness of the year is accomplished through its separate three hundred and sixty-four stations. For the signs and the times and the years and the days the angel Uriel showed to me, whom the Lord of glory hath set for ever over all the luminaries of the heaven, in the heaven and in the world, that they should rule on the face of the heaven and be seen on the earth, and be leaders for the day and the night, i.e. the sun, moon, and stars, and all the ministering creatures which make their revolution in all the chariots of the heaven. In like manner twelve doors Uriel showed me, open in the circumference of the sun's chariot in the heaven, through which the rays of the sun break forth: and from them is warmth diffused over the earth, when they are opened at their appointed seasons. And for the winds and the spirit of the dew when they are opened, standing open in the heavens at the ends. As for the twelve portals in the heaven, at the ends of the earth, out of which go forth the sun, moon, and stars, and all the works of heaven in the east and in the west, There are many windows open to the left and right of them, and one window at its appointed season produces warmth, corresponding as these do to those doors from which the stars come forth according as He has commanded them, and wherein they set corresponding to their number. And I saw chariots in the heaven, running in the world, above those portals in which revolve the stars that never set. And one is larger than all the rest, and it is that that makes its course through the entire world.

An ancient depiction of Enoch observing the celestial bodies, mapping the paths of the stars, the sun, and the moon, surrounded by cosmic patterns and mysterious heavenly movements.

CHAPTER 76

And at the ends of the earth I saw twelve portals open to all the quarters (of the heaven), from which the winds go forth and blow over the earth. Three of them are open on the face (i.e. the east) of the heavens, and three in the west, and three on the right (i.e. the south) of the heaven, and three on the left (i.e. the north). And the three first are those of the east, and three are of the north, and three [after those on the left] of the south, and three of the west. Through four of these come winds of blessing and prosperity, and from those eight come hurtful winds: when they are sent, they bring destruction on all the earth and on the water upon it, and on all who dwell thereon, and on everything which is in the water and on the land. And the first wind from those portals, called the east wind, comes forth through the first portal which is in the east, inclining towards the south: from it come forth desolation, drought, heat, and destruction. And through the second portal in the middle comes what is fitting, and from it there come rain and fruitfulness and prosperity and dew; and through the third portal which lies toward the north come cold and drought. And after these come forth the south winds through three portals: through the first portal of them inclining to the east comes forth a hot wind. And through the middle portal next to it there come forth fragrant smells, and dew and rain, and prosperity and health. And through the third portal lying to the west come forth dew and rain, locusts and desolation. And after these the north winds: from the seventh portal in the east come dew and rain, locusts and desolation. And from the middle portal come in a direct direction health and rain and dew and prosperity; and through the third portal in the west come cloud and hoar-frost, and snow and rain, and dew and locusts. And after these [four] are the west winds: through the first portal adjoining the north come forth dew and hoar-frost, and cold and snow and frost. And from the middle portal come forth dew and rain, and prosperity and blessing; and through the last portal which adjoins the south come forth drought and desolation, and burning and destruction. And the twelve portals of the four quarters of the heaven are therewith completed, and all their laws and all their plagues and all their benefactions have I shown to thee, my son Methuselah.

CHAPTER 77

And the first quarter is called the east, because it is the first: and the second, the south, because the Most High will descend there, yea, there in quite a special sense will He who is blessed for ever descend. And the west quarter is named the diminished, because there all the luminaries of the heaven wane and go down. And the fourth quarter, named the north, is divided into three parts: the first of them is for the dwelling of men: and the second contains seas of water, and the abysses and forests and rivers, and darkness and clouds; and the third part contains the garden of righteousness. I saw seven high mountains, higher than all the mountains which are on the earth: and thence comes forth hoar-frost, and days, seasons, and years pass away. I saw seven rivers on the earth larger than all the rivers: one of them coming from the west pours its waters into the Great Sea. And these two come from the north to the sea and pour their waters into the Erythraean Sea in the east. And the remaining four come forth on the side of the north to their own sea, two of them to the Erythraean Sea, and two into the Great Sea and discharge themselves there [and some say: into the desert]. Seven great islands I saw in the sea and in the mainland: two in the mainland and five in the Great Sea.

CHAPTER 78

And the names of the sun are the following: the first Orjares, and the second Tomas. And the moon has four names: the first name is Asonja, the second Ebla, the third Benase, and the fourth Erae. These are the two great luminaries: their circumference is like the circumference of the heaven, and the size of the circumference of both is alike. In the circumference of the sun there are seven portions of light which are added to it more than to the moon, and in definite measures it is transferred till the seventh portion of the sun is exhausted. And they set and enter the portals of the west, and make their revolution by the north, and come forth through the eastern portals on the face of the heaven. And when the moon rises one-fourteenth part appears in the heaven: [the light becomes full in her]: on the fourteenth day she accomplishes her light. And fifteen parts of light are transferred to her till the fifteenth day (when) her light is accomplished, according to the sign of the year, and she becomes fifteen parts, and the moon grows by (the addition of) fourteenth parts. And in her waning (the moon) decreases on the first day to fourteen parts of her light, on the second to thirteen parts of light, on the third to twelve, on the fourth to eleven, on the fifth to ten, on the sixth to nine, on the seventh to eight, on the eighth to seven, on the ninth to six, on the tenth to five, on the eleventh to four, on the twelfth to three, on the thirteenth to two, on the fourteenth to the half of a seventh, and all her remaining light disappears wholly on the fifteenth. And in certain months the month has twenty-

nine days and once twenty-eight. And Uriel showed me another law:
when light is transferred to the moon, and on which side it is transferred to her by the sun. During all the period during which the moon
is growing in her light, she is transferring it to herself when opposite to
the sun during fourteen days [her light is accomplished in the heaven,
and when she is illumined throughout, her light is accomplished full in
the heaven. And on the first day she is called the new moon, for on
that day the light rises upon her. She becomes full moon exactly on the
day when the sun sets in the west, and from the east she rises at night,
and the moon shines the whole night through till the sun rises over
against her and the moon is seen over against the sun. On the side
whence the light of the moon comes forth, there again she wanes till all
the light vanishes and all the days of the month are at an end, and her
circumference is empty, void of light. And three months she makes of
thirty days, and at her time she makes three months of twenty-nine
days each, in which she accomplishes her waning in the first period of
time, and in the first portal for one hundred and seventy-seven days.
And in the time of her going out she appears for three months (of)
thirty days each, and for three months she appears (of) twenty-nine
each. At night she appears like a man for twenty days each time, and by
day she appears like the heaven, and there is nothing else in her save
her light.

CHAPTER 79

And now, my son, I have shown thee everything, and the law of all the
stars of the heaven is completed. And he showed me all the laws of these
for every day, and for every season of bearing rule, and for every year, and
for its going forth, and for the order prescribed to it every month and
every week: And the waning of the moon which takes place in the sixth
portal: for in this sixth portal her light is accomplished, and after that
there is the beginning of the waning: (And the waning) which takes place
in the first portal in its season, till one hundred and seventy-seven days
are accomplished: reckoned according to weeks, twenty-five (weeks) and
two days. She falls behind the sun and the order of the stars exactly five
days in the course of one period, and when this place which thou seest

has been traversed. Such is the picture and sketch of every luminary which Uriel the archangel, who is their leader, showed unto me.

CHAPTER 80

And in those days the angel Uriel answered and said to me: 'Behold, I have shown thee everything, Enoch, and I have revealed everything to thee that thou shouldst see this sun and this moon, and the leaders of the stars of the heaven and all those who turn them, their tasks and times and departures.

And in the days of the sinners the years shall be shortened, And their seed shall be tardy on their lands and fields, And all things on the earth shall alter, And shall not appear in their time: And the rain shall be kept back And the heaven shall withhold (it). And in those times the fruits of the earth shall be backward, And shall not grow in their time, And the fruits of the trees shall be withheld in their time. And the moon shall alter her order, And not appear at her time.

[And in those days the sun shall be seen and he shall journey in the evening on the extremity of the great chariot in the west]

And shall shine more brightly than accords with the order of light. And many chiefs of the stars shall transgress the order (prescribed). And these shall alter their orbits and tasks, And not appear at the seasons prescribed to them. And the whole order of the stars shall be concealed from the sinners, And the thoughts of those on the earth shall err concerning them, [And they shall be altered from all their ways], Yea, they shall err and take them to be gods. And evil shall be multiplied upon them, And punishment shall come upon them So as to destroy all.'

CHAPTER 81

And he said unto me: 'Observe, Enoch, these heavenly tablets, and read what is written thereon, and mark every individual fact.'

And I observed the heavenly tablets, and read everything which was written (thereon) and understood everything, and read the book of all the deeds of mankind, and of all the children of flesh that shall be upon the earth to the remotest generations. And forthwith I blessed the great Lord the King of glory for ever, in that He has made all the works of the world, And I extolled the Lord because of His patience, and blessed Him because of the children of men.

And after that I said: 'Blessed is the man who dies in righteousness and goodness, concerning whom there is no book of unrighteousness written, and against whom no day of judgement shall be found.'

And those seven holy ones brought me and placed me on the earth before the door of my house, and said to me: 'Declare everything to thy son Methuselah, and show to all thy children that no flesh is righteous in the sight of the Lord, for He is their Creator. One year we will leave thee with thy son, till thou givest thy (last) commands, that thou mayest teach thy children and record (it) for them, and testify to all thy children; and in the second year they shall take thee from their midst.

Let thy heart be strong, for the good shall announce righteousness to the good; the righteous with the righteous shall rejoice, and shall offer congratulation to one another. But the sinners shall die with the sinners, and the apostate go down with the apostate. And those who practice righteousness shall die on account of the deeds of men, and be taken away on account of the doings of the godless.'

And in those days they ceased to speak to me, and I came to my people, blessing the Lord of the world.

CHAPTER 82

And now, my son Methuselah, all these things I am recounting to thee and writing down for thee! and I have revealed to thee everything, and given thee books concerning all these: so preserve, my son Methuselah, the books from thy father's hand, and (see) that thou deliver them to the generations of the world.

I have given Wisdom to thee and to thy children, [And thy children that shall be to thee], that they may give it to their children for generations, this wisdom (namely) that passeth their thought. And those who understand it shall not sleep, but shall listen with the ear that they may learn this wisdom, and it shall please those that eat thereof better than good food.

Blessed are all the righteous, blessed are all those who walk in the way of righteousness and sin not as the sinners, in the reckoning of all their days in which the sun traverses the heaven, entering into and departing from the portals for thirty days with the heads of thousands of the order of the stars, together with the four which are intercalated which divide the four portions of the year, which lead them and enter with them four days. Owing to them men shall be at fault and not reckon them in the whole reckoning of the year: yea, men shall be at fault, and not recognize them accurately. For they belong to the reckoning of the year and are truly recorded (thereon) for ever, one in the first portal and one in the third, and one in the fourth and one in the sixth, and the year is completed in three hundred and sixty-four days. And the account thereof is accurate and the recorded reckoning thereof exact; for the luminaries, and months and festivals, and years and days, has Uriel shown and revealed to me, to whom the Lord of the whole creation of the world hath subjected the host of heaven. And he has power over night and day in the heaven to cause the light to give light to men -sun, moon, and stars, and all the powers of the heaven which revolve in their circular chariots. And these are the orders of the stars, which set in their places, and in their seasons and festivals and months. And these are the names of those who lead them, who watch that they enter at their times, in their orders, in their seasons, in their months, in their periods of domin-ion, and in their positions. Their four leaders who divide the four parts of the year enter first; and after them the twelve leaders of the orders who divide the months; and for the three hundred and sixty (days) there are heads over thousands who divide the days; and for the four inter-calary days there are the leaders which sunder the four parts of the year. And these heads over thousands are intercalated between leader and leader, each behind a station, but their leaders make the division. And these are the names of the leaders who divide the four parts of the year which are ordained: Milki'el, Hel'emmelek, and Mel'ejal, and Narel. And the names of those who lead them: Adnar'el, and Ijasusa'el, and 'Elome'el- these three follow the leaders of the orders, and there is one that follows the three leaders of the orders which follow those leaders of stations that divide the four parts of the year. In the beginning of the year Melkejal rises first and rules, who is named Tam'aini and sun, and all the days of his dominion whilst he bears rule are ninety-one days. And these are the signs of the days which are to be seen on earth in the days of his dominion: sweat, and heat, and calms; and all the trees bear fruit, and leaves are produced on all the trees, and the harvest of wheat, and the rose-flowers, and all the flowers which come forth in the field, but the trees of the winter season become withered. And these are the names of the leaders which are under them: Berka'el, Zelebs'el, and another who is added a head of a thousand, called Hilujaseph: and the days of the dominion of this (leader) are at an end. The next leader after him is Hel'emmelek, whom one names the shining sun, and all the days of his light are ninety-one days. And these are the signs of (his) days on the earth: glowing heat and dryness, and the trees ripen their fruits and produce all their fruits ripe and ready, and the sheep pair and become pregnant, and all the fruits of the earth are gathered in, and everything that is in the fields, and the winepress: these things take place in the days of his dominion. These are the names, and the orders, and the leaders of those heads of thousands: Gida'ljal, Ke'el, and He'el, and the name of the head of a thousand which is added to them, Asfa'el: and the days of his dominion are at an end.

THE BOOK OF DREAM VISIONS

CHAPTER 83

And now, my son Methuselah, I will show thee all my visions which I have seen, recounting them before thee. Two visions I saw before I took a wife, and the one was quite unlike the other: the first when I was learning to write: the second before I took thy mother, (when) I saw a terrible vision. And regarding them I prayed to the Lord. I had laid me down in the house of my grandfather Mahalalel, (when) I saw in a vision how the heaven collapsed and was borne off and fell to the earth. And when it fell to the earth I saw how the earth was swallowed up in a great abyss, and mountains were suspended on mountains, and hills sank down on hills, and high trees were rent from their stems, and hurled down and sunk in the abyss. And thereupon a word fell into my mouth, and I lifted up (my voice) to cry aloud, and said: 'The earth is destroyed.' And my grandfather Mahalalel waked me as I lay near him, and said unto me: 'Why dost thou cry so, my son, and why dost thou make such lamentation?' And I recounted to him the whole vision which I had seen, and he said unto me: 'A terrible thing hast thou seen, my son, and of grave moment is thy dream-vision as to the secrets of all the sin of the earth: it must sink into the abyss and be destroyed with a great destruction. And now, my son, arise and make petition to the Lord of glory, since thou art a believer, that a remnant may remain on the earth, and that He may not destroy the whole earth. My son, from heaven all this will come upon the earth, and upon the earth there will be great destruction. After that I arose and prayed and implored and besought, and wrote down my prayer for the generations of the world, and I will show everything to thee, my son Methuselah. And when I had gone forth below and seen the heaven, and the sun rising in the east, and the moon setting in the west, and a few stars, and the whole earth, and everything as He had known it in the beginning, then I blessed the Lord of judgement and extolled Him because He had made the sun to go forth from the windows of the east, and he ascended and rose on the face of the heaven, and set out and kept traversing the path shown unto him.

CHAPTER 84

And I lifted up my hands in righteousness and blessed the Holy and Great One, and spake with the breath of my mouth, and with the tongue of flesh, which God has made for the children of the flesh of men, that they should speak therewith, and He gave them breath and a tongue and a mouth that they should speak therewith:

Blessed be Thou, O Lord, King, Great and mighty in Thy greatness, Lord of the whole creation of the heaven, King of kings and God of the whole world. And Thy power and kingship and greatness abide for ever and ever, And throughout all generations Thy dominion; And all the heavens are Thy throne for ever, And the whole earth Thy footstool for ever and ever.

For Thou hast made and Thou rulest all things, And nothing is too hard for Thee, Wisdom departs not from the place of Thy throne, Nor turns away from Thy presence. And Thou knowest and seest and hearest everything, And there is nothing hidden from Thee [for Thou seest everything] And now the angels of Thy heavens are guilty of trespass, And upon the flesh of men abideth Thy wrath until the great day of judgement. And now, O God and Lord and Great King, I implore and beseech Thee to fulfil my prayer, To leave me a posterity on earth, And not destroy all the flesh of man, And make the earth without inhabitant, So that there should be an eternal destruction. And now, my Lord, destroy from the earth the flesh which has aroused Thy wrath, But the flesh of righteousness and uprightness establish as a plant of the eternal seed, And hide not Thy face from the prayer of Thy servant, O Lord.'

CHAPTER 85

And after this I saw another dream, and I will show the whole dream to thee, my son. And Enoch lifted up (his voice) and spake to his son Methuselah: 'To thee, my son, will I speak: hear my words-incline thine ear to the dream-vision of thy father. Before I took thy mother Edna, I saw in a vision on my bed, and behold a bull came forth from the earth, and that bull was white; and after it came forth a heifer, and along with this (latter) came forth two bulls, one of them black and the other red. And that black bull gored the red one and pursued him over the earth, and thereupon I could no longer see that red bull. But that black bull grew and that heifer went with him, and I saw that many oxen proceeded from him which resembled and followed him. And that cow, that first one, went from the presence of that first bull in order to seek that red one, but found him not, and lamented with a great lamentation over him and sought him. And I looked till that first bull came to her and quieted her, and from that time onward she cried no more. And after that she bore another white bull, and after him she bore many bulls and black cows. And I saw in my sleep that white bull likewise grow and become a great white bull, and from Him proceeded many white bulls, and they resembled him. And they began to beget many white bulls, which resembled them, one following the other, (even) many.

CHAPTER 86

And again I saw with mine eyes as I slept, and I saw the heaven above, and behold a star fell from heaven, and it arose and eat and pastured amongst those oxen. And after that I saw the large and the black oxen, and behold they all changed their stalls and pastures and their cattle, and began to live with each other. And again I saw in the vision, and looked towards the heaven, and behold I saw many stars descend and cast themselves down from heaven to that first star, and they became bulls amongst those cattle and pastured with them [amongst them]. And I looked at them and saw, and behold they all let out their privy members, like horses, and began to cover the cows of the oxen, and they all became pregnant and bare elephants, camels, and asses. And all the oxen feared them and were affrighted at them, and began to bite with their teeth and to devour, and to gore with their horns. And they began, moreover, to devour those oxen; and behold all the children of the earth began to tremble and quake before them and to flee from them.

CHAPTER 87

And again I saw how they began to gore each other and to devour each other, and the earth began to cry aloud. And I raised mine eyes again to heaven, and I saw in the vision, and behold there came forth from heaven beings who were like white men: and four went forth from that place and three with them. And those three that had last come forth grasped me by my hand and took me up, away from the generations of the earth, and raised me up to a lofty place, and showed me a tower raised high above the earth, and all the hills were lower. And one said unto me: 'Remain here till thou seest everything that befalls those elephants, camels, and asses, and the stars and the oxen, and all of them.'

Enoch witnessing a massive, apocalyptic flood engulfing the earth, with towering waves and dark, stormy skies, as the world beneath is submerged in chaos.

CHAPTER 88

And I saw one of those four who had come forth first, and he seized that first star which had fallen from the heaven, and bound it hand and foot and cast it into an abyss: now that abyss was narrow and deep, and horrible and dark. And one of them drew a sword, and gave it to those elephants and camels and asses: then they began to smite each other, and the whole earth quaked because of them. And as I was beholding in the vision, lo, one of those four who had come forth stoned (them) from heaven, and gathered and took all the great stars whose privy members were like those of horses, and bound them all hand and foot, and cast them in an abyss of the earth.

CHAPTER 89

And one of those four went to that white bull and instructed him in a secret, without his being terrified: he was born a bull and became a man, and built for himself a great vessel and dwelt thereon; and three bulls dwelt with him in that vessel and they were covered in. And again I raised mine eyes towards heaven and saw a lofty roof, with seven water torrents thereon, and those torrents flowed with much water into an enclosure. And I saw again, and behold fountains were opened on the surface of that great enclosure, and that water began to swell and rise upon the surface, and I saw that enclosure till all its surface was covered with water. And the water, the darkness, and mist increased upon it; and as I looked at the height of that water, that water had risen above the height of that enclosure, and was streaming over that enclosure, and it stood upon the earth. And all the cattle of that enclosure were gathered together until I saw how they sank and were swallowed up and perished in that water. But that vessel floated on the water, while all the oxen and elephants and camels and asses sank to the bottom with all the animals, so that I could no longer see them, and they were not able to escape, (but) perished and sank into the depths. And again I saw in the vision till those water torrents were removed from that high roof, and the chasms of the earth were leveled up and other abysses were opened. Then the water began to run down into these, till the earth became visible; but that vessel settled on the earth, and the darkness retired and light appeared. But that white bull which had become a man came out of that vessel, and the three bulls with him, and one of those three was white like that bull, and one of them was red as blood, and one black: and that white bull departed from them. And they began to bring forth beasts of the field and birds, so that there arose different genera: lions, tigers, wolves, dogs, hyenas, wild boars, foxes, squirrels, swine, falcons, vultures, kites, eagles, and ravens; and among them was born a white bull. And they began to bite one another; but that white bull which was born amongst them begat a wild ass and a white bull with it, and the wild asses multiplied. But that bull which was born from him begat a black wild boar and a white sheep; and the former begat many boars, but that sheep begat twelve sheep. And when those twelve sheep had grown, they gave up one of them to the asses, and those asses again gave up that sheep to the wolves, and that sheep grew up among the wolves. And the Lord brought the eleven sheep to live with it and to pasture with it among the wolves: and they multiplied and became many flocks of sheep. And the wolves began to fear them, and they oppressed them until they destroyed their little ones, and they cast their young into a river of much water: but those sheep began to cry aloud on account of their little ones, and to complain unto their Lord. And a sheep which had been saved from the wolves fled and escaped to the wild asses; and I saw the sheep how they lamented and cried, and besought their Lord with all their might, till that Lord of the sheep descended at the voice of the sheep from a lofty abode, and came to them and pastured them. And He called that sheep which had escaped the wolves, and spake with it concerning the wolves that it should admonish them not to touch the sheep. And the sheep went to the wolves according to the word of the Lord, and another sheep met it and went with it, and the two went and entered together into the assembly of those wolves, and spake with them and admonished them not to touch the sheep from henceforth. And thereupon I saw the wolves, and how they oppressed the sheep exceedingly with all their power; and the sheep cried aloud. And the Lord came to the sheep and they began to smite those wolves: and the wolves began to make lamentation; but the sheep became quiet and forthwith ceased to cry out. And I saw the sheep till they departed from amongst the wolves; but the eyes of the wolves were blinded, and those wolves departed in pursuit of the sheep with all their power. And the Lord of the sheep went with them, as their leader, and all His sheep followed Him: and his face was dazzling and glorious and terrible to behold. But the wolves began to pursue those sheep till they reached a sea of water. And that sea was divided, and the water stood on this side and on that before their face, and their Lord led them and placed Himself between them and the wolves. And as those wolves did not yet see the sheep, they proceeded into the midst of that sea, and the wolves followed the sheep, and [those wolves] ran after them into that sea. And when they saw the Lord of the sheep, they turned to flee before His face, but that sea gathered itself together, and became as it had been created, and the water swelled and rose till it covered those wolves. And I saw till all the wolves who pursued those sheep perished and were drowned. But the sheep escaped from that water and went forth into a wilderness, where there was no water and no grass; and they began to open their eyes and to see; and I saw the Lord of the sheep pasturing them and giving them water and grass, and that sheep going and leading them. And that sheep ascended to the summit of that lofty rock, and the Lord of the sheep sent it to them. And after that I saw the Lord of the sheep who stood before them, and His appearance was great and terrible and majestic, and all those sheep saw Him and were afraid before His face. And they all feared and trembled because of Him, and they cried to that sheep with them [which was amongst them]: 'We are not able to stand before our Lord or to behold Him.' And that sheep which led them again ascended to the summit of that rock, but the sheep began to be blinded and to wander from the way which he had showed them, but that sheep wot not thereof. And the Lord of the sheep was wrathful exceedingly against them, and that sheep discovered it, and went down from the summit of the rock, and came to the sheep, and found the greatest part of them blinded and fallen away. And when they saw it they feared and trembled at its presence, and desired to return to their folds. And that sheep took other sheep with it, and came to those sheep which had fallen away, and began to slay them; and the sheep feared its presence, and thus that sheep brought back those sheep that had fallen away, and they returned to their folds. And I saw in this vision till that sheep became a man and built a house for the Lord of the sheep, and placed all the sheep in that house. And I saw till this sheep which had met that sheep which led them fell asleep: and I saw till all the great sheep perished and little ones arose in their place, and they came to a pasture, and approached a stream of water. Then that sheep, their leader which had become a man, withdrew from them and fell asleep, and all the sheep sought it and cried over it with a great crying. And I saw till they left off crying for that sheep and crossed that stream of water, and there arose the two sheep as leaders in the place of those which had led them and fallen asleep (lit. 'had fallen asleep and led them'). And I saw till the sheep came to a goodly place, and a pleasant and glorious land, and I saw till those sheep were satisfied; and that house stood amongst them in the pleasant land. And sometimes their eyes were opened, and sometimes blinded, till another sheep arose and led them and brought them all back, and their eyes were opened.

And the dogs and the foxes and the wild boars began to devour those sheep till the Lord of the sheep raised up [another sheep] a ram from their midst, which led them. And that ram began to butt on either side those dogs, foxes, and wild boars till he had destroyed them all. And that sheep whose eyes were opened saw that ram, which was amongst the sheep, till it forsook its glory and began to butt those sheep, and trampled upon them, and behaved itself unseemly. And the Lord of the sheep sent the lamb to another lamb and raised it to being a ram and leader of the sheep instead of that ram which had forsaken its glory. And it went to it and spake to it alone, and raised it to being a ram, and made it the prince and leader of the sheep; but during all these things those dogs oppressed the sheep. And the first ram pursued that second ram, and that second ram arose and fled before it; and I saw till those dogs pulled down the first ram. And that second ram arose and led the [little] sheep. And those sheep grew and multiplied; but all the dogs, and foxes, and wild boars feared and fled before it, and that ram butted and killed the wild beasts, and those wild beasts had no longer any power among the sheep and robbed them no more of ought. And that ram begat many sheep and fell asleep; and a little sheep became ram in its stead, and became prince and leader of those sheep. And that house became great and broad, and it was built for those sheep: (and) a tower lofty and great was built on the house for the Lord of the sheep, and that house was low, but the tower was elevated and lofty, and the Lord of the sheep stood on that tower and they offered a full table before Him. And again I saw those sheep that they again erred and went many ways, and forsook that their house, and the Lord of the sheep called some from amongst the sheep and sent them to the sheep, but the sheep began to slay them. And one of them was saved and was not slain, and it sped away and cried aloud over the sheep; and they sought to slay it, but the Lord of the sheep saved it from the sheep, and brought it up to me, and caused it to dwell there. And many other sheep He sent to those sheep to testify unto them and lament over them. And after that I saw that when they forsook the house of the Lord and His tower they fell away entirely, and their eyes were blinded; and I saw the Lord of the sheep how He wrought much slaughter amongst them in their herds until those sheep invited that slaughter and betrayed His place. And He gave them over into the hands of the lions and tigers, and wolves and hyenas, and into the hand of the foxes, and to all the wild beasts, and those wild beasts began to tear in pieces those sheep. And I saw that He forsook that their house and their tower and gave them all into the hand of the lions, to tear and devour them, into the hand of all the wild beasts. And I began to cry aloud with all my power, and to appeal to the Lord of the sheep, and to represent to Him in regard to the sheep that they were devoured by all the wild beasts. But He remained unmoved, though He saw it, and rejoiced that they were devoured and swallowed and robbed, and left them to be devoured in the hand of all the beasts. And He called seventy shepherds, and cast those sheep to them that they might pasture them, and He spake to the shepherds and their companions: 'Let each individual of you pasture the sheep henceforward, and everything that I shall command you that do ye. And I will deliver them over unto you duly numbered, and tell you which of them are to be destroyed-and them destroy ye.' And He gave over unto them those sheep. And He called another and spake unto him: 'Observe and mark everything that the shepherds will do to those sheep; for they will destroy more of them than I have commanded them. And every excess and the destruction which will be wrought through the shepherds, record (namely) how many they destroy according to my command, and how many according to their own caprice: record against every individual shepherd all the destruction he effects. And read out before me by number how many they destroy, and how many they deliver over for destruction, that I may have this as a testimony against them, and know every deed of the shepherds, that I may comprehend and see what they do, whether or not they abide by my command which I have commanded them. But they shall not know it, and thou shalt not declare it to them, nor admonish them, but only record against each individual all the destruction which the shepherds effect each in his time and lay it all before me.' And I saw till those shepherds pastured in their season, and they began to slay and to destroy more than they were bidden, and they delivered those sheep into the hand of the lions. And the lions and tigers eat and devoured the greater part of those sheep, and the wild boars eat along with them; and they burnt that tower and demolished that house. And I became exceedingly sorrowful over that tower because that house of the sheep was demolished, and afterwards I was unable to see if those sheep entered that house. And the shepherds and their associates delivered over those sheep to all the wild beasts, to devour them, and each one of them received in his time a definite number: it was written by the other in a book how many each one of them destroyed of them. And each one slew and destroyed many more than was prescribed; and I began to weep and lament on account of those sheep. And thus in the vision I saw that one who wrote, how he wrote down every one that was destroyed by those shepherds, day by day, and carried up and laid down and showed actually the whole book to the Lord of the sheep-(even) everything that they had done, and all that each one of them had made away with, and all that they had given over to destruction. And the book was read before the Lord of the sheep, and He took the book from his hand and read it and sealed it and laid it down. And forthwith I saw how the shepherds pastured for twelve hours, and behold three of those sheep turned back and came and entered and began to build up all that had fallen down of that house; but the wild boars tried to hinder them, but they were not able. And they began again to build as before, and they reared up that tower, and it was named the high tower; and they began again to place a table before the tower, but all the bread on it was polluted and not pure. And as touching all this the eyes of those sheep were blinded so that they saw not, and (the eyes of) their shepherds likewise; and they delivered them in large numbers to their shepherds for destruction, and they trampled the sheep with their feet and devoured them. And the Lord of the sheep remained unmoved till all the sheep were dispersed over the field and mingled with them (i.e. the beasts), and they (i.e. the shepherds) did not save them out of the hand of the beasts. And this one who wrote the book carried it up, and showed it and read it before the Lord of the sheep, and implored Him on their account, and besought Him on their account as he showed Him all the doings of the shepherds, and gave testimony before Him against all the shepherds. And he took the actual book and laid it down beside Him and departed.

CHAPTER 90

And I saw till that in this manner thirty-five shepherds undertook the pasturing (of the sheep), and they severally completed their periods as did the first; and others received them into their hands, to pasture them for their period, each shepherd in his own period. And after that I saw in my vision all the birds of heaven coming, the eagles, the vultures, the kites, the ravens; but the eagles led all the birds; and they began to devour those sheep, and to pick out their eyes and to devour their flesh. And the sheep cried out because their flesh was being devoured by the birds, and as for me I looked and lamented in my sleep over that shepherd who pastured the sheep. And I saw until those sheep were devoured by the dogs and eagles and kites, and they left neither flesh nor skin nor sinew remaining on them till only their bones stood there: and their bones too fell to the earth and the sheep became few. And I saw until that twenty-three had undertaken the pasturing and completed in their several periods fifty-eight times. But behold lambs were borne by those white sheep, and they began to open their eyes and to see, and to cry to the sheep. Yea, they cried to them, but they did not hearken to what they said to them, but were exceedingly deaf, and their eyes were very exceedingly blinded. And I saw in the vision how the ravens flew upon those lambs and took one of those lambs, and dashed the sheep in pieces and devoured them. And I saw till horns grew upon those lambs, and the ravens cast down their horns; and I saw till there sprouted a great horn of one of those sheep, and their eyes were opened. And it looked at them and their eyes opened, and it cried to the sheep, and the rams saw it and all ran to it. And notwithstanding all this those eagles and vultures and ravens and kites still kept tearing the sheep and swooping down upon them and devouring them: still the sheep remained silent, but the rams lamented and cried out. And those ravens fought and battled with it and sought to lay low its horn, but they had no power over it. All the eagles and vultures and ravens and kites were gathered together, and there came with them all the sheep of the field, yea, they all came together, and helped each other to break that horn of the ram. And I saw till a great sword was given to the sheep, and the sheep proceeded against all the beasts of the field to slay them, and all the beasts and the birds of the heaven fled before their face. And I saw that man, who wrote the book according to the command of the Lord, till he opened that book concerning the destruction which those twelve last shepherds had wrought, and showed that they had destroyed much more than their predecessors, before the Lord of the sheep. And I saw till the Lord of the sheep came unto them and took in His hand the staff of His wrath, and smote the earth, and the earth clave asunder, and all the beasts and all the birds of the heaven fell from among those sheep, and were swallowed up in the earth and it covered them. And I saw till a throne was erected in the pleasant land, and the Lord of the sheep sat Himself thereon, and the other took the sealed books and opened those books before the Lord of the sheep. And the Lord called those men the seven first white ones, and commanded that they should bring before Him, beginning with the first star which led the way, all the stars whose privy members were like those of horses, and they brought them all before Him. And He said to that man who wrote before Him, being one of those seven white ones, and said unto him: 'Take those seventy shepherds to whom I delivered the sheep, and who taking them on their own authority slew more than I commanded them.' And behold they were all bound, I saw, and they all stood before Him. And the judgement was held first over the stars, and they were judged and found guilty, and went to the place of condemnation, and they were cast into an abyss, full of fire and flaming, and full of pillars of fire. And those seventy shepherds were judged and found guilty, and they were cast into that fiery abyss. And I saw at that time how a like abyss was opened in the midst of the earth, full of fire, and they brought those blinded sheep, and they were all judged and found guilty and cast into this fiery abyss, and they burned; now this abyss was to the right of that house. And I saw those sheep burning and their bones burning. And I stood up to see till they folded up that old house; and carried off all the pillars, and all the beams and ornaments of the house were at the same time folded up with it, and they carried it off and laid it in a place in the south of the land. And I saw till the Lord of the sheep brought a new house greater and loftier than that first, and set it up in the place of the first which had been folded up: all its pillars were new, and its ornaments were new and larger than those of the first, the old one which He had taken away, and all the sheep were within it. And I saw all the sheep which had been left, and all the beasts on the earth, and all the birds of the heaven, falling down and doing homage to those sheep and making petition to and obeying them in every thing. And thereafter those three who were clothed in white and had seized me by my hand who had taken me up before, and the hand of that ram also seizing hold of me, they took me up and set me down in the midst of those sheep before the judgement took place. And those sheep were all white, and their wool was abundant and clean. And all that had been destroyed and dispersed, and all the beasts of the field, and all the birds of the heaven, assembled in that house, and the Lord of the sheep rejoiced with great joy because they were all good and had returned to His house. And I saw till they laid down that sword, which had been given to the sheep, and they brought it back into the house, and it was sealed before the presence of the Lord, and all the sheep were invited into that house, but it held them not. And the eyes of them all were opened, and they saw the good, and there was not one among them that did not see. And I saw that that house was large and broad and very full. And I saw that a white bull was born, with large horns and all the beasts of the field and all the birds of the air feared him and made petition to him all the time. And I saw till all their generations were transformed, and they all became white bulls; and the first among them became a lamb, and that lamb became a great animal and had great black horns on its head; and the Lord of the sheep rejoiced over it and over all the oxen. And I slept in their midst: and I awoke and saw everything. This is the vision which I saw while I slept, and I awoke and blessed the Lord of righteousness and gave Him glory. Then I wept with a great weeping and my tears stayed not till I could no longer endure it: when I saw, they flowed on account of what I had seen; for everything shall come and be fulfilled, and all the deeds of men in their order were shown to me. On that night I remembered the first dream, and because of it I wept and was troubled-because I had seen that vision.

THE EPISTLE OF ENOCH

CHAPTER 91

The book written by Enoch-[Enoch indeed wrote this complete doctrine of wisdom, (which is) praised of all men and a judge of all the earth] for all my children who shall dwell on the earth. And for the future generations who shall observe uprightness and peace.

Let not your spirit be troubled on account of the times; For the Holy and Great One has appointed days for all things.

And the righteous one shall arise from sleep, [Shall arise] and walk in the paths of righteousness, And all his path and conversation shall be in eternal goodness and grace.

He will be gracious to the righteous and give him eternal uprightness, And He will give him power so that he shall be (endowed) with goodness and righteousness. And he shall walk in eternal light.

And sin shall perish in darkness for ever, And shall no more be seen from that day for evermore.

CHAPTER 92

And now, my son Methuselah, call to me all thy brothers And gather together to me all the sons of thy mother; For the word calls me, And the spirit is poured out upon me, That I may show you everything That shall befall you for ever.'

And there upon Methuselah went and summoned to him all his brothers and assembled his relatives. And he spake unto all the children of right-eousness and said:

'Hear, ye sons of Enoch, all the words of your father, And hearken aright to the voice of my mouth; For I exhort you and say unto you, beloved:

Love uprightness and walk therein. And draw not nigh to uprightness with a double heart, And associate not with those of a double heart,

But walk in righteousness, my sons. And it shall guide you on good paths, And righteousness shall be your companion.

For I know that violence must increase on the earth, And a great chas-tisement be executed on the earth,

Yea, it shall be cut off from its roots, And its whole structure be destroyed.

And unrighteousness shall again be consummated on the earth, And all the deeds of unrighteousness and of violence And transgression shall prevail in a twofold degree.

And when sin and unrighteousness and blasphemy And violence in all kinds of deeds increase, And apostasy and transgression and uncleanness increase,

A great chastisement shall come from heaven upon all these, And the holy Lord will come forth with wrath and chastisement To execute judgement on earth.

In those days violence shall be cut off from its roots, And the roots of unrighteousness together with deceit, And they shall be destroyed from under heaven.

And all the idols of the heathen shall be abandoned, And the temples burned with fire, And they shall remove them from the whole earth,

And they (i.e. the heathen) shall be cast into the judgement of fire, And shall perish in wrath and in grievous judgement for ever.

And the righteous shall arise from their sleep, And wisdom shall arise and be given unto them.

[And after that the roots of unrighteousness shall be cut off, and the sinners shall be destroyed by the sword . . . shall be cut off from the blasphemers in every place, and those who plan violence and those who commit blasphemy shall perish by the sword.]

And now I tell you, my sons, and show you The paths of righteousness and the paths of violence. Yea, I will show them to you again That ye may know what will come to pass. And now, hearken unto me, my sons, And walk in the paths of righteousness, And walk not in the paths of violence; For all who walk in the paths of unrighteousness shall perish for ever.'

CHAPTER 93

And after that Enoch both gave and began to recount from the books. And Enoch said:

' Concerning the children of righteousness and concerning the elect of the world, And concerning the plant of uprightness, I will speak these things, Yea, I Enoch will declare (them) unto you, my sons:

According to that which appeared to me in the heavenly vision, And which I have known through the word of the holy angels, And have learnt from the heavenly tablets.'

And Enoch began to recount from the books and said: ' I was born the seventh in the first week, While judgement and righteousness still endured.

And after me there shall arise in the second week great wickedness, And deceit shall have sprung up; And in it there shall be the first end.

And in it a man shall be saved; And after it is ended unrighteousness shall grow up, And a law shall be made for the sinners.

And after that in the third week at its close A man shall be elected as the plant of righteous judgement, And his posterity shall become the plant of righteousness for evermore.

And after that in the fourth week, at its close, Visions of the holy and righteous shall be seen, And a law for all generations and an enclosure shall be made for them.

And after that in the fifth week, at its close, The house of glory and dominion shall be built for ever.

And after that in the sixth week all who live in it shall be blinded, And the hearts of all of them shall godlessly forsake wisdom.

And in it a man shall ascend; And at its close the house of dominion shall be burnt with fire, And the whole race of the chosen root shall be dispersed.

And after that in the seventh week shall an apostate generation arise, And many shall be its deeds, And all its deeds shall be apostate.

And at its close shall be elected The elect righteous of the eternal plant of righteousness, To receive sevenfold instruction concerning all His creation.

[For who is there of all the children of men that is able to hear the voice of the Holy One without being troubled ? And who can think His thoughts ? and who is there that can behold all the works of heaven ? And how should there be one who could behold the heaven, and who is there that could understand the things of heaven and see a soul or a spirit and could tell thereof, or ascend and see all their ends and think them or do like them ? And who is there of all men that could know what is the breadth and the length of the earth, and to whom has been shown the measure of all of them ? Or is there any one who could discern the length of the heaven and how great is its height, and upon what it is founded, and how great is the number of the stars, and where all the luminaries rest ?]

CHAPTER 94

And after that there shall be another, the eighth week, that of righteousness, And a sword shall be given to it that a righteous judgement
may be executed on the oppressors, And sinners shall be delivered into
the hands of the righteous.

And at its close they shall acquire houses through their righteousness,
And a house shall be built for the Great King in glory for evermore, And
all mankind shall look to the path of uprightness.

And after that, in the ninth week, the righteous judgement shall be
revealed to the whole world, And all the works of the godless shall vanish
from all the earth, And the world shall be written down for destruction.

And after this, in the tenth week in the seventh part, There shall be the
great eternal judgement, In which He will execute vengeance amongst
the angels.

And the first heaven shall depart and pass away, And a new heaven shall
appear, And all the powers of the heavens shall give sevenfold light.

And after that there will be many weeks without number for ever, And
all shall be in goodness and righteousness, And sin shall no more be
mentioned for ever.

Enoch delivering a message of judgment from the heavens, surrounded by light, as
the righteous and wicked face their fate.

CHAPTER 95

And now I say unto you, my sons, love righteousness and walk therein;
For the paths of righteousness are worthy of acceptation, But the paths
of unrighteousness shall suddenly be destroyed and vanish.

And to certain men of a generation shall the paths of violence and of
death be revealed, And they shall hold themselves afar from them, And
shall not follow them.

And now I say unto you the righteous: Walk not in the paths of wickedness, nor in the paths of death, And draw not nigh to them, lest ye be
destroyed.

But seek and choose for yourselves righteousness and an elect life, And walk in the paths of peace, And ye shall live and prosper.

And hold fast my words in the thoughts of your hearts, And suffer them not to be effaced from your hearts;

For I know that sinners will tempt men to evilly-entreat wisdom, So that no place may be found for her, And no manner of temptation may minish.

Woe to those who build unrighteousness and oppression And lay deceit as a foundation; For they shall be suddenly overthrown, And they shall have no peace.

Woe to those who build their houses with sin; For from all their foundations shall they be overthrown, And by the sword shall they fall. [And those who acquire gold and silver in judgement suddenly shall perish.]

Woe to you, ye rich, for ye have trusted in your riches, And from your riches shall ye depart, Because ye have not remembered the Most High in the days of your riches.

Ye have committed blasphemy and unrighteousness, And have become ready for the day of slaughter, And the day of darkness and the day of the great judgement.

Thus I speak and declare unto you: He who hath created you will overthrow you, And for your fall there shall be no compassion, And your Creator will rejoice at your destruction.

And your righteous ones in those days shall be A reproach to the sinners and the godless.

CHAPTER 96

Oh that mine eyes were [a cloud of] waters That I might weep over you, And pour down my tears as a cloud of waters: That so I might rest from my trouble of heart!

Who has permitted you to practice reproaches and wickedness? And so judgement shall overtake you, sinners.

Fear not the sinners, ye righteous; For again will the Lord deliver them into your hands, That ye may execute judgement upon them according to your desires.

Woe to you who fulminate anathemas which cannot be reversed: Healing shall therefore be far from you because of your sins.

Woe to you who requite your neighbour with evil; For ye shall be requited according to your works.

Woe to you, lying witnesses, And to those who weigh out injustice, For suddenly shall ye perish.

Woe to you, sinners, for ye persecute the righteous; For ye shall be delivered up and persecuted because of injustice, And heavy shall its yoke be upon you.

CHAPTER 97

Be hopeful, ye righteous; for suddenly shall the sinners perish before you, And ye shall have lordship over them according to your desires.

[And in the day of the tribulation of the sinners, Your children shall mount and rise as eagles, And higher than the vultures will be your nest, And ye shall ascend and enter the crevices of the earth, And the clefts of the rock for ever as coneys before the unrighteous, And the sirens shall sigh because of you-and weep.]

Wherefore fear not, ye that have suffered; For healing shall be your portion, And a bright light shall enlighten you, And the voice of rest ye shall hear from heaven.

Woe unto you, ye sinners, for your riches make you appear like the righteous, But your hearts convict you of being sinners, And this fact shall be a testimony against you for a memorial of (your) evil deeds.

Woe to you who devour the finest of the wheat, And drink wine in large bowls, And tread under foot the lowly with your might.

Woe to you who drink water from every fountain, For suddenly shall ye be consumed and wither away, Because ye have forsaken the fountain of life.

Woe to you who work unrighteousness And deceit and blasphemy: It shall be a memorial against you for evil.

Woe to you, ye mighty, Who with might oppress the righteous; For the day of your destruction is coming.

In those days many and good days shall come to the righteous-in the day of your judgement.

CHAPTER 98

Believe, ye righteous, that the sinners will become a shame And perish in the day of unrighteousness. Be it known unto you (ye sinners) that the Most High is mindful of your destruction, And the angels of heaven rejoice over your destruction.

What will ye do, ye sinners, And whither will ye flee on that day of judgement, When ye hear the voice of the prayer of the righteous?

Yea, ye shall fare like unto them, Against whom this word shall be a testimony: "Ye have been companions of sinners."

And in those days the prayer of the righteous shall reach unto the Lord, And for you the days of your judgement shall come.

And all the words of your unrighteousness shall be read out before the Great Holy One, And your faces shall be covered with shame, And He will reject every work which is grounded on unrighteousness.

Woe to you, ye sinners, who live on the mid ocean and on the dry land, Whose remembrance is evil against you.

Woe to you who acquire silver and gold in unrighteousness and say: "We have become rich with riches and have possessions; And have acquired everything we have desired.

And now let us do what we purposed: For we have gathered silver, And many are the husbandmen in our houses." And our granaries are (brim) full as with water, Yea and like water your lies shall flow away; For your riches shall not abide But speedily ascend from you;

For ye have acquired it all in unrighteousness, And ye shall be given over to a great curse.

CHAPTER 99

And now I swear unto you, to the wise and to the foolish, For ye shall have manifold experiences on the earth.

For ye men shall put on more adornments than a woman, And coloured garments more than a virgin: In royalty and in grandeur and in power, And in silver and in gold and in purple, And in splendour and in food they shall be poured out as water.

Therefore they shall be wanting in doctrine and wisdom, And they shall perish thereby together with their possessions; And with all their glory and their splendour, And in shame and in slaughter and in great destitution, Their spirits shall be cast into the furnace of fire.

I have sworn unto you, ye sinners, as a mountain has not become a slave, And a hill does not become the handmaid of a woman, Even so sin has not been sent upon the earth, But man of himself has created it, And under a great curse shall they fall who commit it.

And barrenness has not been given to the woman, But on account of the deeds of her own hands she dies without children.

I have sworn unto you, ye sinners, by the Holy Great One, That all your evil deeds are revealed in the heavens, And that none of your deeds of oppression are covered and hidden.

And do not think in your spirit nor say in your heart that ye do not know and that ye do not see that every sin is every day recorded in heaven in the presence of the Most High. From henceforth ye know that all your oppression wherewith ye oppress is written down every day till the day of your judgement. Woe to you, ye fools, for through your folly shall ye perish: and ye transgress against the wise, and so good hap shall not be your portion. And now, know ye that ye are prepared for the day of destruction: wherefore do not hope to live, ye sinners, but ye shall depart and die; for ye know no ransom; for ye are prepared for the day of the great judgement, for the day of tribulation and great shame for your spirits. Woe to you, ye obstinate of heart, who work wickedness and eat blood: Whence have ye good things to eat and to drink and to be filled? From all the good things which the Lord the Most High has placed in abundance on the earth; therefore ye shall have no peace. Woe to you who love the deeds of unrighteousness: wherefore do ye hope for good hap unto yourselves? know that ye shall be delivered into the hands of the righteous, and they shall cut off your necks and slay you, and have no mercy upon you. Woe to you who rejoice in the tribulation of the righteous; for no grave shall be dug for you. Woe to you who set at nought the words of the righteous; for ye shall have no hope of life. Woe to you who write down lying and godless words; for they write down their lies that men may hear them and act godlessly towards (their) neighbour. Therefore they shall have no peace but die a sudden death.

CHAPTER 100

Woe to you who work godlessness, And glory in lying and extol them: Ye shall perish, and no happy life shall be yours.

Woe to them who pervert the words of uprightness, And transgress the eternal law, And transform themselves into what they were not [into sinners]: They shall be trodden under foot upon the earth.

In those days make ready, ye righteous, to raise your prayers as a memorial, And place them as a testimony before the angels, That they may place the sin of the sinners for a memorial before the Most High.

In those days the nations shall be stirred up, And the families of the nations shall arise on the day of destruction.

And in those days the destitute shall go forth and carry off their children, And they shall abandon them, so that their children shall perish through them: Yea, they shall abandon their children (that are still) sucklings, and not return to them, And shall have no pity on their beloved ones.

And again I swear to you, ye sinners, that sin is prepared for a day of unceasing bloodshed. And they who worship stones, and grave images of gold and silver and wood (and stone) and clay, and those who worship impure spirits and demons, and all kinds of idols not according to knowledge, shall get no manner of help from them.

And they shall become godless by reason of the folly of their hearts, And their eyes shall be blinded through the fear of their hearts And through visions in their dreams.

Through these they shall become godless and fearful; For they shall have wrought all their work in a lie, And shall have worshiped a stone: Therefore in an instant shall they perish.

But in those days blessed are all they who accept the words of wisdom, and understand them, And observe the paths of the Most High, and walk in the path of His righteousness, And become not godless with the godless; For they shall be saved.

Woe to you who spread evil to your neighbours; For you shall be slain in Sheol.

Woe to you who make deceitful and false measures, And (to them) who cause bitterness on the earth; For they shall thereby be utterly consumed.

Woe to you who build your houses through the grievous toil of others, And all their building materials are the bricks and stones of sin; I tell you ye shall have no peace.

Woe to them who reject the measure and eternal heritage of their fathers And whose souls follow after idols; For they shall have no rest.

Woe to them who work unrighteousness and help oppression, And slay their neighbours until the day of the great judgement.

For He shall cast down your glory, And bring affliction on your hearts, And shall arouse His fierce indignation And destroy you all with the sword; And all the holy and righteous shall remember your sins.

CHAPTER 101

And in those days in one place the fathers together with their sons shall be smitten And brothers one with another shall fall in death Till the streams flow with their blood.

For a man shall not withhold his hand from slaying his sons and his sons' sons, And the sinner shall not withhold his hand from his honoured brother: From dawn till sunset they shall slay one another.

And the horse shall walk up to the breast in the blood of sinners, And the chariot shall be submerged to its height.

In those days the angels shall descend into the secret places And gather together into one place all those who brought down sin And the Most High will arise on that day of judgement To execute great judgement amongst sinners.

And over all the righteous and holy He will appoint guardians from amongst the holy angels To guard them as the apple of an eye, Until He makes an end of all wickedness and all sin, And though the righteous sleep a long sleep, they have nought to fear.

And (then) the children of the earth shall see the wise in security, And shall understand all the words of this book, And recognize that their riches shall not be able to save them In the overthrow of their sins.

Woe to you, Sinners, on the day of strong anguish, Ye who afflict the righteous and burn them with fire: Ye shall be requited according to your works.

Woe to you, ye obstinate of heart, Who watch in order to devise wickedness: Therefore shall fear come upon you And there shall be none to help you.

Woe to you, ye sinners, on account of the words of your mouth, And on account of the deeds of your hands which your godlessness as wrought, In blazing flames burning worse than fire shall ye burn.

And now, know ye that from the angels He will inquire as to your deeds in heaven, from the sun and from the moon and from the stars in reference to your sins because upon the earth ye execute judgement on the righteous. And He will summon to testify against you every cloud and mist and dew and rain; for they shall all be withheld because of you from descending upon you, and they shall be mindful of your sins. And now give presents to the rain that it be not withheld from descending upon you, nor yet the dew, when it has received gold and silver from you that it may descend. When the hoar-frost and snow with their chilliness, and all the snow-storms with all their plagues fall upon you, in those days ye shall not be able to stand before them.

CHAPTER 102

Observe the heaven, ye children of heaven, and every work of the Most High, and fear ye Him and work no evil in His presence. If He closes the windows of heaven, and withholds the rain and the dew from descending on the earth on your account, what will ye do then? And if He sends His anger upon you because of your deeds, ye cannot petition Him; for ye spake proud and insolent words against His righteousness: therefore ye shall have no peace. And see ye not the sailors of the ships, how their ships are tossed to and fro by the waves, and are shaken by the winds, and are in sore trouble? And therefore do they fear because all their goodly possessions go upon the sea with them, and they have evil forebodings of heart that the sea will swallow them and they will perish therein. Are not the entire sea and all its waters, and all its movements, the work of the Most High, and has He not set limits to its doings, and confined it throughout by the sand? And at His reproof it is afraid and dries up, and all its fish die and all that is in it; But ye sinners that are on the earth fear Him not. Has He not made the heaven and the earth, and all that is therein? Who has given understanding and wisdom to everything that moves on the earth and in the sea. Do not the sailors of the ships fear the sea? Yet sinners fear not the Most High.

CHAPTER 103

In those days when He hath brought a grievous fire upon you, Whither will ye flee, and where will ye find deliverance? And when He launches forth His Word against you Will you not be affrighted and fear?

And all the luminaries shall be affrighted with great fear, And all the earth shall be affrighted and tremble and be alarmed.

And all the angels shall execute their commands And shall seek to hide themselves from the presence of the Great Glory, And the children of earth shall tremble and quake; And ye sinners shall be cursed for ever, And ye shall have no peace.

Fear ye not, ye souls of the righteous, And be hopeful ye that have died in righteousness.

And grieve not if your soul into Sheol has descended in grief, And that in your life your body fared not according to your goodness, But wait for the day of the judgement of sinners And for the day of cursing and chastisement.

And yet when ye die the sinners speak over you: "As we die, so die the righteous, And what benefit do they reap for their deeds?

Behold, even as we, so do they die in grief and darkness, And what have they more than we? From henceforth we are equal.

And what will they receive and what will they see for ever? Behold, they too have died, And henceforth for ever shall they see no light."

I tell you, ye sinners, ye are content to eat and drink, and rob and sin, and strip men naked, and acquire wealth and see good days. Have ye seen the righteous how their end falls out, that no manner of violence is found in them till their death? "Nevertheless they perished and became as though they had not been, and their spirits descended into Sheol in tribulation."

CHAPTER 104

Now, therefore, I swear to you, the righteous, by the glory of the Great and Honoured and Mighty One in dominion, and by His greatness I swear to you.

I know a mystery And have read the heavenly tablets, And have seen the holy books, And have found written therein and inscribed regarding them:

That all goodness and joy and glory are prepared for them, And written down for the spirits of those who have died in righteousness, And that manifold good shall be given to you in recompense for your labours, And that your lot is abundantly beyond the lot of the living.

And the spirits of you who have died in righteousness shall live and rejoice, And their spirits shall not perish, nor their memorial from before the face of the Great One Unto all the generations of the world: wherefore no longer fear their contumely.

Woe to you, ye sinners, when ye have died, If ye die in the wealth of your sins, And those who are like you say regarding you: 'Blessed are the sinners: they have seen all their days.

And how they have died in prosperity and in wealth, And have not seen tribulation or murder in their life; And they have died in honour, And judgement has not been executed on them during their life."

Know ye, that their souls will be made to descend into Sheol And they shall be wretched in their great tribulation.

And into darkness and chains and a burning flame where there is grievous judgement shall your spirits enter; And the great judgement shall be for all the generations of the world. Woe to you, for ye shall have no peace.

Say not in regard to the righteous and good who are in life: "In our troubled days we have toiled laboriously and experienced every trouble, And met with much evil and been consumed, And have become few and our spirit small.

And we have been destroyed and have not found any to help us even with a word: We have been tortured [and destroyed], and not hoped to see life from day to day.

We hoped to be the head and have become the tail: We have toiled laboriously and had no satisfaction in our toil; And we have become the food of the sinners and the unrighteous, And they have laid their yoke heavily upon us.

They have had dominion over us that hated us and smote us; And to those that hated us we have bowed our necks But they pitied us not.

We desired to get away from them that we might escape and be at rest, But found no place whereunto we should flee and be safe from them.

And are complained to the rulers in our tribulation, And cried out against those who devoured us, But they did not attend to our cries And would not hearken to our voice.

And they helped those who robbed us and devoured us and those who made us few; and they concealed their oppression, and they did not remove from us the yoke of those that devoured us and dispersed us and murdered us, and they concealed their murder, and remembered not that they had lifted up their hands against us.

CHAPTER 105

I swear unto you, that in heaven the angels remember you for good before the glory of the Great One: and your names are written before the glory of the Great One. Be hopeful; for aforetime ye were put to shame through ill and affliction; but now ye shall shine as the lights of heaven, ye shall shine and ye shall be seen, and the portals of heaven shall be opened to you. And in your cry, cry for judgement, and it shall appear to you; for all your tribulation shall be visited on the rulers, and on all who helped those who plundered you. Be hopeful, and cast not away your hopes for ye shall have great joy as the angels of heaven. What shall ye be obliged to do? Ye shall not have to hide on the day of the great judgement and ye shall not be found as sinners, and the eternal judgement shall be far from you for all the generations of the world. And now

fear not, ye righteous, when ye see the sinners growing strong and pros-
pering in their ways: be not companions with them, but keep afar from
their violence; for ye shall become companions of the hosts of heaven.
And, although ye sinners say: "All our sins shall not be searched out and
be written down," nevertheless they shall write down all your sins every
day. And now I show unto you that light and darkness, day and night, see
all your sins. Be not godless in your hearts, and lie not and alter not the
words of uprightness, nor charge with lying the words of the Holy Great
One, nor take account of your idols; for all your lying and all your
godlessness issue not in righteousness but in great sin. And now I know
this mystery, that sinners will alter and pervert the words of righteousness in many ways, and will speak wicked words, and lie, and practice great deceits, and write books concerning their words. But when
they write down truthfully all my words in their languages, and do not
change or minish ought from my words but write them all down truthfully -all that I first testified concerning them. Then, I know another
mystery, that books will be given to the righteous and the wise to
become a cause of joy and uprightness and much wisdom. And to them
shall the books be given, and they shall believe in them and rejoice over
them, and then shall all the righteous who have learnt therefrom all the
paths of uprightness be recompensed.'

CHAPTER 106

In those days the Lord bade (them) to summon and testify to the children of earth concerning their wisdom: Show (it) unto them; for ye are
their guides, and a recompense over the whole earth. For I and My son
will be united with them for ever in the paths of uprightness in their
lives; and ye shall have peace: rejoice, ye children of uprightness. Amen.

BONUS: FRAGMENT OF THE BOOK OF NOAH

CHAPTER 107

And after some days my son Methuselah took a wife for his son Lamech, and she became pregnant by him and bore a son. And his body was white as snow and red as the blooming of a rose, and the hair of his head and his long locks were white as wool, and his eyes beautiful. And when he opened his eyes, he lighted up the whole house like the sun, and the whole house was very bright. And thereupon he arose in the hands of the midwife, opened his mouth, and conversed with the Lord of right-eousness. And his father Lamech was afraid of him and fled, and came to his father Methuselah. And he said unto him: 'I have begotten a strange son, diverse from and unlike man, and resembling the sons of the God of heaven; and his nature is different and he is not like us, and his eyes are as the rays of the sun, and his countenance is glorious. And it seems to me that he is not sprung from me but from the angels, and I fear that in his days a wonder may be wrought on the earth. And now, my father, I am here to petition thee and implore thee that thou mayest go to Enoch, our father, and learn from him the truth, for his dwelling-place is amongst the angels.' And when Methuselah heard the words of his son, he came to me to the ends of the earth; for he had heard that I was there, and he cried aloud, and I heard his voice and I came to him. And I said unto him: 'Behold, here am I, my son, wherefore hast thou come to me?' And he answered and said: 'Because of a great cause of anxiety have I come to thee, and because of a disturbing vision have I approached. And now, my father, hear me: unto Lamech my son there hath been born a son, the like of whom there is none, and his nature is not like man's nature, and the colour of his body is whiter than snow and redder than the bloom of a rose, and the hair of his head is whiter than white wool, and his eyes are like the rays of the sun, and he opened his eyes and thereupon lighted up the whole house. And he arose in the hands of the midwife, and opened his mouth and blessed the Lord of heaven. And his father Lamech became afraid and fled to me, and did not believe that he was sprung from him, but that he was in the likeness of the angels of heaven; and behold I have come to thee that thou mayest make known to me the truth.' And I, Enoch, answered and said unto him: 'The Lord will do a new thing on the earth, and this I have already seen in a vision, and make known to thee that in the generation of my father Jared some of the angels of heaven transgressed the word of the Lord. And behold they commit sin and transgress the law, and have united themselves with women and commit sin with them, and have married some of them, and have begot children by them. And they shall produce on the earth giants not according to the spirit, but according to the flesh, and there shall be a great punishment on the earth, and the earth shall be cleansed from all impurity. Yea, there shall come a great destruction over the whole earth, and there shall be a deluge and a great destruction for one year. And this son who has been born unto you shall be left on the earth, and his three children shall be saved with him: when all mankind that are on the earth shall die he and his sons shall be saved. And now make known to thy son Lamech that he who has been born is in truth his son, and call his name Noah; for he shall be left to you, and he and his sons shall be saved from the destruction, which shall come upon the earth on account of all the sin and all the unrighteousness, which shall be consummated on the earth in his days. And after that there shall be still more unrighteousness than that which was first consummated on the earth; for I know the mysteries of the holy ones; for He, the Lord, has showed me and informed me, and I have read them in the heavenly tablets.

Noah standing before the ark, under dark clouds, as rain begins to fall and animals gather around him.

CHAPTER 108

And I saw written on them that generation upon generation shall transgress, till a generation of righteousness arises, and transgression is destroyed and sin passes away from the earth, and all manner of good comes upon it. And now, my son, go and make known to thy son Lamech that this son, which has been born, is in truth his son, and that this is no lie.' And when Methuselah had heard the words of his father Enoch-for he had shown to him everything in secret-he returned and showed them to him and called the name of that son Noah; for he will comfort the earth after all the destruction.

CHAPTER 109

Another book which Enoch wrote for his son Methuselah and for those who will come after him, and keep the law in the last days. Ye who have done good shall wait for those days till an end is made of those who work evil; and an end of the might of the transgressors. And wait ye indeed till sin has passed away, for their names shall be blotted out of the book of life and out of the holy books, and their seed shall be destroyed for ever, and their spirits shall be slain, and they shall cry and make lamentation in a place that is a chaotic wilderness, and in the fire shall they burn; for there is no earth there. And I saw there something like an invisible cloud; for by reason of its depth I could not look over, and I saw a flame of fire blazing brightly, and things like shining mountains circling and sweeping to and fro. And I asked one of the holy angels who was with me and said unto him: 'What is this shining thing? for it is not a heaven but only the flame of a blazing fire, and the voice of weeping and crying and lamentation and strong pain.' And he said unto me: 'This place which thou seest-here are cast the spirits of sinners and blasphemers, and of those who work wicked-ness, and of those who pervert everything that the Lord hath spoken through the mouth of the prophets-(even) the things that shall be. For some of them are written and inscribed above in the heaven, in order that the angels may read them and know that which shall befall the sinners, and the spirits of the humble, and of those who have afflicted their bodies, and been recompensed by God; and of those who have been put to shame by wicked men: Who love God and loved neither gold nor silver nor any of the good things which are in the world, but gave over their bodies to torture. Who, since they came into being, longed not after earthly food, but regarded everything as a passing breath, and lived accordingly, and the Lord tried them much, and their spirits were found pure so that they should bless His name. And all the blessings destined for them I have recounted in the books. And he hath assigned them their recompense, because they have been found to be such as loved heaven more than their life in the world, and though they were trodden under foot of wicked men, and experienced abuse and reviling from them and were put to shame, yet they blessed Me. And now I will summon the spirits of the good who belong to the generation of light, and I will transform those who were born in darkness, who in the flesh were not recompensed with such honour as their faithfulness deserved. And I will bring forth in shining light those who have loved My holy name, and I will seat each on the throne of his honour. And they shall be resplendent for times without number; for righteousness is the judgement of God; for to the faithful He will give faithfulness in the habitation of upright paths. And they shall see those who were born in darkness led into darkness, while the righteous shall be resplendent. And the sinners shall cry aloud and see them resplendent, and they indeed will go where days and seasons are prescribed for them.'

2 ENOCH

THE BOOK OF THE SECRETS OF ENOCH (SLAVONIC ENOCH)

TRANSLATION: FRANCIS I. ANDERSEN

THE BOOK OF THE SECRETS OF ENOCH

CHAPTER 1A

A wise man and a great artisan whom the LORD took away.

And he loved him so that he might see the highest realms;

And of the most wise and great and inconceivable and unchanging kingdom of God almighty, and of the most marvelous and glorious and shining and many-eyed station of the LORD's servants, and of the LORD's immovable throne, and of the ranks and organization of the bodiless armies, and of the indescribable composition of the multitude of elements, singing of the army of the cherubim, and of the light without measure, to be an eyewitness.

CHAPTER 1

At that time he said, When 165 years were complete for me, I fathered my son Methusala; and after that I lived 200 years.

I completed all the years of my life, 365 years. In the first month, on the assigned day of the first month, I was in my house alone.

And I lay on my bad sleeping. And, while I slept, a great distress entered my heart, and I was weeping with my eyes in a dream. And I could not figure out what this distress might be, |nor| what might be happening to me. Then two huge men appeared to me, the like of which I had never seen on earth.

Their faces were like the shining sun;

their eyes were like burning lamps;

from their mouths fire was coming forth;

their clothing was various singing;

their wings were more glistening than gold;

their hands were whiter than snow.

And they stood at the head of my bed and called me by my name.

Then I awake from my sleep, and saw those men, standing in front of me, in actuality.

Then I bowed down to them; and I was terrified; and the appearance of my face was changed because of fear. Then those men said to me, "Be brave, Enoch! In truth, do not fear! The eternal God has sent us to you. And behold, you will ascend with us to heaven today. And tell your sonseverything that they must do in your house while they are without you on the earth. And let no one search for you until the LORD returns you to them." And I hurried and obeyed them; and I went out of my house and I shut the doors as I had been ordered. And I called my sons, Methusalam and Regim and Gaidad. And I declared to them all the marvels that those men had told me.

A depiction of Enoch being approached by two radiant angels, ascending from Earth into the heavens.

CHAPTER 2

"Listen, my children! I do not know where I am going,

nor what will confront me. Now, my children, I say to you:

Do not turn away from God.

Walk before his face, and keep his commandments.

Do not abhor the prayers of your salvation, so that the LORD will not curtail the work of your hands.

And do not be ungenerous with the LORD's gifts, and the LORD will not be ungenerous with his donations and love-gifts in your storehouses.

And bless the LORD with the firstborn of your herds and the firstborn of your children, and the blessing will be on you forever.

And do not turn away from the LORD, and do not worship vain gods, gods who did not created the heaven and the earth or any other created thing; for they will perish, and so will those who worship them.

And may God make your hearts true in reverence for him.

And now, my children, no one must search for me until the LORD returns me to you."

CHAPTER 3

And it came about, when I had spoken to my sons, those med called me. And they took me up onto their wings, and carried me up to the first heaven, and placed me on the clouds. And, behold, they were moving. And there I perceived the air higher up, and higher still I saw the ether. And they placed me on the first heaven. And they showed me a vast ocean, much bigger than the earthly ocean.

CHAPTER 4

They led before my face the elders, the rulers of the stellar orders.

And they showed me the 200 angels who govern the stars and the heavenly combinations. And they fly with their wings, and do the rounds of all the planets.

CHAPTER 5

And there I perceived the treasuries of the snow and the ice, and the angels who guard their terrible storehouses, and the treasury of the clouds, from which they come out and go in.

CHAPTER 6

And they showed me the treasuries of the dew, like olive oil.

And the appearance of its image was like every kind of earthly flower , only more numerous; and the angels who guard their treasuries, how they are shut and opened.

CHAPTER 7

And those men picked me up and brought me up to the second heaven. And they showed me, and I saw a darkness greater than earthly darkness. And there I perceived prisoners under guard, hanging up, waiting for the measureless judgment. And those angels have the appearance of darkness itself, more than earthly darkness. And unceasingly they made weeping, all the day long. And I said to the men who were with me, "Why are these ones being tormented unceasingly?"

Those men answered me, "These are those who turned away from the LORD, who did not obey the LORD's commandments, but of their own will plotted together and turned away with their prince and with those who are under restraint in the fifth heaven." And I felt very sorry for them; and those angels bowed down to me and said to me, "Man of God, pray for us to the LORD!"

And I answered them and said, "Who am I, a mortal man, that I should pray for angels? Who knows where I am going and what will confront me? Or who indeed will pray for me?"

CHAPTER 8

And those men took me from there, and they brought me up to the third heaven, and set me down. Then I looked downward, and I saw Paradise. And that place is inconceivably pleasant.

And I saw the trees in full flower. And their fruits were ripe and pleasant-smelling, with every food in yield and giving off profusely a pleasant fragrance.

And in the midst (of them was) the tree of life, at that place where the LORD takes a rest when he goes into paradise. And that tree is indescribable for pleasantness and fine fragrance, and more beautiful than any (other) created thing that exists.

And from every direction it has an appearance which is good-looking and crimson, and with the form of fire. And it covers the whole of Paradise. And it has something of every orchard tree and of every fruit. And its root is in Paradise at the exit that leads to the earth.

And paradise is in between the corruptible and the incorruptible. And two streams come forth, one a source of honey and milk, and a source which produces oil and wine. And it is divided into 4 parts, and they go around with a quiet movement. And they come out into the paradise of Edem, between the corruptible and the incorruptible. And from there they pass along and divide into 40 parts. And it proceeds in descent along the earth, and they have a revolution in their cycle, just like the other atmospheric elements.

And there is no unfruitful tree there, and every tree is well fruited, and every place is blessed.

And there are 300 angels, very bright, who look after Paradise; and with never-ceasing voice and pleasant singing they worship the LORD every day and hour. And I said, "How very pleasant is this place!" And those men said to me:

CHAPTER 9

"This place, Enoch, has been prepared for the righteous,

who suffer every kind of calamity in their life

and who afflict their souls,

and who avert their eyes from injustice,

and who carry out righteous judgment,

and who give bread to the hungry,

and who cover the naked with clothing,

and who lift up the fallen

and who help the injured and the orphans,

and who walk without a defect before the face of the LORD,

and who worship him only –

even for them this place has been prepared as an eternal inheritance."

CHAPTER 10

And those men carried me

to the northern region; and they showed me there a very frightful place;

and all kinds of torture and torment are in that place, cruel darkness and lightless gloom. And there is no light there, and a black fire blazes up perpetually, with a river of fire that comes out over the whole place, fire here, freezing ice there, and it dries up and it freezes;

and very cruel places of detention and dark and merciless angels, carrying instruments of atrocities torturing without pity.

And I said, "Woe, woe! How very frightful this place is!" And those men said to me, "This place, Enoch, has been prepared for those who do not glorify God, who practice on the earth the sin of witchcraft, enchantments, divinations, trafficking with demons, who boast about their evil deeds and who steal the souls of men secretly, seizing the poor by the throat, taking away their possessions, enriching themselves from the possessions of others, defrauding them; who, when they are able to provide sustenance, bring about the death of the hungry by starvation; and, when they are able to provide clothing, take away the last garment of the naked; who do not acknowledge their Creator, but bow down to idols which have no souls, which can neither see nor hear, vain gods; constructing images, and bowing down to vile things made by hands – for all these this place has been prepared as an eternal reward."

CHAPTER 11

And those men took me and they carried me up to the fourth heaven. And they showed me there all the movements and sequences, and all the rays of solar and lunar light. And I measured their movements and I compared their light. And I saw that the sun has a light seven times greater than the moon. And I saw his circle and his wheels on which he always goes, going past always like the wind with quite marvelous speed. And his coming and his return give him no rest, day and night.

And 4 great stars, each star having 1000 stars under it, on the right hand side of the sun's chariot, and 4 on the left-hand side, each one having 1000 stars under it, all together 8000, going with the sun perpetually.

And 150,000 angels accompany him in the daytime, and at night 1000. And 100 angels go in front of the sun's chariot, six-winged, in flaming fire; and the sun blazes up and sets the 100 angels on fire.

CHAPTER 12

And flying spirits, the solar elements, called phoenixes and khalkedras, strange and wonderful. For their form was that of a lion, their tail that of a ..., and their head that of a crocodile. Their appearance was multicolored, like a rainbow. Their size was 900 measures. Their wings were those of angels, but they have 12 wings each. They accompany and run with the sun, carrying heat and dew, whatever is commanded from God.

Thus he goes through a cycle, and he goes down and he rises up across the sky and beneath the earth with the light of his rays. And he was there, on the track, unceasingly.

CHAPTER 13

And those men carried me away to the east.

And they showed methe solar gates through which the sun comes out according to the appointment of the seasons and according to the phases of the moon, for the entire year, and according to the numbers on the horologe, day and night. And I saw 6 open gates, each gate having 61 stadia and a quarter of a stadium. And I measured carefully and I figured out their size to be so much – through which the sun comes out and goes off to the west.

And it becomes even and goes through all the months.

And the 1st gate he comes out for 42 days,

the second 35 days,

the third 35 days,

the fourth 35 days,

the fifth 35 days,

the sixth 42 days.

And then once more he does an about-turn and goes back the other way from the sixth gate, according to the round of the seasons:

And he goes in through the fifth gate 35 days,

the 4th 35 days,

the 3rd 35 days,

the second 35 days.

And so the whole year are completed, according to the cycle of the four seasons.

CHAPTER 14

And then those men carried me away to the west of the heaven, and they showed me six large open gates, corresponding to the circuit of the eastern gates, opposite them, where the sun sets according to the number of the days, 365 and ¼.

Thus he goes back once again to the eastern gates, under the earth. And when he goes out from the western gates, he takes off his light, the splendor which is his radiance, and four hundred angels take his crown and carry it to the LORD. For, since his shining crown is with God, with 400 angels guarding it, the sunturns his chariot aroundand goes back under the earth on wheels, without the great light which is his great radiance and ornament. For seven great hours in night. And the chariot spends half its time under the earth. And when he comes to the eastern approaches, in the 8th hour of the night, the 400 angels, bring back the crown, and crown him. And his brightness and the shining of his crown are seen before sunrise. And the sun blazes out more than fire does.

CHAPTER 15

And then the solar elements, called phoenixes and khalkedras, burst into song. That is why every bird flaps its wings, rejoicing at the giver of light. And they burst into song at the LORD's command:

The light-giver is coming,

to give radiance to the whole world;

and the morning watch appears,

which is the sun's rays.

And the sun comes out over the face of the earth,

and retrieves his radiance,

to give light to all the face of the earth.

And they showed me this calculation of the sun's movement, and the gates by which he goes in and goes out; for these are the great gates which God created to be an annual horologe.

This is why the sun has the greater heat; and the cycle for him goes on for 28 years, and begins once more from the start.

CHAPTER 16

And another calculation those men showed me, that of the moon, and all the movements and phases;

12 big gates, crowned from the west to the east, through which the moon goes in and goes out, in accordance with the regular seasons.

She goes in by the first western gate, in the place of the sun –

by the 1ˢᵗ gate for 31 days exactly,

the 2ⁿᵈ for 35 days exactly,

the 3ʳᵈ for 30 days exactly,

the 4ᵗʰ for 30 days exactly,

the 5ᵗʰ for 31 days extraordinarily,

the 6ᵗʰ for 31 days exactly,

the 7ᵗʰ for 30 days exactly,

the 8ᵗʰ for 31 days exactly,

the 9ᵗʰ for 31 days accurately,

the 10ᵗʰ for 30 days exactly,

the 11ᵗʰ for 31 days exactly,

the 12ᵗʰ for 28 days exactly.

Thus likewise by the western gates in accordance with the cycle, and in accordance with the number of the eastern gates.

And thus she goes, and completes the solar year 365 and ½ of one day.

But the lunar year has 354, making 12 months, in accordance with 29 days. And it lacks 12 days of the solar cycle, which are the lunar epacts for each year. Also, the great cycle contains 532 years.

It passes by the quarters for three years, and the fourth completes it exactly. For this reason they are taken away, outside heaven, for three years; and they are not added to the number of the days, because these ones change the seasons of the year – two new moons in augmentation, two others in diminution.

And when the western gates are completed, she turns around and goes to the eastern ones with her light. Thus she goes, day and night, in accordance with the heavenly cycles, lower than all the cycles, swifter than the heavenly winds, and spirits and elements and flying angels, with 6 wings to each angel. And the moon has a sevenfold intercalation, and a period of revolution of 19 years. And she begins once again from the start.

CHAPTER 17

In the middle of the heaven I saw armed troops, worshiping the LORD with tympani and pipes and unceasing voices, and pleasant, and various songs, which it is impossible to describe. And every mind would be quite astonished, so marvelous and wonderful is the singing of these angels. And I was delighted, listening to them.

CHAPTER 18

And those men took me up on their wings and placed me on the fifth heaven. And I saw there many innumerable armies called Grigori. And their appearance was like the appearance of a human being, and their size was larger than that of large giants. And their faces were dejected, and the silence of their mouths was perpetual. And there was no liturgy in the fifth heaven. I said to the men who were with me, "What is the explanation that these ones are so very dejected, and their faces miserable, and their mouths silent? And is there no liturgy in this heaven?" And those men answered me, "These are the Grigori, who turned aside from the LORD, 200 myriads, together with their prince Satanail. And similar to them are those who went down as prisoners in their train, who are in the second heaven, imprisoned in great darkness.

And three of them descended to the earth from the LORD's Throne onto the place Ermon. And they broke the promise on the shoulder of Mount Ermon. And they saw the daughters of men, how beautiful they were; and they took wives for themselves, and the earth was defiled by their deeds.

Whoin the entire time of this age acted lawlessly and practiced miscegenation and gave birth to giants and great monsters and great enmity.

And that is why God has judged them with a great judgment; and they mourn their brothers, and they will be outrages on the great day of the LORD." And I said to the Grigori, "I have seen your brothers and their deeds and their torments and their great prayers; and I have prayed for them. But the LORD has sentenced them under the earth until heaven and earth are ended forever." And I said, "Why are you waiting for your brothers? And why don't you perform the liturgy before the face of the LORD? Start up your liturgy, and perform the liturgy before the face of the LORD, so that you do not enrage your LORD to the limit."

And they responded to my recommendations, and they stood in four regiments in this heaven. And behold, while I was standing with those men, 4 trumpets trumpeted in unison with a great sound, and the Grigori burst into singing in unison. And their voice rose in front of the face of the LORD, piteously and touchingly.

A depiction of Enoch traveling through the seven heavens, encountering various angelic beings and celestial wonders. with Enoch moving towards a divine, glowing destination.

CHAPTER 19

And those men took me from there, and they carried me up to the 6ᵗʰheaven. And I saw there 7 groups of angels, brilliant and very glorious. And their faces were more radiant than the radiance of the sun, and there was no difference between their faces or in their dimensions of in the style of their clothing.

And these groups carry out and carefully study the movements of the stars, and the revolution of the sun and the phases of the moon, and the well-being of the cosmos.

And when they see any evil activity, they put the commandments and instructions in order, and the sweet choral singing and every kind of glorious praise. These are the archangels who are over the angels; and they harmonize all existence, heavenly and earthly; and angels who are over seasons and years, and angels who are over rivers and the ocean, and angels who are over the fruits of the earth and over every kind of grass, and who give every kind of food to every kind of living thing; and angels who record all human souls, and all their deeds, and their lives before the face of the LORD.

And in the midst of them are 7 phoenixes and 7 cherubim and 7 six-winged beings, having but one voice and singing in unison. And their song is not to be reported; and the LORD is delighted by his footstool.

CHAPTER 20

And those men lifted me up from there, and they carried me up to the 7thheaven. And I saw there an exceptionally great light, and all the fiery armies of the great archangels, and the incorporeal forces and the dominions and the origins and the authorities, the cherubim and the seraphim and the many-eyed thrones; and 5 regiments and the shining *otanim* stations. And I was terrified, and I trembled with a great fear.

And those men picked me up and led me into their midst. And they said to me, "Be brave, Enoch! Don't be frightened!"

And they showed me the LORD, from a distance, sitting on his exceedingly high throne. For what is God, and it is called in the Hebrew language Aravoth. And all the heavenly armies came and stood on the ten steps, corresponding to their ranks, and they did obeisance to the LORD.

And then they went to their places in joy and merriment and in immeasurable light, singing songs with soft and gentle voices, while presenting the liturgy to him gloriously.

CHAPTER 21

And they do not leave by night, nor depart by day, standing in front of the face of the LORD, and carrying out his will – cherubim and seraphim standing all around his throne, six-winged and many-eyed; they cover his entire throne, singing with gentle voice, in front of the face of the LORD.

Holy, Holy, Holy, LORD Sabaoth,

Heaven and earth are full of his glory.

And when I had seen all these things, those men said to me, "Enoch, up to this point we have been commanded to travel with you." And the men went away from me, and from then on I did not see them anymore. But I, I remained alone at the edge of the seventh heaven. And I became terrified; and I fell on my face, and I said in myself, "Woe to me! What has happened to me?"

And the LORD sent one of his glorious ones, the Archangel Gabriel. And he said to me, "Be brave, Enoch! Don't be frightened! Stand up, and come with me and stand in front of the face of the LORD forever."

And I answered him and said, "Woe to me, my LORD! My soul has departed from me from fear and horror. And call the two men who brought me to this place, because I have put my confidence in them, and with them I will go before the face of the LORD." And Gabriel carried me up, like a leaf carried up by the wind. He moved me along and put me down in front of the face of the LORD. And I saw the eighth heaven, which is called in the Hebrew language Muzaloth, the changer of the seasons, of dry and of wet, and the 12 zodiacs, which are above the seventh heaven. And I saw the ninth heaven, which in the Hebrew language is called Kukhavim, where the heavenly houses of the 12 zodiacs are.

CHAPTER 22

And on the 10th heaven, Aravoth, I saw the view of the face of the LORD, like iron made burning hot in a fire brought out, and it emits sparks and is incandescent. Thus even I saw the face of the LORD. But the face of the LORD is not to be talked about, it is so very marvelous and supremely awesome and supremely frightening. Who am I to give an account of the incomprehensible being of the LORD, and of his face, so extremely strange and indescribable? And how many are his commands, and his multiple voice, and the LORD's throne, supremely great and not made by hands, and the choir stalls all around him, the cherubim and the seraphim armies, and their never-silent singing.

Who can give an account of his beautiful appearance, never changing and indescribable, and his great glory?

And I fell down flat and did obeisance to the LORD. And the LORD, with his own mouth, said to me, "Be brave, Enoch! Don't be frightened! Stand up, and stand in front of my face forever." And Michael, the LORD's archistratig, lifted me up and brought me in front of the face of the LORD. And the LORD said to his servants, sounding them out, "Let Enoch join in and stand in front of my face forever!" And the LORD's glorious ones did obeisance and said, "Let Enoch yield in accordance with your word, O LORD!"

And the LORD said to Michael, "Go, and extract Enoch from earthly clothing. And anoint him with my delightful oil, and put him into the clothes of my glory." And so Michael did, just as the LORD had said to him. He anointed me and clothed me. And the appearance of that oil is greater than the greatest light, and its ointment is like sweet dew, and its fragrance myrrh; and it is like the rays of the glittering sun. And I looked at myself, and I had become like one of his glorious ones, and there was no observable difference. And the LORD summoned one of his archangels, Vrevoil by name, who was swifter in wisdom than the other archangels, and who records all the LORD's deeds. And the LORD said to Vrevoil, "Bring out the books from my storehouses, and fetch a pen for speed-writing, and give it to Enoch and read him the books." And Vrevoil hurried and brought me the books, a knife, and ink. And he gave me the pen for speed writing from his hand.

CHAPTER 23

And he was telling me all the things of heaven and earth and sea and all the elements and the movements and their courses, and the living thunder, the sun and the moon and the stars, their courses and their changes, and seasons and years and days and hours, and the coming of the clouds and the blowing of the winds, and the number of the angels and the songs of the armed troops; and every kind of human thing, and every kind of language, and singing, and human life and rules and instructions and sweet voiced singing, and everything that it is appropriate to learn.

And Vrevoil instructed me for 30 days and 30 nights, and his mouth never stopped speaking. And, as for me, I did not rest, writing all the symbols and all the creatures. And when I had finished 30 days and 30 nights, Vrevoil said to me, "These things, whatever I have taught you, whatever you have learned, and whatever we have written down, you sit down and write – all the souls of men, whatever of them are not yet born, and their places, prepared for eternity.

For all the souls are prepared for eternity, before the composition of the earth." And I sat down for a second period of 30 days and 30 nights, and I wrote everything accurately. And I wrote 366 books.

A depiction of Enoch standing before the magnificent throne of God in the highest heaven.

CHAPTER 24

And the Lord called me; and he said to me, "Enoch, sit to the left of me with Gabriel." And I did obeisance to the LORD.

And the LORD spoke to me: "Enoch, whatever you see and whatever things are standing still or moving about were brought to perfection by me. And I myself will explain it to you.

Before anything existed at all, from the very beginning, whatever exists I created from the non-existent, and from the invisible the visible.

For not even to my angels have I explained my secrets, nor related to them their origin, nor my endlessness and inconceivableness, as I devise the creatures, as I am making them known to you today. For, before any visible things had come into existence,

I, the ONE, moved around in the invisible things, like the sun,

from east to west and from west to east.

But the sun has rest in himself; yet I did not find rest, because everything was not yet created. And I thought up the idea of establishing a foundation, to create a visible creation.

CHAPTER 25

"And I commanded the lowest things: 'Let one of the invisible things descend visibly!' And Adoil descended, extremely large. And I looked at him, and, behold, in his belly he had a great light. And I said to him, 'Disintegrate yourself, Adoil, and let what is born from you become visible.' And he disintegrated himself, and there came out a very great light. And I was in the midst of the light. And light out of light is carried thus. And the great age came out, and it revealed all the creation which I had thought up to create. And I saw how good it was.

And I placed for myself a throne, and I sat down on it. And then to the light I spoke: 'You go up higher, and be solidified, and become the foundation for the highest things.

And there is nothing higher than the light, except nothing itself. And again I bowed myself, and I looked upward from my throne.

CHAPTER 26

And I called out a second time into the very lowest things, and I said, 'Let one of the invisible things come out visibly, solid.'

Arkhas came out, solid and heavy and very red.And I said, 'Open yourself up, Arkhas, and let what is born from you become visible!' And he disintegrated himself. There came out an age, dark, very large, carrying the creation of all lower things. And I saw how good it was.

And I said to him, 'Come down low and become solid! And become the foundation of the lowest things!' And he came down and became solid. And he became the foundation of the lowest things. And there is nothing lower than the darkness, except nothing itself.

CHAPTER 27

"And I gave the command: 'Let there be taken some of the light and some of the darkness.' And I said, 'Become thickened, and be wrapped around with light!' And I spread it out, and it became water.

And I spread it out above the darkness, below the light. And thus I made the solid waters, that is to say, the Bottomless. And I made a foundation of light around the water. And I created seven great circles inside it, and I gave them an appearance of crystal, wet and dry, that is to say glass and ice, and to be the circuit for water and the other elements. And I pointed out to each one his route, to the seven stars, each one of them in his own heaven, so that they might travel accordingly.

And I saw how good it was. And I made a division between the light and between the darkness, that is to say, in the middle of the waters, this way and that way. And I said to the light that it should be day, and to the darknessI commanded that it should be night. And evening came, and again morning came, that is the first day.

CHAPTER 28

"And thus I made solid the heavenly circles. AndI said, 'Let the lower water, which is below heaven, collect itself into one collection, and let its waves become dry.' And it happened like that.

And from the waves I created rocks, solid and big. And from the rocks I assembled the dry land; and I called the dry land Earth.

And what was in the middle of the earth I called chasm, that is to say, Bottomless. The sea I gathered into one place, and I bound it with a yoke. And I said to the sea: 'Behold, I give you an eternal boundary. And you will not break through from your own waters.' And so I fixed the solid structure and established it above the waters.

This first-created day I named for myself. Then evening came and again morning, and it was the second day.

CHAPTER 29

"And for all my own heavens I shaped a shape from the fiery substance. My eye looked at the solid and very hard rock. And from the flash of my eye I took the substance of lightning, both fire in water and water in fire; neither does this one extinguish that one, nor does that one dry out this one. That is why lightning is sharper and brighter than the shining of the sun, and softer than water, more solid than the hardest rock.

And from the rock I cut off a great fire, and from the fire I created the ranks of the bodiless armies – the myriad angels – and their weapons are fiery and their clothes are burning flames. And I gave orders that each should stand in his own rank.

But one from the order of the archangels deviated, together with the division that was under his authority. He thought up the impossible idea, that he might place his throne higher than the clouds which are above the earth, and that he might become equal to my power.

And I hurled him out from the height, together with his angels. And he was flying around in the air, ceaselessly above the Bottomless.

And thus I created the entire heavens. And the third day came."

CHAPTER 30

"And on the third day I commanded the earth to make trees grow, large and fruit-bearing; and the mountains – all kinds ofsweet grass and all kinds ofsown seed. And I laid out paradise as a garden, and I enclosed it; and I placed armed guards, angels aflame with fire. And thus I created the renewal of the earth.

And then evening came and morning came – the fourth day.

And on the fourth day I commanded: 'Let there be great lamps on the heavenly circles.'

On the first, the highest circle, I placed the star Kronos;

on the 2nd, lower down, I placed Afridit;

on the 3rd Arris;

on the 4th the sun;

on the 5th Zeous;

on the 6th Ermis;

and on the 7th, the lowest, the moon.

And with the lowest stars I beautified the air below.

And I appointed the sun over the illumination of the day, but the moon and stars over the illumination of the night. And the sun goes in accordance with each animal, and the twelve animals are the succession of the months. And I assigned their names and the animals of their seasons, and their connection with the newborn, and their horoscopes, and how they revolve. Then evening came and morning came – the fifth day.

And on the 5th day I commanded the sea to engender fishes and feathered birds of many different kinds, and every kind of reptile that creeps on the earth and that walks on the earth of four legs and that flies through the air – male sex and female – and every kind of soul that breathes the breath of all living things. And evening came and morning came – the sixth day.

And on the sixth day I commanded my wisdom to create man out of the seven components:

his flesh from earth;

his blood from and from the sun;

his eyes from the bottomless sea;

his bones from stone;

his reason from the mobility of angels and from clouds;

his veins and hair from grass of the earth;

his spirit from my spirit and from wind.

And I gave him 7 properties:

hearing to the flesh;

sight to the eyes;

smell to the spirit;

touch to the veins;

taste to the blood;

to the bones– endurance ;

to the reason– sweetness.

Behold, I have thought up an ingenious poem to recite:

From invisible and visible substances I created man.

From both his natures come both death and life.

And as my image he knows the word like no other creature.

But even at his greatest he is small,

and again at his smallest he is great.

And on the earth I assigned him to be a second angel, honored and

great and glorious. And I assigned him to be a king, to reign the earth, to have my wisdom. And there was nothing comparable to him on earth, even among my creatures that exist. And I assigned to him a name from the four components:

from East – (A)

from West – (D)

from North − (A)⎣⎡⎣⎡⎣ |South| − (M)

from South − (M) ⎣⎡⎣⎡ |North| − (A).

And I assigned to him four special stars, and called his name Adam.

And I gave him his free will; and I pointed out to him the two ways − light and darkness. And I said to him, 'This is good for you, but that is bad'; so that I might come to know whether he has love toward me or abhorrence, and so that it might become plain who among his race loves me.

Whereas I have come to know his nature, he does not know his own nature. That is why ignorance is more lamentable than the sin such as it is in him to sin. And I said, 'After sin there is nothing for it but death.'

And I assigned a shade for him; and I imposed sleep upon him, and he fell asleep. And while he was sleeping, I took from him a rib. And I created for him a wife, so that death might come by his wife.

And I took his last word, and I called her name Mother, that is to say, Euva.

A depiction of God revealing the creation of the world to Enoch, with scenes of the
Earth forming.

CHAPTER 31

"Adam – Mother; earthly and life. And I created a garden in Edem, in
the east, so that he might keep the agreement and preserve the
commandment.

And I created for him an open heaven, so that he might look upon the
angels, singing the triumphal song. And the light which is never darkened was perpetually in paradise. And the devil understood how I
wished to create another world, so that everything could be subjected to
Adam on the earth, to rule and reign over it. The devil is of the lowest
places. And he will become a demon, because he fled from heaven;

Sotona, because his name was Satanail. In this way he became different from the angels. His nature did not change, but his thought did, since his consciousness of righteous and sinful things changed. And he became aware of his condemnation and of the sin which he sinned previously. And that is why he thought up the scheme against Adam. In such a form he entered paradise, and corrupted Eve. But Adam he did not contact.

But on account of her nescience I cursed him. But those whom I had blessed previously, them I did not curse; and those whom I had not blessed previously, even them I did not curse— neither mankind I cursed, nor the earth, nor any other creature, but only mankind's evil fruit-bearing.

This is why the fruit of doing good is sweat and exertion.

CHAPTER 32

"And I said, 'You are earth, and into the earth once again you will go, out of which I took you. And I will not destroy you, but I will send you away to what I took you from. Then I can take you once again at my second coming.' And I blessed all my creatures, visible and invisible. And Adam was in paradise for 5 hours and a half.

And I blessed the 7th day in which I rested from all my doings.

CHAPTER 33

"On the eighth day I likewise appointed, so that the 8th day might be the 1st, the first-created of my week, and that it should revolve in the revolution of 7000; so that the 8000 might be in the beginning of a time not reckoned and unending, neither years, nor months, nor weeks, nor days, nor hours like the first day of the week, so also that the eighth day of the week might return continually.

And now, Enoch, whatever I have told you, and whatever you have understood, and whatever you have seen in the heavens, and whatever you have seen on the earth, and whatever I have written in the books —

by my supreme wisdom all these things I planned to accomplish. And I created them for the highest foundation to the lowest, and to the end.

And there is no adviser and no successor to my creation. I am self-eternal and not made by hands. My thought is without change. My wisdom is my adviser and my deed is my word. And my eyes look at all things.If I look at all things, then they stand still and shake with terror; but, if I should turn my face away, then all things would perish.

Apply your mind, Enoch, and acknowledge the One who is speaking. And you take the books which you yourself have written.

And I give you Samoila and Raguila, who brought you up to me. And you go down onto the earth and tell your sons all that I have told you and everything that you have seen, from the lowest heavens up to my throne.

I created all the armies and all their forces. And there is no one who opposes me or who is insubordinate to me; for all submit themselves to my sole rule and work my sole dominion.

And give them the books in your handwriting, and they will read them and they will acknowledge me as the Creator of everything. And they will understand that there is no other God except myself.

And let them distribute the books in your handwriting,

children to children and family to family and kinsfolk to kinsfolk.

And I will give you, Enoch, my mediator, my archistratig, Michael, on account of your handwritings and the handwritings of your fathers – Adam and Sith and Enos and Kainan and Maleleil and Ared your father. And they will not be destroyed until the final age. So I have commanded my angels, Ariukh and Pariukh, whom I have appointed on the earth as their guardians, and I have commanded the seasons, so that they might preserve them so that they might no perish in the future flood which I shall create in your generation.

CHAPTER 34

"For I know the wickedness of mankind, how they will not carry the yoke which I have placed on them.

But they will cast off my yoke, and they will accept a different yoke. And they will sow worthless seed, worship vain gods, and they renounced my uniqueness.

And all the world will be reduced to confusion by iniquities and wickednesses and fornications and the worship of the evil one.

And that is why I shall bring down the flood onto the earth, and the earth itself will collapse in great darkness.

CHAPTER 35

"And I will leave a righteous man from your tribe, together with all his house, who will act in accordance with my will.

And from his seed another generation will arise, the last of many, but even out of those the majority will be very insatiable.

And I shall raise up for that generation someone who will reveal to them the books in your handwriting and those of your fathers. And he will have to point out to them the guard tower of the earth, truthful men, and those who carry out my will, who do not invoke my name invalidly.

And you will tell that generation; and they, when they have read them, will be more glorified in the end than in the beginning."

CHAPTER 36

"And now, Enoch, I am giving you a waiting period of 30 days to set your house in order to instruct your sons about everything from me personally, so that they may obey what is said to them by you. And they will read and understand that there is no other God apart from myself, so that they may carry out all your instructions and study the books in your handwriting.

And after 30 days I shall send for you my angel, and he will take you up from the earth and from your sons to me."

CHAPTER 37

And the LORD called one of the senior angels, terrifying and frightful, and he made him stand with me. And the appearance of that angel was as white as snow, and his hands like ice, having the appearance of great frigidity. And he chilled my face, because I could not endure the terror of the LORD, just as it is not possible to endure the fire of a stove and the heat of the sun and the frost of death.

And the LORD said to me, "Enoch, if your face had not been chilled here, no human being would be able to look at your face."

CHAPTER 38

And the LORD said to those men who had brought me up at the first, "Let Enoch descend onto the earth with you. And wait for him until the specified day." And they placed me at highttime on my bed. And Methusalam was anticipating my arrival, mounting strict guard at my bed and he was terrified when he heard my arrival. And I said to him, "Let all the members of my household come down." Then I said to them:

CHAPTER 39

"O my children, my beloved ones! Give heed, my children, to whatever is in accordance with the will of the LORD. I have been sent today to you from the lips of the LORD, to speak to you whatever has been and whatever is now and whatever will be until the day of judgment. Listen, my children, it is not from my own lips that I am reporting to you today, but form the lips of the LORD I have been sent to you. For you hear my words, out of my lips, a human being created exactly equal to yourselves; but I have heard from the fiery lips of the LORD. For the lips of the LORD are a furnace of fire, and his angels are the flames which come out. But you, my children, see my face, a human being created just like yourselves; but I am one who has seen the face of the LORD, like iron made burning hot by a fire, and it is brought out and it emits sparks and it is incandescent. But you gaze into my eyes, a human being equal in significance to yourselves; but I have gazed into the eyes of the LORD, shining like the rays of the sun and terrifying the eyes of a human being. But you, my children, see the right hand of one who helps you, a human being created identical to yourselves; but I have seen the right hand of the LORD, helping me and filling heaven.

But you see the scope of my activity, the same as your own; but I have seen the scope of the LORD, without limit and without analogy, and to which there is no end.

For you hear the sayings of my lips, but I have heard the LORD speaking like loud thunder, when there is a continual disturbance in the clouds. And now, my children, listen to the discourses of your earthly father. Frightening and dangerous it is to stand before the face of an earthly king, terrifying and very dangerous it is, because the will of the king is death and the will of the king is life. How much more terrifying it is to stand before the face of the King of earthly kings and of the heavenly armies, who can endure that endless misery?

CHAPTER 40

"And now therefore, my children, I know everything; for either form the lips of the LORD or else my eyes have seen from the beginning even to the end, and from the end to the recommencement.

I know everything, and everything I have written down in books, the heavens and their boundaries and their contents. And all the armies and their movements I have measured. And I have recorded the stars and the multitude of multitudes innumerable. What human being can see their cycles and their phases?

For not even the angels know their number. But I have

written down all their names. The solar circle I have measured, and its rays I have counted; and its entrances in all the months, and its departures, and all its movements – their names I have written down. The lunar circle I have measured, and its movements which are in accordance with each day, and the diminution which it undergoes during each day and night in accordance with all the hours.

I appointed 4 seasons, and from the seasons I created 4 cycles, and in the cycles I appointed the year, and I appointed months, and from the months I counted days, and from the days I measured off the hours and I counted them and wrote them down. And everything that is nourished on the earth I have investigated and written down, and every seed, sown and not sown, which grows form the earth, and all the garden plants, and all the grasses, and all the flowers, and their delightful fragrances and their names.

And the dwelling places of the clouds, their organization and their wings, and how they carry the rain and the raindrops – all this I investigated.

And I wrote down the rumble of the thunder and the lightning: and they showed me the keys and their keepers, and the places where they go, where they go in and where they go out, by measure. They are raised by means of a chain, and they are lowered by means of a chain, so that he does not drop the clouds of anger with terrible injuries and violence, and destroy everything on the earth.

I wrote down the treasuries of the snow, and the storehouses of the cold, and the frosty winds. And I observed how, depending on the season, their custodians fill up the clouds with them, and their treasuries are not emptied.

I wrote down the sleeping chambers of the winds, and I observed and I saw how their custodians carry scales and measures. And first they place them on the scales, and secondly in the measure, and it is my measure that they release them skillfully into all the earth, lest the earth should be rocked by violent gusts.

I measured all the earth, and its mountains and hills and fields and woods and stones and rivers, and everything that exists. I wrote down the height from the earth to the seventh heaven, and the depth to the lowermost hell, and the place of condemnation, and the supremely large hell, open and weeping.

And I saw how the prisoners were in pain, looking forward to endless punishment; and I recorded all those who have been condemned by the judge, and all their sentences and all their corresponding deeds.

CHAPTER 41

"I saw all those from the age of my ancestors, with Adam and Eve. And I sighed and burst into tears. Concerning their disreputable depravity, 'Oh how miserable for me is my incapacity and that of my ancestors!'

And I thought in my heart and I said, 'How blessed is the person who has not been born, or who, having been born, has not sinned before the face of the LORD, so that he will not come into this place nor carry the yoke of this place.'

A depiction of Enoch receiving divine instructions and prophecies about the future from God, with visions of the final judgment.

CHAPTER 42

"And I saw the key-holders and the guards of the gates of hell standing, as large as serpents, with their faces like lamps that have been extinguished, and their eyes aflame, and their teeth naked down to their breasts.

And I said to their faces, 'It would have been better if I had not seen you, nor heard about your activities, nor that any member of my tribe had been brought to you. To what a small extent they have sinned in this life, but in the eternal life they will suffer forever.'

And I ascended to the east, into the paradise of Edem, where rest is prepared for the righteous. And it is open as far as the 3rd heaven; but it is closed off from this world.

And the guards are appointed at the very large gates of the east of the sun, angels of flame, singing victory songs, never silent, rejoicing at the arrival of the righteous.

When the last one arrives, he will bring out Adam, together with the ancestors; and he will bring them in there, so that they may be filled with joy; just as a person invites his best friends to have dinner with him and they arrive with joy, and they talk together in front of that man's palace, waiting with joyful anticipation to have dinner with delightful enjoyments and riches that cannot be measured, and joy and happiness in eternal light and life; and I say to you, my children: Happy is the person who reverences the name of the LORD, and who serves in front of his face always, and who organizes his gifts with fear, offerings of life, and who in this life lives and dies correctly!

Happy is he who carries out righteous judgment, not for the sake of payment, but for justice, not expecting anything whatever as a result; and the result will be that judgment without favoritism will follow for him.

Happy is he who clothes the naked with his garment , and to the hungry gives his bread! Happy is he who judges righteous judgment for orphan and widow, and who helps anyone who has been treated unjustly!

Happy is he who turns aside from the secular path of this vain world, and walks in the right paths, and who lives that life which is without end!

Happy is he who sows right seed, for he shall harvest sevenfold!

Happy is he in whom is the truth, so that he may speak the truth to his neighbor!

Happy is he who has compassion on his lips and gentleness in his heart!

Happy is he who understands all the works of the LORD, performed by the LORD, and glorifies him! For the works of the LORD are right, but the works of mankind − some are good, but others are evil; and by their works those who speak lying blasphemies are recognized.

CHAPTER 43

"I, my children, every just deed and every just decree and every just decision I have checked out and written down, just as the LORD commanded me.

And in all these things I discovered differences. For, just as one year is more honorable than another year, so one person is more honorable than another person—

some again because of much poverty;

some again because of wisdom of the heart;

some again because of singular intelligence;

some again because of craftiness;

some again because of silence of the lips;

some again because of purity;

some again because of strength;

some again because of handsome appearance;

some again because of youth;

some again because of a penetrating mind;

some again because of bodily appearance;

some again because of abundant feelings.

Even though these sayings are heard on every side, nevertheless there is no one better than he who fears God. He will be the most glorious in that age.

CHAPTER 44

"The LORD with his own two hands created mankind; in a facsimile of his own face, both small and great, the LORD created |them|.

And whoever insults a person's face, insults the face of a king, and treats the face of the LORD with repugnance.

He who treats with contempt the face of any person treats the face of the LORD with contempt.

He who expresses anger to any person without provocation will reap anger in the great judgment. He who spits on any person's face, insultingly, will reap the same at the LORD's great judgment.

Happy is the person who does not direct his heart with malice toward any person, but who helps the condemned, and lifts up those who have been crushed, and shows compassion on the needy.

Because on the day of the great judgment, every weight and every measure and every set of scales will be just as they are in the market.

That is to say, each will be weighed in the balance, and each will stand in the market, and each will find out his own measure and in accordance with that measure men teach shall receive his own reward.

CHAPTER 45

"If anyone is prompt in performing a good oblation in front of the face of the LORD, than the LORD will be prompt to accept it on his account, and he will not perform righteous judgment for him.

If anyone makes lamps numerous in front of the face of the LORD, then the LORD will make his treasure stores numerous in the highest kingdom.

Does the LORD demand bread or lamps or sheep or oxen or any kind of sacrifices at all? This is nothing, but he demands pure hearts, and by means of all those things he tests people's hearts.

CHAPTER 46

"Listen, my people, and give heed to the utterance of my lips! If to an earthly king someone should bring some kinds of gifts, if he is thinking treachery in his heart, and the king perceives it, will he not be angry with his gifts?

And will he not hand him over for judgment? If any person seduces another person into untruth by fair speech, but his heart is evil, will he not be conscious of his heart, and will he not judge himself in himself, whether or not his judgment be true?

And when the LORD sends out the great light, in that light there will be true judgment, without favoritism, for true and untrue alike; and no one will be able to hide himself then.

CHAPTER 47

"And now, my children, place the thought on your hearts, and give heed to the sayings of your father which I am making known to you from the lips of the LORD. And receive these books in your father's handwriting, and read them. And in them you will learn all the deeds of the LORD. there have been many books since the beginning of creation, and there will be until the end of the age; but not one of them will make things as plain to you as the books in my handwriting. If you hold on firmly to them, you will not sin against the LORD.

For there is no other besides the LORD, neither in heaven, nor on the earth, nor in the deepest places, nor in the one foundation.

The LORD is the one who laid the foundations upon the unknown things, and he is the one who spread out the heavens above the visible and the invisible things. And the earth he solidified above the waters, and the waters he based upon the unfixed things; and he alone created the uncountable creatures. And who is it who has counted the dust of the earth or the sand of the sea of the drops of rain of the dew of the clouds or the blowing of the wind?

Who is it who has plaited the land and the sea together with indissoluble bonds, and cut the stars out of fire, and decorated the sky and put in the midst of them...

CHAPTER 48

"... the sun, so that he might travel along the seven celestial circles, which are appointed with 182 thrones so that he might descend to the shortest day, and once more 182 so that he might descend to the longest day.

He also has two great thrones where he pauses when he turns around in this direction and in the other direction, higher than the lunar thrones. From the month Tsivan, from the 17th day, he descends until the month Theved; and from the 17th day of Theved he ascends.

And in this way the sun moves along all the celestial circles. When he comes close to the earth, then the earth is merry and makes its fruit grow. But when he goes away, then the earth laments, and the trees and all fruits have no productivity. All this is by measurement, and by the most precise measurement of the hours. He fixed it by measure, by his own wisdom, visible and invisible. From the invisible things and the visible things he created all the visible things; he himself is invisible.

Thus I am making it known to you, my children; you must hand over the books to your children, and throughout all your generations, and to your relatives, and all nations who are discerning so that they may fear God, and so that they may accept them. And they will be more enjoyable than any delightful food on earth.

And they will read them and adhere to them. But those who are undiscerning and who do not understand the LORD neither fear God nor accept them, but renounce them, and regard themselves as burdened by them −. Happy is who puts their yoke on and carries it around; for he will plow on the day of the great judgment.

CHAPTER 49

"For I am swearing to you, my children − But look! I am not swearing by any oath at all, neither by heaven nor by earth nor by any other creature which the LORD created. For the LORD said, 'There is no oath in me, nor any unrighteousness, but only truth.' So, if there is no truth in human beings, then let them make an oath by means of the words 'Yes, Yes!' or, if it should be the other way around, 'No, No!'

And I make an oath to you – 'Yes, Yes!' – that even before any person was in his mother's womb, individually a place I prepared for each soul, as well as a set of scales and a measurement of how long he intends him to live in this world, so that each person may be investigated with it. Yes, children, do not deceive yourselves; ahead of the time a place has been prepared there for each human soul.

CHAPTER 50

"I have set down the achievements of each person in the writings, and no one can |hide himself who is born on the earth, nor his achievement be kept secret. I see everything, as if in a mirror.

Now therefore, my children, in patience and meekness abide for the number of your days, so that you may inherit the final endless age that is coming.

Every assault and every persecution and every evil word. If the injury and persecution happen to you on account of the LORD, then endure them all for the sake of the LORD. And if you are able to take vengeance with a hundredfold revenge, do not take vengeance, neither on one who is close to you nor on one who is distant from you. For the LORD is the one who takes vengeance, and he will be the avenger for you on the day of the great judgment, so that there may be no acts of retribution here from human beings, but only form the LORD.

Let each one of you put up with the loss of his gold and silver on account of a brother, so that he may receive a full treasury in that age.

Widows and orphans and foreigners |do no distress, so that God's anger does not come upon you;|...

CHAPTER 51

"... stretch out your hands in accordance with your strength.

Help a believer in affliction, and then affliction will not find you, in your treasuries and in the time of your work. Every kind of afflictive and burdensome yoke, if it comes upon you for the sake of the LORD, carry everything and put it off. And thus you will find your reward on the day of judgment.

In the morning of the day and in the middle of the day and in the evening of the day it is good to go to the LORD's temple. For every kind of spirit glorifies him and every kind of creature, visible and invisible, praises him.

CHAPTER 52

"Happy is the person who opens his lips for praise, and praises the LORD with his whole heart. And cursed is every person who opens his heart for insulting, and insults the poor and slanders his neighbor, because that person slanders God.

Happy is he who opens his lips, both blessing and praising God.

Cursed is he who opens his lips for cursing and blasphemy, before the face of the LORD all his days.

Happy — who blesses all the works of the LORD.

Cursed — who despises any of the LORD's creatures.

Happy — who looks carefully to the raising up of the works of his own hand.

Cursed — who looks |and is jealous| to destroy another.

Happy — who preserves the foundations of his most ancient fathers.

Cursed — he who breaks down the institutions of his ancestors and fathers.

Happy — who cultivates the love of peace.

Cursed — who disturbs those who are peaceful by means of love.

Happy is he who even though he does not speak peace with his tongue, nevertheless in his heart there is peace toward all.

Cursed – who with his tongue speaks peace, but in his heart there is no peace but a sword.

For all these things will be weighed in the balances and exposed in the books on the great judgment day.

A depiction of Enoch returning to Earth, teaching his sons and the people.

CHAPTER 53

"So now, my children, do not say, 'Our father is with God, and he will stand in front of God for us, and he will pray for us concerning our sins.' For there is no helper there – not even for any one person who has sinned. See how I have written down all the deeds of every person before the creation, and I am writing down what is done among all persons forever. And no one can contradict my handwriting; because the LORD sees all the evil thoughts of mankind, how vain they are, where they lie in the treasuries of the heart.

So now, my children, pay close attention to all your father's sayings, whatever I say to you, so that you will not be sorry, saying, 'Our father warned us...'

CHAPTER 54

"... at that time, about this ignorance of ours, so that they may be for your inheritance of peace. The books which I have given to you, do not hide them. To all who wish, recite them, so that they may know about the extremely marvelous works of the LORD.

CHAPTER 55

"For behold, my children, the prescribed day has arrived and the appointed time confronts me. It urges me on to my departure; the angels who wish to go with me are standing on the earth, waiting for what they have been told. Tomorrow morning I shall go up to the highest heaven, into my eternal inheritance. That is why I am commanding you, my children, so that you may do all that is well-pleasing before the face of the LORD."

CHAPTER 56

Methusalam answered his father and said, "What is pleasing in your eyes, Enoch? Let us prepare food in front of your face, so that you may bless our houses and your children and all your household; and people will be glorified by you. And thus, after that, you will go away, as the LORD wills."

Enoch answered his son and said, "Listen, child! Since the time when the LORD anointed me with the ointment of his glory, food has not come into me, and earthly pleasure my soul does not remember; nor do I desire anything earthly.

CHAPTER 57

"But, call your brothers, and all the members of your households, and the elders of the people, so that I may speak to them and depart, as it has been predetermined for me."

And Methusalam hurried and summoned his brothers, Regim and Riman and Ukhan and Khermion and Gaidad, and the elders of all the people. And he summoned them before the face of his father Enoch, and they prostrated themselves in front of his face, and Enoch looked upon them. And he blessed them; and he spoke to them, saying:

CHAPTER 58

"Listen, In the days of our father Adam, the LORD came down onto the earth. And he inspected all his creatures which he himself had created in the beginning of the thousand ages and when after all those he had created Adam.

And the LORD summoned all the animals of the earth and all the reptiles of the earth and all the birds that fly in the air, and he brought them all before the face of our father Adam, so that he might pronounce names for all the quadrupeds; and named everything that lives on the earth.

And the LORD appointed him over everything, and he subjected everything to him in subservience under his hand, both the dumb and the deaf, to be commanded and for submission and for every servitude. So also to every human being. The LORD created mankind to be the lord of all his possessions. And the LORD will not judge a single animal soul for the sake of man; but human souls he will judge for the sake of the souls of their animals.

In the great Age there is a special place for human beings. And just as every human soul is according to number, so also it is with animal souls. And not a single soul which the LORD has created will perish until the great judgment. And every kind of animal soul will accuse the human beings who have fed them badly.

CHAPTER 59

"He who acts lawlessly with the soul of an animal acts lawlessly with his own soul. For a person brings one of the clean animals to make a sacrifice on account of sin, so that he may have healing for his soul. If he brings it to the sacrifice from clean animals and birdsand cereals, then there is healing for that person, and he will heal his soul.

Everything that has been given to you for food, bind by four legs, so as to perform the healing properly. And there is healing and he will heal his soul. And he who puts to death any kind of animal without bonds, and acts lawlessly with his own flesh. And he who does any kind of harm whatsoever to any kind of animal in secret, it is an evil custom, and he acts lawlessly with his own soul."

CHAPTER 60

"He who does harm to a human soul creates harm for his own soul, and there is for him no healing of his flesh, nor any forgiveness for eternity.

He who carries out the murder of a human soul causes the death of his own soul, and murders his own body; and there is no healing for him for eternity.

He who lies in wait for a person with any kind of trap, he himself will be entangles in it; and there is no healing for him for eternity.

He who lies in wait for a person in judgment, his retribution will not be slackened in the great judgment for eternity.

He who acts perversely, or says anything against any soul, righteousness will not be created for him for eternity.

CHAPTER 61

"So now, my children, keep your hearts from every unrighteous deed which the LORD hates.

And just as a person makes request for his own soul from God, in the same manner let him behave toward every living soul, because in the great age I will find out everything. Many shelters have been prepared for people, good ones for the good, but bad ones for the bad, many, without number.

Happy is he who enters into the blessed houses; for in the bad ones there is no rest, nor returning.

Listen, my children, old and young! A person, when he places vow upon his heart to bring gifts before the face of the LORD from his own works, and his hands did not make that thing, then the LORD will turn away his face form the works of his hands, and he will not find the works of his hands. But even if his hands did make it, but his heart is complaining, the illness of his heart will not cease; making complaint without ceasing, he shall not have even a single benefit.

CHAPTER 62

"Happy is the person who, in his suffering, brings gifts before the face of the LORD, ⟨and⟩ sacrifices them and then receives remission of sins. But if, before the time comes, he should retract his vows, there is no repentance for him.

If the time specified elapses, and then he does it, he will not be accepted, and there is no repentance after death. Because everything before the time and after the time which a person does, both are a scandal before men and a sin before God.

CHAPTER 63

"A person, when he clothes the naked or gives his bread to the hungry, then he will obtain a reward.

If his heart should murmur, it is a twofold evil that he creates for himself. It is a loss that he creates in respect to that which he gives, and he will not have any obtaining of remuneration because of it.

And the poor man, when his heart is satisfied or his body is clothed, and he performs an act of contempt, then he will ruin all his endurance of poverty, and he will not obtain the reward for his good deeds.

For the LORD detests every kind of contemptuous person, and every person who makes himself out to be great, and every untruthful word, stimulated by injustice; and it will be cut out with the blade of the sword of death, and thrown into the fire. And it will burn; and this cutting out has no healing unto eternity."

CHAPTER 64

When Enoch had spoken to his sons and to the princes of the people, and all his people, near and far, having heard that the LORD was calling Enoch, they consulted one another, saying,

"Let us go, let us kiss Enoch."

And they came together, up to 2000 men, and they arrived at the place

Akhuzan where Enoch was, and his sons.

And the elders of the people and all the community came and prostrated themselves and kissed Enoch.

And they said to him, "O our father, Enoch! May you be blessed by the LORD, the eternal king! And now, bless your sons, and all the people, so that we may be glorified in front of your face today.

For you will be glorified in front of the face of the LORD for eternity, because you are the one whom the LORD chose in preference to all the people upon the earth; and he appointed you to be the one who makes a written record of all his creation, visible and invisible, and the one who carried away the sin of mankind and the helper of your own household."

CHAPTER 65

"Listen, my children! Before ever anything existed, and before ever any created thing was created, the LORD created the whole of his creation, visible and invisible.

And however much time there was went by. Understand how, on account of this, he constituted man in his own form, in accordance with a similarity.

And he gave him

eyes to see,

and ears to hear,

and heart to think,

and reason to argue.

And the LORD set everything forth for the sake of man, and he created the whole of creation for his sake. And he divided it into times:

And from time he established years;

and from the years he settled months;

and from the months he settled days;

and from the day she settled 7;

and in those he settled the hours;

and the hour she measured exactly,

so that a person might think about time, and so that he might count the years and the months and the days and the hours and the perturbations and the beginnings and the endings, and that he might keep count of his own life form the beginning onto death, and think of his sins, and so that he might write his own achievement, both evil and good.

For no achievement is hidden in front of the LORD, so that every person might know his own achievement and so that he might not transgress any one of his commandments at all and so that he might hold onto what my hand has written in generation and generation.

And when the whole of creation, visible and invisible, which the LORD has created, shall come to an end, then each person will go to

the LORD's great judgment. •|And| then |all| time will perish, and afterward there will be neither years nor months nor days nor hours. They will be dissipated, and after that they will not be reckoned.

But they will constitute a single age. And all the righteous, who escape from the LORD's great judgment, will be collected together into the great age. And the great age will come about for the righteous, and it will be eternal.

And after that there will be among them neither weariness nor sickness nor affliction nor worry nor want nor debilitation nor night nor darkness.

But they will have a great light, a great indestructible light, and paradise, great and incorruptible. For everything corruptible will pass away, and the incorruptible will come into being, and will be the shelter of the eternal residences."

CHAPTER 66

"Now therefore, my children, guard your souls from every kind of injustice, such as the LORD hates.

And walk in front of his face with fear, and worship him alone. And every kind of oblation present justly in front of the face of the LORD; but what is unjust the LORD detests.

For the LORD sees everything that a person thinks in his heart. Then reason advises him. For every thought is presented before the LORD.

If you look upon the sky, behold, the LORD is there; for the LORD created the sky. If you look upon the earth, then the LORD is there; for the LORD founded the earth, and placed upon it all his creatures. If you meditate upon the depths of the ocean and on all that is beneath the earth, then the LORD is there. Because the LORD created all things.

Do not bow down to anything created by man, nor to anything created by God, so committing apostasy against the LORD of all creation. For no kind of deed is hidden from the face of the LORD.

Walk, my children,

in long-suffering,

in meekness,

in affliction,

in distress,

in faithfulness,

in truth,

in hope,

in weakness,

in derision,

in assaults,

in temptation,

in deprivation,

in nakedness,

having love for one another, until you go out from this age of suffering, so that you may become inheritors of the never-ending age.

How happy are the righteous who shall escape the LORD's great judgment; for they will be made to shine seven times brighter than the sun.

For in that age everything is estimated sevenfold — light and darkness and food and enjoyment and misery and paradise and torture. All this I have put down in writing, so that you might read it and think about it."

CHAPTER 67

And when Enoch had spoken to his people, the LORD sent the gloom onto the earth, and it became dark and covered the men who were standing with Enoch.

And the angels hurried and grasped Enoch and carried him up to the highest heaven, where the LORD received him and made him stand in front of his face for eternity. Then the darkness departed from the earth, and it became light.

And the people looked, but they could not figure out how Enoch had been taken away. And they glorified God. And they found a scroll on which was inscribed: THE INVISIBLE GOD. And then they went to their homes.

CHAPTER 68

Enoch was born of the 6th day of the month Tsivan, and he lived for 365 years.

And he was taken up to heaven in the month of Nitsan, on the 1st day. And he remained in heaven for 50 days, writing down all notes about all the creatures which the LORD had created.

And he wrote 366 books and he handed them over to his sons. And he remained on the earth for 30 days, talking with them.

And then he was taken up to heaven again in the month of Tsivan, on the very same 6th day on which he was even born, and at the very same hour.

And just as every person has as his nature the darkness of this present life, so also he has his conception and birth and departure from his life. In which he was conceived, in that hour also he is born, in that also departs.

And Methusalam and his brothers and all the sons of Enoch hurried, and they constructed an altar at the place Akhuzan, where Enoch had been taken up.

And they obtained sheep and oxen, and they summoned all the people, and they sacrificed sacrifices in front of the face of the LORD.

And the people came to them to the festival, and brought offerings for the sons of Enoch. And they made a festival, rejoicing and making merriment for three days, praising God who had given them such a sign through Enoch, his own favored servant, even so that they might hand it on to their own sons, form generation to generation, from age to age. AMEN.

CHAPTER 69

And on the third day, in the time of the evening, the elders of the people spoke to Methusalam, saying, "Stand in front of the face of the LORD and in front of the face of all the people and in front of the face of the altar of the LORD, and you will be glorified in your people."

And Methusalam answered his people: "Wait, O men, until ⟨the LORD⟩ , the God of my father Enoch, shall himself raise up for himself a priest over his own people."

And the people waited until that night in vain at the place Akhuzan.

And Methusalam remained near the altar and prayed to the LORD and said, "O LORD, the only One of the whole world, who has taken away my father Enoch, you raise up a priest foryourpeople, and give their heart understanding to fear your glory and to perform everything in accordance with your will."

Methusalam fell asleep, and the LORD appeared to him in a night vision and said to him, "Listen, Methusalam! I am the LORD, the God of your father Enoch. Give heed to the voice of these people and stand in frontof my altar, and I shall glorify you in front of the face of all the people, and you will be glorified all the days of your life, and I shall bless you."

And Methusalam got up from his sleep and blessed the LORD who had appeared to him.

And the elders of the people hurried to Methusalam,

and the LORD God directed Methusalam's heart to give heed to the voice of the people. And he said to them, "The LORD God is the one who has given grace to these people in front of my eyes today."

And Sarkhasan and Kharmis and Zazas, the elders of the people, hurried and attired Methusalam in the designated garments and place a blazing crown on his head.

And the people hurried, and they brought sheep and oxen and some birds, all of them having passed inspection, for Methusalam to sacrifice in the name of the LORD and in the name of the people.

And Methusalam came up to the LORD's altar, and his face was radiant, like the sun at midday rising up, with all the people in procession behind him.

And Methusalam stood in front of the altar of the LORD, with all the people standing around the place of sacrifice.

And when the elders of the people had taken sheep and oxen, they tied their four legs together, and place them at the head of the altar.

And they said to Methusalam, "Pick the knife! And slaughter

them in the required manner in the face of the LORD."

And Methusalam stretched out his hands to heaven and he called out to the LORD thus, saying, "Acceptme, O LORD! Who am I, to stand at the head of your place of sacrifice and over the head of these people?

And now, O LORD, look upon your servantandupon all these people. Now all the inquiries, let them come to pass! And give a blessing to your servant in front of the face of all the people, so that they may realize that you are the one who has appointedmeto be priest over your people."

And it happened, when Methusalam had prayed, that the altar was shaken, and the knife rose up from the altar, and leaped into Methusalam's hand in front of the face of all the people. And the people trembled and glorified God.

And Methusalam was honored in front of the face of the LORD and in front of the face of all the people from that day.

And Methuselam took the knife and slaughtered all that had been brought by the people. Andthe peoplerejoiced greatly, and they made merry in front of the face of the LORD and in front of the face of Methusalam on that day.

And then the people went off to their own shelters, each one of them.

CHAPTER 70

And Methusalam began to stand at the altar in front of the face of the LORD, and all the people, from that day for 10 years, hoping in an eternal inheritance, and having thoroughly taught all the earth and all his own people.

And there was not one single person turning himself away in vanity from the LORD during all the days that Methusalam lived.

And the LORD blessed Methusalam and was gratified by his sacrifices and by his gifts and by every kind of service which he performed in front of the face of the LORD.

And when the time of the departure days of Methusalam arrived, the LORD appeared to him in a night vision and said to him, "Listen, Methusalam! I am the LORD, the God of your father Enoch. I want you to know that the days of your life have come to an end, and the day of your rest has come close.

Call Nir, the second son of your son Lamekh, born after Noe, and invest him in the garments of your consecration. And make him stand at my altar. And tell him everything that will happen in his days, for the time of the destruction of all the earth, and of every human being and of everything that lives on the earth, is drawing near.

For in his days there will be a very great breakdown on the earth, for each one has begun to envy his neighbor, and people against people have destroyed boundaries, and the nation wages war. And all the earth is filled with vileness and blood and every kind of evil.

Andeven more than that, they have abandoned their LORD, and they will do obeisance to unreal gods, and to the vault above the sky, and to what moves above the earth, and to the waves of the sea. And the adversary will make himself great and will be delighted with his deeds, to my great provocation.

And all the earth will change its seasons anticipating the time of destruction. And all the races will change on the earth by my conflagration.

Then I shall give the command. The Bottomless will be poured out over the earth, and the great storages of the waters of heaven will come down onto the earth.

And the whole constitution of the earth will perish, and all the earth will quake, and it will be deprived of its strength from that day. Then I will preserve the son of your son Lamekh, his first son, Noe. And from his seed I will raise up another world, and his seed will exist forever, until the second destruction when once again mankind will have committed sin in front of my face."

And Methusalam leaped up from his sleep, and his dream was very disturbing. And he summoned all the elders of the people, and recounted to them all that the LORD had said to him and all the vision that had been revealed to him by the LORD. And all the people were disturbed by his vision. And they answered him, "The LORD is lord, and he will act in accordance with his own will. And now, Methusalam, *you* do everything just as the LORD has told you."

And Methusalam summoned Nir, the son of Lamekh, Noe's younger brother, and he invested him with the vestments of priesthood in front of the face of all the people, and made him stand at the head of the altar of the LORD. And he taught him everything that he would have to do among the people.

And Methusalam spoke to the people:"Here is Nir. He will be in front of your face from the present day as a prince and a leader."

And the people said to Methusalam, "Let it be soin accordance with your word. And you will be the voice of the LORD, just as he said to you."

And when Methusalam had spoken to the people in front of the altar, his spirit was convulsed, and, having knelt on his knees, he stretched out his hands to heaven, and prayed to the LORD. And, as he was praying to him, his spirit went out in accordance with the LORD.

And Nir and all the people hurried and constructed a sepulcher for Methusalam in the place Akhuzan, very thoughtfully adorned with all holy things, with lamps.

And Nir came with many praises, and the people lifted up Methusalam's body, glorifyingGod; they performed the service for him at the sepulcher which they had made for him and they covered him over.

And they said, "Blessed was Methusalam in front of the face of the LORD and in front of the face of all the people!" And when they wanted to go away to their own places, Nir said to the people, "Hurry up today and bring sheep and bulls and turtledoves and pigeons, so that you may make a sacrifice in front of the face of the LORD today.

And then go away to your houses." And the people gave heed to Nir the priest, and they hurried and they brought them and tied them up at the head of the altar. And Nir took the knife of sacrifice, and slaughtered all that had been brought to be sacrificed in front of the face of the LORD. And all the people made merry in front of the face of the LORD, and on that day they glorified the LORD, the God of heaven and earth, of Nir. And from that day there was peace and order over all the earth in the days of Nir – 202 years.

And then the people turned away from the LORD, and they began to be envious one against another, and people went to war against people, and race rose up against race and struggled and insulted one another.

Even if the lips were the same, nevertheless the hearts chose different things. For the devil became ruler for the third time. The first was before paradise, the second time was in paradise; the third time was after paradise, continuing right up to the Flood.

And there arose disputation and great turbulence. And Nir the priest heard and was greatly aggrieved. And he said in his heart, "In truth I have come to understand how the time has arrived and the saying which the LORD said to Methusalam, the father of my father Lamekh."

CHAPTER 71

Behold, the wife of Nir, whose name was Sopanim, being sterile and never having at any time given birth to a child by Nir –

And Sopanim was in the time of her old age, and in the day of her death. She conceived in her womb, but Nir the priest had not slept with her, nor had he touched her, from the day that the LORD had appointed him to conduct the liturgy in front of the face of the people.

And when Sopanim saw her pregnancy, she was ashamed and embarrassed, and she hid herself during all the days until she gave birth. And not one of the people knew about it.

And when 282 days had been completed, and the day of birth had begun to approach, and Nir remembered his wife, and he called her to himself in his house, so that he might converse with her.

And Sopanim came to Nir, her husband; and, behold, she was pregnant, and the day appointed for giving birth was drawing near.

And Nir saw her, and he became very ashamed. And he said to her, "What is this that you have done, O wife? And why have you disgraced me in front of the face of these people? And now, depart from me, and go where you began the disgrace of your womb, so that I might not defile my hand on account of you, and sin in front of the face of the LORD."

And Sopanim spoke to Nir, her husband, saying, "O my lord! Behold, it is the time of my old age, and the day of my death has arrived. I do not understand how my menopause and the barrenness of my womb have been reversed."

And Nir did not believe his wife, and for the second time he said to her, "Depart from me, or else I might assault you, and commit a sin in front of the face of the LORD."

And it came to pass, when Nir had spoken to his wife, Sopanim, that Sopanim fell down at Nir's feet and died.

Nir was extremely distressed, and he said in his heart, "Could this have happened because of my word, since by word and thought a person can sin in front of the face of the LORD?

Now may God have mercy upon me! I know in truth in my heart that my hand was not upon her. And so I say, 'Glory to you, O LORD, because no one among mankind knows about this deed which the LORD has done.'"

And Nir hurried, and he shut the door of his house, and he went to Noe his brother, and he reported to him everything that had happened in connection with his wife.

And Noe hurried. He came with Nir his brother; he came into Nir's house, because of the death of Sopanim, and they discussed between themselves how her womb was at the time of giving birth. And Noe said to Nir, "Don't let yourself be sorrowful, Nir, my brother! For the LORD today has covered up our scandal, in that nobody from the people knows this.

Now, let us go quickly and let us bury her secretly, and the LORD will cover up the scandal of our shame." And they placed Sopanim on the bed, and they wrapped her around with black garments, and shut her in the house, prepared for burial. They dug a grave in secret.

And a child came out from the dead Sopanim. And he sat on the bed at her side. And Noe and Nir came in to bury Sopanim, and they saw the child sitting beside the dead Sopanim, and wiping his clothing. And Noe and Nir were very terrified with a great fear, because the child was fully developed physically, like a three-year-old. And he spoke with his lips, and he blessed the LORD.

And Noe and Nir looked at him, and behold, the badge of priesthood was on his chest, and it was glorious in appearance. And Noe and Nir said, "Behold, God is renewing the priesthood from blood related to us, just as he pleases." And Noe and Nir hurried, and they washed the child, and they dressed him in the garments of priesthood, and they gave him the holy bread and he ate it. And they called his name Melkisedek.

And Noe and Nir lifted up the body of Sopanim, and divested her of the

black garments, and they washed her, and they clothed her in exceptionally bright garments, and they built a shrine for her.

Noe and Nir and Melkisedek came, and they buried her publicly. And
Noe said to his brother Nir, "Look after this child in secret until the
time, because people will become treacherous in all the earth, and they
will begin to turn away from God, and having become totally ignorant,
they will put him to death."

And then Noe went away to his own place.

And great lawlessness began to become abundant over all the earth in
the days of Nir. And Nir began to worry excessively, especially about the
child, saying,

"How miserable it is for me, eternal LORD, that in my days all lawlessness has begun to become abundant over the earth. And I realize how
much nearer out end is, over all the earth, on account of the lawlessness
of the people.

And now, LORD, what is the vision about this child, and what is his
destiny, and what will I do for him? Is it possible that he too will be
joined with us in the destruction?" And the LORD heeded Nir, and
appeared to him in a night vision. He said to him, "Nir, the great lawlessness which has come about on the earth among the multitude I shall not
tolerate.

And behold, I desire now to send out a great destruction onto the earth,
and everything that stands on the earth shall perish.

But, concerning the child, don't be anxious, Nir; because in a short while
I shall send my archistratig, Michael. And he will take the child, and put
him in the paradise of Edem, in the Paradise where Adam was formerly
for 7 years, having heaven open all the time up until when he sinned.

And this child will not perish along with those who are perishing in this
generation, as I have revealed it, so that Melkisedek will be the priest to
all holy priests, and I will establish him so that

he will be the head of the priests of the future." And Nir arose from his
sleep and blessed the LORD who had appeared to him, saying,

"Blessed be the LORD, the God of my fathers,

who has told me how he has made a great priest in my day,

in the womb of Sopanim, my wife.

Because I had no child in this tribe who might become the great

priest, but this is

my son and your servant, and you are the great God.

Therefore honor him together with your servants and great priests, with Sit, and Enos, and Rusi, and Amilam, and Prasidam, and Maleleil, and Serokh, and Arusan, and Aleem, and Enoch, and Methusalam, and me, your servant Nir.

And behold, Melkisedek will be the head of the 13 priests who existed before. And afterward, in the last generation, there will be another Melkisedek, the first of 12 priests. And the last will be the head of all, a great archpriest, the Word and Power of God, who will perform miracles, greater and more glorious than all the previous ones. He, Melkisedek, will be priest and king in the place Akhuzan, that is to say, in the center of the earth, where Adam was created, and there will be his final grave. And in connection with that archpriest it is written how he also will be buried there, where the center of the earth is, just as Adam also buried his own son there – Abel, whom his brother Cain murdered; for he lay for 3 years unburied, until he saw a bird called Jackdaw, how it buried his own young.

I know that great confusion has come and in confusion this generation will come to an end; and everyone will perish, except that Noe, my brother, will be preserved. And afterward there will be a planting from his tribe, and there will be other people, and there will be another Melkisedek, the head of priests reigning over the people, and performing the liturgy for the LORD."

CHAPTER 72

And when the child had been 40 days in Nir's tent, the LORD said to Michael, "Go down onto the earth to Nir the priest, and take my child Melkisedek, who is with him, and place him in the paradise of Edem for preservation. For the time is approaching, and I will pour out all the water onto the earth, and everything that is on the earth will perish."

Michael hurried, and he came down when it was night, and Nir was sleeping on his bed. And Michael appeared to him, and said to him, "Thus says the LORD: 'Nir! Send the child to me whom I entrusted to you.'"

And Nir did not realize who was speaking to him, and his heart was confused. And he said, "When the people find out about the child, then they will seize him and kill him, because the heart of these people is deceitful in front of the face of the LORD." Nir said to the one who was speaking, "The child is not with me, and I don't know who you are."

And he who was speaking to me answered, "Don't be frightened, Nir! I am the LORD's archistratig. The LORD has sent me, and behold, I shall take your child today. I will go with him and I will place him in the paradise of Edem, and there he will be forever.

And when the twelfth generation shall come into being, and there will be one thousand and seventy years, and there will be born in that generation a righteous man. And the LORD will tell him that he should to out to that mountain where stands the ark of Noe, your brother. And he will find there another Melkisedek, who has been living there for 7 years, hiding himself from the people who sacrifice to idols, so that they might not kill him. He will bring him out, and he will be the first priest and king in the city Salim in the style of this Melkisedek, the originator of the priests. The years will be completed up to that time – 3 thousand and 4 hundred and 32 – from the beginning and the creation of Adam. And from that Melkisedek the priests will be 12 in number until the great Igumen, that is to say, Leader, will bring out everything visible and invisible."

And Nir understood the first dream and believed it. And having answered Michael he said, "Blessed be the LORD who has glorified you today for me! And now, bless your servant Nir! For we are coming close to departure from this world. And take the child, and do to him just as the LORD said to you." And Michael took the child on the same night on which he had come down; and he took him on his wings, and he placed him in the paradise of Edom. And Nir got up in the morning. He went into his tent and he did not find the child. And there was instead of joy very great grief, because he had no other son except this one.

Thus Nir ended his life. And after him there was no priest among the people. And from that time great confusion arose on the earth.

CHAPTER 73

And the LORD called Noe onto the mount Ararat, between Assyria and Armenia, in the land of Arabia, beside the ocean. And he said to him, "Make there an ark with 300 lakets in length and in width 50 lakets and in height 30. And two stories in the middle, and its doors of one laket.

And of their lakets 300, but of ours also 15 thousand; and so of theirs 50, but of ours 2000 and 500, and so of theirs 30, but of ours 900, and of theirs one laket, but of ours 50." In agreement with this numeral the Jews keep their measurements of Noe's ark, just as the LORD said to him, and they carry out all their measurements in the same way, and all their regulations, even up to the present.

The LORD God opened the doors of heaven. Rain came onto the earth for 150 days, and all flesh died.

And Noe was in the year 500. He fathered 3 sons: Sim, Kham, Afet. After 100 years, after the birth of his three sons, he went into the ark in the month, according to the Hebrews, Iuars, according to the Egyptians, Famenoth, on the 18th day. And the ark floated for 40 days. And in all they were in the ark for 120 days.

And he went into the ark, a son of 600 years, and in the six hundred first year of his life he went out from the ark in the month Farmout according to the Egyptians, but according to the Hebrews Nisan, on the 28th day. After the Flood he lived 350 years, and he died. He lived in all 950 years, according to the LORD our God.

And to him be glory, from the beginning and now

and until the end of the whole era. AMEN+

A depiction of Enoch's final ascension into heaven, surrounded by celestial light, leaving Earth behind.

3 ENOCH

THE HEBREW BOOK OF PALACES
(SEFER HEKHALOT)

AUTHOR: RABBI ISHMAEL.
TRANSLATION: HUGO
ODEBERG

THE HEBREW BOOK OF PALACES (SEFER HEKHALOT)

CHAPTER 1

INTRODUCTION : R. Ishmael ascends to heaven to behold the vision of the Merkaba and is given in charge to Metatron

AND ENOCH WALKED WITH GOD: AND HE WAS NOT; FOR GOD TOOK HIM

(Gen. V. 24)

Rabbi Ishmael said:

When I ascended on high to behold the vision of the Merkaba and had entered the six Halls, one within the other:

As soon as I reached the door of the seventh Hall I stood still in prayer before the Holy One, blessed be He, and, lifting up my eyes on high (i.e. towards the Divine Majesty), I said:

"Lord of the Universe, I pray thee, that the merit of Aaron, the son of Amram, the lover of peace and pursuer of peace, who received the crown of priesthood from Thy Glory on the mount of Sinai, be valid for me in this hour, so that Qafsiel*, the prince, and the angels with him may not get power over me nor throw me down from the heavens".

Forthwith the Holy One, blessed be He, sent to me Metatron, his Servant ('Ebed) the angel, the Prince of the Presence, and he, spreading his wings, with great joy came to meet me so as to save me from their hand.

And he took me by his hand in their sight, saying to me: "Enter in peace before the high and exalted King3 and behold the picture of the Merkaba".

Then I entered the seventh Hall, and he led me to the camp(s) of Shekina and placed me before 6the Holy One, blessed be He, to behold the Merkaba.

As soon as the princes of the Merkaba and the flaming Seraphim perceived me, they fixed their eyes upon me. Instantly trembling and shuddering seized me and I fell down and was benumbed by the radiant image of their eyes and the splendid appearance of their faces; until the Holy One, blessed be He, rebuked them, saying:

"My servants, my Seraphim, my Kerubim and my 'Ophanniml Cover ye your eyes before Ishmael, my son, my friend, my beloved one and my glory, that he tremble not nor shudder!"

Forthwith Metatron the Prince of the Presence, came and restored my spiritand put me upon my feet.

After that (moment) there was notin me strength enough to say a song before the Throne of Glory of the glorious King, the mightiest of all kings, the most excellent of all princes, until after the hour had passed.

After one hour (had passed) the Holy One, blessed be He, opened to me the gates of Shekina, the gates of Peace, the gates of Wisdom, the gates of Strength, the gates of Power, the gates of Speech (Dibbur), the gates of Song, the gates of Qedushsha, the gates of Chant.

And he enlightened my eyes and my heart by words of psalm, song, praise, exaltation, thanksgiving, extolment, glorification, hymn and eulogy. And as I opened my mouth, uttering a song before the Holy One, blessed be He, the Holy Chayyoth beneath and above the Throne of Glory answered and said : "HOLY " and "BLESSED BE THE GLORY OF YHWH FROM HIS PLACE !"

A depiction of Rabbi Ishmael ascending to heaven, meeting the angel Metatron.

CHAPTER 2

The highest classes of angels make inquiries about R. Ishmael which are answered by Metatron R. Ishmael said;

In that hour the eagles of the Merkaba, the flaming 'Ophannim and the Seraphim of consuming fire asked Metatron, saying to him:

"Youth! Why sufferest thou one born of woman to enter and behold the Merkaba? From which nation, from which tribe is this one? What is his character?"

Metatron answered and said to them: "From the nation of Israel whom the Holy One, blessed be He, chose for his people from among seventy tongues (nations), from the tribe of Levi, whom he set aside as a contribution to his name and from the seed of Aaron whom the Holy One, blessed be He, did choose for his servant and put upon him the crown of priesthood on Sinai".

Forthwith they spake and said: "Indeed, this one is worthy to behold the Merkaba ". And they said: "Happy is the people that is in such a case!".

CHAPTER 3

Metatron has 70 names, but God calls him ' Youth '

R. Ishmael said:

In that hour I asked Metatron, the angel, the Prince of the Presence: "What is thy name?"

He answered me: "I have seventy names, corresponding to the seventy tongues of the world and all of them are based upon the name Metatron, angel of the Presence; but my King calls me Youth' (Na'ar)"

CHAPTER 4

Metatron is identical with Enoch who was translated to heaven at the time of the Deluge

R. Ishmael said :

I asked Metatron and said to him: "Why art thou called by the name of thy Creator, by seventy names? Thou art greater than all the princes, higher than all the angels, beloved more than all the servants, honoured above all the mighty ones in kingship, greatness and glory : why do they call thee ' Youth ' in the high heavens ?"

He answered and said to me: " Because I am Enoch, the son of Jared.

For when the generation of the flood sinned and were confounded in their deeds, saying unto God: 'Depart from us, for we desire not the knowledge of thy ways' (Job xxi. 14), then the Holy One, blessed be He, removed me from their midst to be a witness against them in the high heavens to all the inhabitants of the world, that they may not say: 'The Merciful One is cruel".

What sinned all those multitudes, their wives, their sons and their, daughters, their horses, their mules and their cattle and their property, and all the birds of the world, all of which the Holy One, blessed be He, destroyed from the world together with them in the waters of the flood?

Hence the Holy One, blessed be He, lifted me up in their lifetime before their eyes to be a witness against them to the future world. And the Holy One, blessed be He, assigned me for a prince and a ruler among the ministering angels.

In that hour three of the ministering angels, 'UZZA, 'AZZA and 'AZZAEL came forth and brought charges against me in the high heavens, saying before the Holy One, blessed be He:

"Said not the Ancient Ones (First Ones) rightly before Thee: Do not create man! ' " The Holy One, blessed be He, answered and said unto them: "I have made and I will bear, yea, I will carry and will deliver".

As soon as they saw me, they said before Him: "Lord of the Universe! What is this one that he should ascend to the height of heights? Is not he one from among the sons of [the sons of] those who perished in the days of the Flood? "What doeth he in the Raqia'?"

Again, the Holy One, blessed be He, answered and said to them: "What are ye, that ye enter and speak in my presence? I delight in this one more than in all of you, and hence he shall be a prince and a ruler over you in the high heavens."

Forthwith all stood up and went out to meet me, prostrated themselves before me and said:

"Happy art thou and happy is thy father for thy Creator doth favour thee".

And because I am small and a youth among them in days, months and years, therefore they call me "Youth" (Na'ar).

Enoch transforming into the angel Metatron, glowing with divine light and gaining wings.

CHAPTER 5

The idolatry of the generation of Enosh causes God to remove the Shekina from earth. The idolatry inspired by 'Azza, 'Uzza and 'Azziel

R. Ishmael said; Metatron, the Prince of the Presence, said to me;

From the day when the Holy One, blessed be He, expelled the first Adam from the Garden of Eden (and onwards), Shekina was dwelling upon a Kerub under the Tree of Life.

And the ministering angels were gathering together and going down from heaven in parties, from the Raqia in companies and from the heavens in camps to do His will in the whole world.

And the first man and his generation were sitting outside the gate of the Garden to behold the radiant appearance of the Shekina.

For the silendour of the Shekina traversed the world from one end to the other (with a splendour) 365,000 times (that) of the globe of the sun. And everyone who made use of the splendour of the Shekina, on him no flies and no gnats did rest, neither was he ill nor suffered he any pain. No demons got power over him, neither were they able to injure him.

When the Holy One, blessed be He, went out and went in; from the Garden to Eden, from Eden to the Garden, from the Garden to Raqia and from Raqia to the Garden of Eden then all and everyone beheld the splendour of His Shekina and they were not injured; until the time of the generation of Enosh who was the head of all idol worshippers of the world.

And what did the generation of Enosh do? They went from one end of the world to the other, and each one brought silver, gold, precious stones and pearls in heaps like unto mountains and hills making idols out of them throughout all the world. And they erected the idols in every quarter of the world: the size of each idol was 1000 parasangs.

And they brought down the sun, the moon, planets and constellations, and placed them before the idols on their right hand and on their left, to attend them even as they attend the Holy One, blessed be He, as it is written (1 Kings xxii. 19): "And all the host of heaven was standing by him on his right hand and on his left".

What power was in them that they were able to bring them down? They would not have been able to bring them down but for 'Uzza, 'Azza and 'Azziel who taught them sorceries whereby they brought them down and made use of them

In that time the ministering angels brought charges (against them) before the Holy One, blessed be He, saying before him: "Master of the World! What hast thou to do with the children of men? As it is written (Ps. viii. 4) 'What is man (Enosh) that thou art mindful of him?' 'Mah Adam' is not written here, but 'Mah Enosh', for he (Enosh) is the head of the idol worshippers.

Why hast thou left the highest of the high heavens, the abode of thy glorious Name, and the high and exalted Throne in 'Araboth Raqia' in the highest and art gone and dwellest with the children of men who worship idols and equal thee to the idols.

Now thou art on earth and the idols likewise. What hast thou to do with the inhabitants of the earth who worship idols?"

Forthwith the Holy One, blessed be He, lifted up His Shekina from the earth, from their midst. In that moment came the ministering angels, the troops of hosts and the armies of 'Araboth in thousand camps and ten thousand hosts : they fetched trumpets and took the horns in their hands and surrounded the Shekina with all kinds of songs.And He ascended to the high heavens, as it is written: "God is gone up with a shout, the Lord with the sound of a trumpet ".

CHAPTER 6

Enoch lifted up to heaven together with the Shekina.

Angels protests answered by God

R. Ishmael said: Metatron, the Angel, the Prince of the Presence, said to me :

When the Holy One, blessed be He, desired to lift me up on high, He first sent 'Anaphiel H (H = Tetragrammaton) the Prince, and he took me from their midst in their sight and carried me in great glory upon a a fiery chariot with fiery horses, servants of glory. And he lifted me up to the high heavens together with the Shekina.

As soon as I reached the high heavens, the Holy Chayyoth, the 'Ophannim, the Seraphim, the Kerubim, the Wheels of the Merkaba (the Galgallim), and the ministers of the consuming fire, perceiving my smell from a distance of 365,000 myriads of parasangs, said: "What smell of one born of woman and what taste of a white drop (is this) that ascends on high, and (lo, he is merely) a gnat among those who 'divide flames (of fire)'?"

The Holy One, blessed be He, answered and spake unto them: "My servants, my hosts, my Kerubim, my 'Ophannim, my Seraphim! Be ye not displeased on account of this! Since all the children of men have denied me and my great Kingdom and are gone worshipping idols, I have removed my Shekina from among them and have lifted it up on high. But this one whom I have taken from among them is an ELECT ONE among (the inhabitants of) the world and he is equal to all of them in faith, righteousness and perfection of deed and I have taken him for (as) a tribute from my world under all the heavens".

CHAPTER 7

Enoch raised upon the wings of the Shekina to the place

of the Throne, the Merkaba and the angelic hosts

R. Ishmael said: Metatron, the Angel, the Prince of the Presence, said to me;

When the Holy One, blessed be He, took me away from the generation of the Flood, he lifted me on the wings of the wind of Shekina to the highest heaven and brought me into the great palaces of the 'Araboth Raqia' on high, where are the glorious Throne of Shekina, the Merkaba, the troops of anger, the armies of vehemence, the fiery Shin'anim', the flaming Kerubim, and the burning 'Ophannim, the flaming servants, the flashing Chashmattim and the lightening Seraphim. And he placed me (there) to attend the Throne of Glory day after day.

CHAPTER 8

The gates (of the treasuries of heaven)

opened to Metatron

R. Ishmael said : Metatron, the Prince of the Presence, said to me :

Before He appointed me to attend the Throne of Glory, the Holy One, blessed be He, opened to me

three hundred thousand gates of Understanding

three hundred thousand gates of Subtlety

three hundred thousand gates of Life

three hundred thousand gates of grace and loving-kindness

three hundred thousand gates of love

three hundred thousand gates of Tora

three hundred thousand gates of meekness

three hundred thousand gates of maintenance

three hundred thousand gates' of mercy

three hundred thousand gates of fear of heaven

In that hour the Holy One, blessed be He, added in me wisdom unto wisdom, understanding unto understanding, subtlety unto subtlety, knowledge unto knowledge, mercy unto mercy, instruction unto instruction, love unto love, loving-kindness unto loving-kindness, goodness unto goodness,

meekness unto meekness, power unto power, strength unto strength, might unto might, brilliance unto brilliance, beauty unto beauty, splendour unto splendour, and I was honoured and adorned with all these good and praiseworthy things more than all the children of heaven.

CHAPTER 9

Enoch receives blessings from the Most High and

is adorned with angelic attributes

R. Ishmael said : Metatron, the Prince of the Presence, said to me :

After all these things the Holy One, blessed be He, put His hand upon me and blessed me with 5360 blessings.

And I was raised and enlarged to the size of the length and width of the world.

And He caused 72 wings to grow on me, 36 on each side. And each wing was as the whole world.

And He fixed on me 365 eyes : each eye was as the great luminary.

And He left no kind of splendour, brilliance, radiance, beauty in (of) all the lights of the universe that He did not fix on me.

CHAPTER 10

God places Metatron on a throne at the door of the seventh

Hall and announces through the Herald, that Metatron

henceforth is God's representative and ruler over all the

princes of kingdoms and all the children of heaven, save

the eight high princes called YHWH by the name of their King

R. Ishmael said : Metatron, the Prince of the Presence, said to me ;

All these things the Holy One, blessed be He, made for me:He made me a Throne, similar to the

Throne of Glory. And He spread over me a curtain of splendour and brilliant appearance, of beauty, grace and mercy, similar to the curtain of the Throne of Glory; and on it were fixed all kinds of lights in the universe.

And He placed it at the door of the Seventh Hall and seated me on it.

And the herald went forth into every heaven, saying:This is Metatron, my servant. I have made him into a prince and a ruler over all the princes of my kingdoms and over all the children of heaven, except the eight great princes, the honoured and revered ones who are called YHWH, by the name of their King.

And every angel and every prince who has a word to speak in my presence (before me) shall go into his presence (before him) and shall speak to him (instead).

And every command that he utters to you in my name do ye observe and fulfil. For the Prince of Wisdom and the Prince of Understanding have I committed to him to instruct him in the wisdom of heavenly things and of earthly things, in the wisdom of this world and of the world to come.

Moreover, I have set him over all the treasuries of the palapes of Araboih and over all the stores of life that I have in the high heavens.

CHAPTER 11

God reveals all mysteries and secrets to Metatron

R. Ishmael said : Metatron, the angel, the Prince of the Presence, said

to me:

Henceforth the Holy One, blessed be He, revealed to me all the mysteries of Tora and all the secrets of wisdom and all the depths of the Perfect Law; and all living beings' thoughts of heart and all the secrets of the universe and all the secrets of Creation were revealed unto me even as they are revealed unto the Maker of Creation.

And I watched intently to behold the secrets of the depth and the wonderful mystery. Before a man did think in secret, I saw (it) and before a man made a thing I beheld it.

And there was no thing on high nor in the deep hidden from me.

CHAPTER 12

God clothes Metatron in a garment of glory, puts a royal

crown on his head and calls him "the Lesser YHWH"

R. Ishmael said: Metatron, the Prince of the Presence, said to me:

By reason of the love with which the Holy One, blessed be He, loved me more than all the children of heaven. He made me a garment of glory on which were fixed all kinds of lights, and He clad me in it.

And He made me a robe of honour on which were fixed all kinds of beauty, splendour, brilliance and majesty.

And he made me a royal crown in which were fixed forty-nine costly stones like unto the light of the globe of the sun.

For its splendour went forth in the four quarters of the Araboth Raqia', and in (through) the seven heavens, and in the four quarters of the world. And he put it on my head.

And He called me THE LESSER YHWH in the presence of all His heavenly household; as it is written: "For my name is in him".

A depiction of the Angel Metatron seated on a grand throne, surrounded by angels, showing his power and authority in heaven.

CHAPTER 13

God writes with a flaming style on Metatron's crown the

cosmic letters by which heaven and earth were created

R. Ishmael said: Metatron, the angel, the Prince of the Presence, the Glory of all heavens, said to

me:

Because of the great love and mercy with which the Holy One, blessed be He, loved and cherished me more than all the children of heaven. He wrote with his ringer with a flaming style upon the crown on my head the letters by which were created heaven and earth, the seas and rivers, the mountains and hills, the planets and constellations, the lightnings, winds, earthquakes and voices (thunders), the snow and hail, the storm-wind and the tempest ; the letters by which were created all the needs of the world and all the orders of Creation.

And every single letter sent forth time after time as it were lightnings, time after time as it were torches, time after time as it were flames of fire, time after time (rays) like [as] the rising of the sun and the moon and the planets.

CHAPTER 14

All the highest princes, the elementary angels and the

planetary and sideric angels fear and tremble at the sight

of Metatron crowned

R. Ishmael said: Metatron, the Angel, the Prince of the Presence, said to me:

When the Holy One, blessed be He, put this crown on my head, (then) trembled before me all the Princes of Kingdoms who are in the height of Araboth Raqiaf and all the hosts of every heaven; and even the princes (of) the 'Elim, the princes (of) the 'Er'ellim and the princes (of) the Tafsarim, who are greater than all the ministering angels who minister before the Throne of Glory, shook, feared and trembled before me when they beheld me.

Even Sammael, the Prince of the Accusers, who is greater than all the princes of kingdoms on high; feared and trembled before me. And even the angel of fire, and the angel of hail, and the angel of the wind, and the angel of the lightning, and the angel of anger, and the angel of the thunder, and the angel of the snow, and the angel of the rain; and the angel of the day, and the angel of the night, and the angel of the sun and the angel of the moon, and the angel of the planets and the angel of the constellations who rule the world under their hands, feared and trembled and were affrighted before me, when they beheld me.

These are the names of the rulers of the world:

Gabriel, the angel of the fire, Baradiel, the angel of the hail, Ruchiel who is appointed over the wind, Baraqiel who is appointed over the lightnings, Za'amiel who is appointed over the vehemence, Ziqiel who is appointed over the sparks, Zi'iel who is appointed over the commotion, Zdaphiel who is appointed over the storm-wind, Ra'amiel who is appointed over the thunders, Rctashiel who is appointed over the earthquake, Shalgiel who is appointed over the snow, Matariel who is appointed over the rain, Shimshiel who is appointed over the day, Lailiel who is appointed over the night, Galgalliel who is appointed over the globe of the sun, 'Ophanniel who is appointed over the globe of the moon, Kokbiel who is appointed over the planets, Rahatiel who is appointed over the constellations.

And they all fell prostrate, when they saw me. And they were not able to behold me because of the majestic glory and beauty of the appearance of the shining light of the crown of glory upon my head.

CHAPTER 15

Metatron transformed into fire

R. Ishmael said: Metatron, the angel, the Prince of the Presence, the Glory of all heavens, said to me:

As soon as the Holy One, blessed be He, took me in (His) service to attend the Throne of Glory and the Wheels (Galgallim) of the Merkaba and the needs of Shekina, forthwith my flesh was changed into flames, my sinews into flaming fire, my bones into coals of burning juniper, the light of my eye-lids into splendour of lightnings, my eye-balls into fire-brands, the hair of my head into dot flames, all my limbs into wings of burning fire and the whole of my body into glowing fire.

And on my right were divisions 6 of fiery flames, on my left fire-brands were burning, round about me storm wind and tempest were blowing and in front of me and behind me was roaring of thunder with earthquake.

CHAPTER 16

Probably additional

Metatron divested of his privilege of presiding on a

Tlirone of his own on account of Acher's misapprehension

in taking him for a second Divine Power

R. Ishmael said: Metatron, the Angel, the Prince of the Presence, the Glory of all heaven, said to me;

At first I was sitting upon a great Throne at the door of the Seventh Hall ; and I was judging the children of heaven, the household on high by authority of the Holy One, blessed be He. And I divided Greatness, Kingship, Dignity, Rulership, Honour and Praise, and Diadem and Crown of Glory unto all the princes of kingdoms, while I was presiding (lit. sitting) in the Celestial Court (Yeshiba), and the princes of kingdoms were standing before me, on my right and on my left by authority of the Holy One, blessed be He.

But when Acher came to behold the vision of the Merkaba and fixed his eyes on me, he feared and trembled before me and his soul was affrighted even unto departing from him, because of fear, horror and dread of me, when he beheld me sitting upon a throne like a king with all the ministering angels standing by me as my servants and all the princes of kingdoms adorned with crowns surrounding me:

In that moment he opened his mouth and said: "Indeed, there are two Divine Powers in heaven!"

Forthwith Bath Qol (the Divine Voice) went forth from heaven from before the Shekina and said: "Return, ye backsliding children, except Acher!"

Then came 'Aniyel, the Prince, the honoured, glorified, beloved, wonderful, revered and fearful one, in commission from the Holy One, blessed be He and gave me sixty strokes with lashes of fire and made me stand on my feet.

CHAPTER 17

The princes of the seven heavens, of the sun, moon,

planets and constellations and their suites of angels

R. Ishmael said : Metatron, the angel, the Prince of the Presence, the glory of all heavens, said to me:

Seven (are the) princes, the great, beautiful, revered, wonderful and honoured ones who are appointed over the seven heavens. And these are they: MIKAEL, GABRIEL, SHATQIEL, SHACHAQIEL, BAKARIEL, BAD ARIEL, PACHRIEL.

And every one of them is the prince of the host of (one) heaven. And each one of them is accompanied by 496,000 myriads of ministering angels.

MIKAEL, the great prince, is appointed over the seventh heaven, the highest one, which is in the 'Araboth.

GABRIEL, the prince of the host, is appointed over the sixth heaven which is in Makon.

SHATAQIEL, prince of the host, is appointed over the fifth heaven which is in Ma'on. SHAHAQi'EL, prince of the host, is appointed over the fourth heaven which is in Zebul.

BAD ARIEL, prince of the host, is appointed over the third heaven which is in Shehaqim. BARAKIEL, prince of the host, is appointed over the second heaven which is in the height of (Merom) Raqia.

PAZRIEL, prince of the host, is appointed over the first heaven which is in Wilon, which is in Shamayim.

Under them is GALGALLIEL, the prince who is appointed over the globe (galgal) of the sun, and with him are 96 great and honoured angels who move the sun in Raqia'.

Under them is 'OPHANNIEL, the prince who is set over the globe ('ophari) of the moon. And with him are 88 angels who move the globe of the moon 354 thousand parasangs every night at the time when the moon stands in the East at its turning point. And when is the moon sitting in the East at its turning point? Answer: in the fifteenth day of every month.

Under them is RAHATIEL, the prince who is appointed over the constellations. And he is accompanied by 72 great and honoured angels. And why is he called RAHATIEL? Because he makes the stars run (marhit) in their orbits and courses 339 thousand parasangs every night from the East to the West, and from the West to the East. For the Holy One, blessed be He, has made a tent for all of them, for the sun, the moon, the planets and the stars in which they travel at night from the West to the East.

Under them is KOKBIEL, the prince who is appointed over all the planets. And with him are 365,000 myriads of ministering angels, great and honoured ones who move the planets from city to city and from province to province in the Raqia' of heavens.

And over them are SEVENTY-TWO PRINCES OF KINGDOMS on high corresponding to the 72 tongues of the world. And all of them are crowned with royal crowns and clad in royal garments and wrapped in royal cloaks. And all of them are riding on royal horses and they are holding royal sceptres in their hands. And before each one of them when he is travelling in Raqia', royal servants are running with great glory and majesty even as on earth they (princes) are travelling in chariot(s) with horsemen and great armies and in glory and greatness with praise, song and honour.

CHAPTER 18

The order of ranks of the angels and the homage

received by the higher ranks from the lower ones

R. Ishmael said: Metatron, the Angel, the Prince of the Presence, the glory of all heaven, said to me:

THE ANGELS OF THE FIRST HEAVEN, when(ever) they see their prince, they dismount from their horses and fall on their faces.

And THE PRINCE OF THE FIRST HEAVEN, when he sees the prince of the second heaven, he dismounts, removes the crown of glory from his head and falls on his face.

And THE PRINCE OF THE SECOND HEAVEN, when he sees the Prince of the third heaven, he removes the crown of glory from his head and falls on his face.

And THE PRINCE OF THE THIRD HEAVEN, when he sees the prince of the fourth heaven, he removes the crown of glory from his head and falls on his face.

And THE PRINCE OF THE FOURTH HEAVEN, when he sees the prince of the fifth heaven, he removes the crown of glory from his head and falls on his face.

And THE PRINCE OF THE FIFTH HEAVEN, when he sees the prince of the sixth heaven, he removes the crown of glory from his head and falls on his face.

And THE PRINCE OF THE SIXTH HEAVEN, when he sees the prince of the seventh heaven, he removes the crown of glory from his head and falls on his face.

And THE PRINCE OF THE SEVENTH HEAVEN, when he sees THE SEVENTY-TWO PRINCES OF KINGDOMS, he removes the crown of glory from his head and falls on his face.

And the seventy-two princes of kingdoms, when they see THE DOOR KEEPERS OF THE FIRST HALL IN THE ARABOTH RAQIA in the highest, they remove the royal crown from their head and fall on their faces.

And THE DOOR KEEPERS OF THE FIRST HALL, when they see the door keepers of the second Hall, they remove the crown of glory from their head and fall on their faces.

And THE DOOR KEEPERS OF THE SECOND HALL, when they see the door keepers of the third Hall, they remove the crown of glory from their head and fall on their faces.

And THE DOOR KEEPERS OF THE THIRD HALL, when they see the door keepers of the fourth Hall, they remove the crown of glory from their head and fall on their faces.

And THE DOOR KEEPERS OF THE FOURTH HALL, when they see the door keepers of the fifth Hall, they remove the crown of glory from their head and fall on their faces.

And THE DOOR KEEPERS OF THE FIFTH HALL, when they see the door keepers of the sixth Hall, they remove the crown of glory from their head and fall on their faces.

And THE DOOR KEEPERS OF THE SIXTH HALL, when they see the DOOR KEEPERS OF THE SEVENTH HALL, they remove the crown of glory from their head and fall on their faces.

And the door keepers of the seventh Hall, when they see THE FOUR GREAT PRINCES, the honoured ones, WHO ARE APPOINTED OVER THE FOUR CAMPS OF SHEKINA, they remove the crown(s) of glory from their head and fall on their faces.

And the four great princes, when they see TAG'AS, the prince, great and honoured with song (and) praise, at the head of all the children of heaven, they remove the crown of glory from their head and fall on their faces.

And Tag' as, the great and honoured prince, when he sees BARATTIEL, the great prince of three fingers in the height of 'Araboth, the highest heaven, he removes the crown of glory from his head and falls on his face.

And Barattiel, the great prince, when he sees HAMON, the great prince, the fearful and honoured, pleasant and terrible one who maketh all the children of heaven to tremble, when the time draweth nigh (that is set) for the saying of the '(Thrice) Holy', as it is written: "At the noise of the tumult (hamon) the peoples are fled; at the lifting up of thyself the nations are scattered" he removes the crown of glory from his head and falls on his face.

And Hamon, the great prince, when he sees TUTRESIEL, the great prince, he removes the crown of glory from his head and falls on his face.

And Tutresiel H', the great prince, when he sees ATRUGIEL, the great prince, he removes the crown of glory from his head and falls on his face.

And Atrugiel the great prince, when he sees NA'ARIRIEL H', the great prince, he removes the crown of glory from his head and falls on his face.

And Na'aririel H', the great prince, when he sees SASNIGIEL H', the great prince, he removes the crown of glory from his head and falls on his face.

And Sasnigiel H', when he sees ZAZRIEL H', the great prince, he removes the crown of glory from his head and falls on his face.

And Zazriel H', the prince, when he sees GEBURATIEL H', the prince, he removes the crown of glory from his head and falls on his face.

And Geburatiel H', the prince, when he sees 'ARAPHIEL H', the prince, he removes the crown of glory from his head and falls on his face.

And 'Araphiel H', the prince, when he sees 'ASHRUYLU, the prince, who presides in all the sessions of the children of heaven, he removes the crown of glory from his head and falls on his face.

And Ashruylu H, the prince, when he sees GALLISUR H', THE PRINCE, WHO REVEALS ALL THE SECRETS OF THE LAW (Tora), he removes the crown of glory from his head and falls on his face.

And Gallisur H', the prince, when he sees ZAKZAKIEL H', the prince who is appointed to write down the merits of Israel on the Throne of Glory, he removes the crown of glory from his head

and falls on his face.

And Zakzakiel H', the great prince, when he sees 'ANAPHIEL H', the prince who keeps the keys of the heavenly Halls, he removes the crown of glory from his head and falls on his face. Why is he called by the name of 'Anaphiel ? Because the bough of his honour and majesty and his crown and his splendour and his brilliance covers (overshadows) all the chambers of 'Araboth Raqia on high even as the Maker of the World (doth overshadow them). Just as it is written with regard to the Maker of the World (Hab. iii. 3): "His glory covered the heavens, and the earth was full of his praise", even so do the honour and majesty of 'Anaphiel cover all the glories of 'Araboth the highest.

And when he sees SOTHER 'ASHIEL H', the prince, the great, fearful and honoured one, he removes the crown of glory from his head and falls on his face. Why is he called Sother Ashiel? Because he is appointed over the four heads of the fiery river over against the Throne of Glory; and every single prince who goes out or enters before the Shekina, goes out or enters only by his permission.

For the seals of the fiery river are entrusted to him. And furthermore, his height is 7000 myriads of parasangs. And he stirs up the fire of the river ; and he goes out and enters before the Shekina to expound what is written (recorded) concerning the inhabitants of the world. According as it is written: "the judgement was set, and the books were opened".

And Sother 'Ashiel the prince, when he sees SHOQED CHOZI, the great prince, the mighty, terrible and honoured one, he removes the crown of glory from his head and falls upon his face. And why is he called Shoqed Chozi? Because he weighs all the merits (of man) in a balance in the presence of the Holy One, blessed be He.

Andwhen he sees ZEHANPURYU H',the great prince, the mighty and terrible one, honoured, glorified and feared in all the heavenly household, he removes the crown of glory from his head and falls on his face. Why is he called Zehanpuryu? Because he rebukes the fiery river and pushes it back to its place.

Andwhen he sees 'AZBUGA H', the great prince, glorified, revered, honoured, adorned, wonderful, exalted, beloved and feared among allthe great princes who know the mystery of the Throne of Glory, he removes the crown of glory from his head and falls on his face. Why is he called 'Azbuga? Because in the future he will gird (clothe) the righteous and pious of the world with the garments of life and wrap them in the cloak of life, that they may live in them an eternal life.

And when he sees the two great princes, the strong and glorified ones who are standing above him, he removes the crown of glory from his head and falls on his face. And these are the names of the two princes:

SOPHERIEL H' (WHO) KILLETH, (Sopheriel H' the Killer), the great prince, the honoured, glorified, blameless, venerable, ancient and mighty one; (and) SOPHERIEL H' (WHO) MAKETH ALIVE (Sopheriel H' the Lifegiver), the great prince, the honoured, glorified, blameless, ancient and mighty one.

Why is he called Sopheriel H' who killeth (Sopheriel H' the Killer)? Because he is appointed over the books of the dead: [so that] everyone, when the day of his death draws nigh, he writes him in the books of the dead.

Why is he called Sopheriel H' who maketh alive (Sopheriel H' the Lifegiver)? Because he is appointed over the books of the living (of life), so that every one whom the Holy One, blessed be He, will bring into life, he writes him in the book of the living (of life), by authority of MAQOM.

Thou might perhaps say: "Since the Holy One, blessed be He, is sitting on a throne, they also are sitting when writing". (Answer): The Scripture teaches us: "And all the host of heaven are standing by him".

"The host of heaven " (it is said) in order to show us, that even the Great Princes, none like whom there is in the high heavens, do not fulfil the requests of the Shekina otherwise than standing. But how is it (possible that) they (are able to) write, when they are standing?

It is like this:

One is standing on the wheels of the tempest and the other is standing on the wheels of the storm-wind.

The one is clad in kingly garments, the other is clad in kingly garments.

The one is wrapped in a mantle of majesty and the other is wrapped in a mantle of majesty.

The one is crowned with a royal crown, and the other is crowned with a royal crown.

The one's body is full of eyes, and the other's body is full of eyes.

The appearance of one is like unto the appearance of lightnings, and the appearance of the other is like unto the appearance of lightnings.

The eyes of the one are like the sun in its might, and the eyes of the other are like the sun in its might.

The one's height is like the height of the seven heavens, and the other's height is like the height of the seven heavens.

The wings of the one are as (many as) the days of the year, and the wings of the other are as (many as) the days of the year.

The wings of the one extend over the breadth of Raqia', and the wings of the other extend over the breadth of Raqia.

The lips of the one, are as the gates of the East, and the lips of the other are as the gates of the East.

The tongue of the one is as high as the waves of the sea, and the tongue of the other is as high as the waves of the sea.

From the mouth of the one a flame goes forth, and from the mouth of the other a flame goes forth.

From the mouth of the one there go forth lightnings and from the mouth of the other there go forth lightnings.

From the sweat of the one fire is kindled, and from the perspiration of the other fire is kindled.

From the one's tongue a torch is burning, and from the tongue of the other a torch is burning.

On the head of the one there is a sapphire stone, and upon the head of the other there is a sapphire stone.

On the shoulders of the one there is a wheel of a swift cherub, and on the shoulders of the other there is a wheel of a swift cherub.

One has in his hand a burning scroll, the other has in his hand a burning scroll.

The one has in his hand a flaming style, the other has in his hand a flaming style.

The length of the scroll is 3000 myriads of parasangs ; the size of the style is 3000 myriads of parasangs; the size of every single letter that they write is 365 parasangs.

CHAPTER 19

Rikbiel, the prince of the wheels of the Merkaba. The

surroundings of the Merkaba. The commotion among

the angelic hosts at the time of the Qedushsha

R. Ishmael said: Metatron, the Angel, the Prince of the Presence,

said to me:

Above 2 these three angels, these great princes there is one Prince, distinguished, honoured, noble, glorified, adorned, fearful, valiant, strong, great, magnified, glorious, crowned, wonderful, exalted, blameless, beloved, lordly, high and lofty, ancient and mighty, like unto whom there is none among the princes. His name is RIKBIEL H', the great and revered Prince who is standing by the Merkaba.

And why is he called RIKBIEL? Because he is appointed over the wheels of the Merkaba, and they are given in his charge.

And how many are the wheels? Eight; two in each direction. And there are four winds compassing them round about. And these are their names: "the Storm-Wind", "the Tempest", "the Strong Wind", and "the Wind of Earthquake".

And under them four fieryrivers are continually running, one fiery river on each side. And round about them, between the rivers, four clouds are planted (placed), and these they are: "clouds of fire", "clouds of lamps", "clouds of coal", "clouds of brimstone" and they are standing over against [their] wheels.

And the feet of the Chayyoth are resting upon the wheels. And between one wheel and the other earthquake is roaring and thunder is thundering.

And when the time draws nigh for the recital of the Song, (then) the multitudes of wheels are moved, the multitude of clouds tremble, all the chieftains (shallishim) are made afraid, all the horsemen (parashim) do rage, all the mighty ones (gibborim) are excited, all the hosts (seba'im) are afrighted, all the troops (gedudim) are in fear, all the appointed ones (memunnim) haste away, all the princes (sarim) and armies (chayyelim) are dismayed, all the servants (mesharetim) do faint and all the angels (mal'akim) and divisions (degalim) travail with pain.

And one wheel makes a sound to be heard to the other and one Kerub to another, one Chayya. to another, one Seraph to another (saying) "Extol to him that rideth in 'Araboth, by his name Jah and rejoice before him!"

CHAPTER 20

CHAYYLIEL, the prince of the Chayyoth

R. Ishmael said: Metatron, the angel, the Prince of the Presence, said to me :

Above these there is one great and mighty prince. His name is CHAYYLIEL H', a noble and revered prince, a glorious and mighty prince, a great and revered prince, a prince before whom all the children of heaven do tremble, a prince who is able to swallow up the whole earth in one moment (at a mouthful).

And why is he called CHAYYLIEL H'? Because he is appointed over the Holy Chayyoth and smites the Chayyoth with lashes of fire: and glorifies them, when they give praise and glory and rejoicing and he causes them to make haste to say "Holy" and "Blessed be the Glory of H' from his place!" (i.e. the Qedushshd).

CHAPTER 21

The Chayyoth

R. Ishmael said: Metatron, the angel, the Prince of the Presence, said to me:

Four (are) the Chayyoth corresponding to the four winds. Each Chayya is as the space of the whole world. And each one has four faces ; and each face is as the face of the East.

Each one has four wings and each wing is like the cover (roof) of the universe.

And each one has faces in the middle of faces and wings in the middle of wings. The size of the faces is (as the size of) 248 faces, and the size of the wings is (as the size of) 365 wings.

And every one is crowned with 2000 crowns on his head. And each crown is like unto the bow in the cloud. And its splendour is like unto the splendour of the globe of the sun. And the sparks that go forth from every one are like the splendour of the morning star (planet Venus) in the East.

CHAPTER 22A

KERUBIEL, the Prince of the Kembim.

Description of the Kerubim

R. Ishmael said; Metatron, the angel, the Prince of the Presence, said to me :

Above these la there is one prince, noble, wonderful, strong, and praised with all kinds of praise. His name is KERUBIEL H', a mighty prince, full of power and strength a prince of highness, and Highness (is) with him, a righteous prince, and righteousness (is) with him, a holy prince, and holiness (is) with him, a prince glorified in (by) thousand hosts, exalted by ten thousand armies.

At his wrath the earth trembles, at his anger the camps are moved, from fear of him the foundations are shaken, at his rebuke the Araboth do tremble.

His stature is full of (burning) coals. The height of his stature is as the height of the seven heavens the breadth of his stature is as the wideness of the seven heavens and the thickness of his stature is as the seven heavens.

The opening of his mouth is like a lamp of fire. His tongue is a consuming fire. His eyebrows are like unto the splendour of the lightning. His eyes are like sparks of brilliance. His countenance is like a burning fire.

And there is a crown of holiness upon his head on which (crown) the Explicit Name is graven, and hghtnings go forth from it. And the bow of Shekina is between his shoulders.

And his sword is like unto a lightning; and upon his loins there are arrows like unto a flame, and upon his armour and shield there is a consuming fire, and upon his neck there are coals of burning juniper and (also) round about him (there are coals of burning juniper).

And the splendour of Shekina is on his face ; and the horns of majesty on his wheels; and a royal diadem upon his skull.

And his body is full of eyes. And wings are covering the whole of his high stature (lit. the height of his stature is all wings).

On his right hand a flame is burning, and on his left a fire is glowing; and coals are burning from it. And firebrands go forth from his body. And hghtnings are cast forth from his face. With him there is alway thunder upon (in) thunder, by his side there is ever earthquake upon (in) earthquake.

And the two princes of the Merkaba are together with him.

Why is he called KERUBIEL H', the Prince. Because he is appointed over the chariot of the Kerubim. And the mighty Kerubim are given in his charge. And he adorns the crowns on their heads and polishes the diadem upon their skull.

He magnifies the glory of their appearance. And he glorifies the beauty of their majesty. And he increases the greatness of their honour. He causes the song of their praise to be sung. He intensifies their beautiful strength. He causes the brilliance of their glory to shine forth. He beautifies their goodly mercy and lovingkindness. He frames the fairness of their radiance. He makes their merciful beauty even more beautiful. He glorifies their upright majesty. He extols the order of their praise, to stablish the dwellingplace of him "who dwelleth on the Kerubim".

And the Kerubim are standing by the Holy Chayyoth, and their wings are raised up to their heads (lit. are as the height of their heads)

and Shekina is (resting) upon them

and the brillianceof the Glory is upon their faces

and song and praise in their mouth

and their hands are under their wings

and their feet are covered by their wings

and horns of glory are upon their heads

and the splendour of Shekina on their face

and Shekina is (resting) upon them

and sapphire stones are round about them

and columns of fire on their four sides

and columns of firebrands beside them.

There is one sapphire on one side and another sapphire on another side and under the sapphires there are coals of burning juniper.

And one Kerub is standing in each direction but the wings of the Kerubim compass each other above their skulls in glory; and they spread them to sing with them a song to him that inhabiteth the clouds and to praise with them the fearful majesty of the king of kings.

And KERUB IEL H', the prince who is appointed over them, he arrays them in comely, beautiful and pleasant orders and he exalts them in all manner of exaltation, dignity and glory. And he hastens them in glory and might to do the will of their Creator every moment. For above their lofty heads abides continually the glory of the high king "who dwelleth on the Kerubim".

CHAPTER 22B

Additional

And there is a court before the Throne of Glory,

which no seraph nor angel can enter, and it is 36,000 myriads of parasangs, as it is written: "and the Seraphim are standing above him" (the last word of the scriptural passage being 'Lamech-Vav' [numerical value: 36]).

As the numerical value Lamech-Vav (36) the number of the bridges there.

And there are 24 myriads of wheels of fire. And the ministering angels are 12,000 myriads. And there are 12,000 rivers of hail, and 12,000 treasuries of snow. And in the seven Halls are chariots of fire and flames, without reckoning, or end or searching.

R. Ishmael said to me: Metatron, the angel, the Prince of the Presence, said to me:

How are the angels standing on high? Pie said: Like a bridge that is placed over a river so that

every one can pass over it, likewise a bridge is placed from the beginning of the entry to the end.

And three ministering angels surround it and utter a song before YHWH, the God of Israel. And there are standing before it lords of dread and captains of fear, thousand times thousand and ten thousand times ten thousand in number and they sing praise and hymns before YHWH, the God of Israel.

Numerous bridges are there: bridges of fire and numerous bridges of hail. Also numerous rivers of hail, numerous treasuries of snow and numerous wheels offire.

And how many are the ministering angels? 12,000 myriads: six (thousand myriads) above and six (thousand myriads] below. And 12,000 are the treasuries of snow, six above and six below. And 24 myriads of wheels of fire, 12 (myriads] above and 12 (myriads] below. And they surround the bridges and the rivers of fire and the rivers of hail. And there are numerous ministering angels, forming entries, for all the creatures that are standing in the midst thereof, corresponding to (over against) the paths of Raqia Shamayim.

What doeth YHWH, the God of Israel, the King of Glory? The Great and Fearful God, mighty in strength, doth cover his face.

In Araboth are 660,000 myriads of angels of glory standing over against the Throne of Glory and the divisions offlaming fire. And the King of Glory doth cover His face; for else the (Araboth Raqia 1 would be rent asunder in its midst because of the majesty, splendour, beauty, radiance, loveliness, brilliancy, brightness and excellency of the appearance of (the Holy One,) blessed be He.

There are numerous ministering angelsperforming his will, numerous kings, numerous princes in the 'Araboth of his delight, angels who are revered among the rulers in heaven, distinguished, adorned with song and bringing love to remembrance: (who) are affrighted by the splendour of the Shekina, and their eyes are dazzled by the shining beauty of their King, their faces grow black and their strength doth fail.

There go forth rivers ofjoy, streams of gladness, rivers of rejoicing, streams of triumph, rivers of love, streams of friendship (another reading:) of commotion and they flow over and go forth before the Throne of Glory and wax great and go through the gates of the paths of 'Araboth Raqia at the voice of the shouting and musick of the CHAYYOTH, at the voice of the rejoicing of the timbrels of his 'OPHANNIM and at the melody of the cymbals of His Kerubim. And they wax great and go forth with commotion with the sound of the hymn: "HOLY, HOLY, HOLY, IS THE LORD OF HOSTS; THE WHOLE EARTH IS FULL OF HIS GLORY!"

CHAPTER 22C

R. Ishmael said: Metatron, the Prince of the Presence said to me:

What is the distance between one bridge and another? 12 myriads ofparasangs. Their ascent is 12 myriads of parasangs, and their descent 12 myriads ofparasangs.

(The distance) between the rivers of dread and the rivers offear is 22 myriads of parasangs; between the rivers of hail and the rivers of darkness 36 myriads of parasangs; between the chambers of lightnings and the clouds of compassion 42 myriads of parasangs; between the clouds of compassion and the Merkaba 84 myriads ofparasangs; between the Merkaba and the Kerubim 148 myriads of parasangs; between the Kerubim and the 'Ophannim 24 myriads of parasangs; between the Ophannim and the chambers of chambers 24 myriads of parasangs; between the chambers of chambers and the Holy Chayyoth 40,000 myriads ofparasangs; between one wing (of the Chayyoth) and another 12 myriads of parasangs; and the breadth of each one wing is of that same measure; and the distance between the Holy Chayyoth and the Throne of Glory is 30,000 myriads ofparasangs.

And from the foot of the Throne to the seat there are 40,000 myriads of parasangs. And the name of Him that sitteth on it: let the name be sanctified!

And the arches of the Bow are set above the 'Araboth, and they are 1000 thousands and 10,000 times ten thousands (of parasangs) high. Their measure is after the measure of the 'Irin and Qaddishin (Watchers and Holy Ones). As it is written (Gen. ix. 13) "My bow I have set in the cloud". It is not written here "I will set" but "I have set", (i.e.) already; clouds that surround the Throne of Glory. As His clouds pass by, the angels of hail (turn into) burning coal.

And a fire of the voice goes down from by the Holy Chayyoth. And because of the breath of that voice they "run" (Ezek. i. 14) to another place, fearing lest it command them to go; and they "return" lest it injure them from the other side. Therefore "they run and return" (Ezek. i. 14).

And these arches of the Bow are more beautiful and radiant than the radiance of the sun during the summer solstice. And they are whiter than a flaming fire and they are great and beautiful.

Above the arches of the Bow are the wheels of the 'Ophannim. Their height is 1000 thousand and 10,000 times 10,000 units of measure after the measure of the Seraphim and the Troops (Gedudim).

CHAPTER 23

The winds blowing

under the wings of the Kembim

R. Ishmael said; Metatron, the Angel, the Prince of the Presence, said to me :

There are numerous winds blowing under the wings of the Kerubim. There blows "the Brooding Wind", as it is written: " and the wind of God was brooding upon the face of the waters ".

There blows "the Strong Wind", as it is said: "and the Lord caused the sea to go back by a strong east wind all that night".

There blows "the East Wind"as it is written: "the east wind brought the locusts".

There blows "the Wind of Quails" as it is written: "And there went forth a wind from the Lord and brought quails".

There blows "the Wind of Jealousy" as it is written: "And the wind of jealousy came upon him".

There blows the "Wind of Earthquake" as it is written: "and after that the wind of the earthquake ; but the Lord was not in the earthquake".

There blows the "Wind of H' " as it is written: "and he carried me out by the wind of H' and set me down".

There blows the "Evil Wind " as it is written: "and the evil wind departed from him".

There blow the "Wind of Wisdom" Sand the "Wind of Understanding" and the "Wind of Knowledge" and the "Wind of the Fear of H'" as it is written: "And the wind of H'shall rest upon him; the wind of wisdom and understanding, the wind of counsel and might, the wind of knowledge and of the fear.

There blows the "Wind of Rain", as it is written: "the north wind bringeth forth rain".

There blows the "Wind of Lightnings ", as it is written: "he maketh lightnings for the rain and bringeth forth the wind out of his treasuries ".

There blows the "Wind, Breaking the Rocks", as it is written: "the Lord passed by and a great and strong wind (rent the mountains and brake in pieces the rocks before the Lord)".

There blows the "Wind of Assuagement of the Sea", as it is written: "and God made a wind to pass over the earth, and the waters assuaged".

There blows the "Wind of Wrath", as it is written: "and behold there came a great wind from the wilderness and smote the four corners of the house and it fell".

There blows the " Storm-Wind ", as it is written: "Storm-wind, fulfilling his word".

And Satan is standing among these winds, for "storm-wind " is nothing else but "Satan", and all these winds do not blow but under the wings of the Kerubim, as it is written: "and he rode upon a cherub and did fly, yea, and he flew swiftly upon the wings of the wind".

And whither go all these winds? The Scripture teaches us, that they go out from under the wings of the Kerubim and descend on the globe of the sun, as it is written: " The wind goeth toward the south and turneth about unto the north; it tumeth about continually in its course and the wind 14 returneth again to its circuits ". And from the globe of the sun they return and descend upon the rivers and the seas, upon] the mountains and upon the hills, as it is written: "For lo, he that formeth the mountains and createth the wind".

And from the mountains and the hills they return and descend to the seas and the rivers; and from the seas and the rivers they return and descend upon (the) cities and provinces; and from the cities and provinces they return and descend into the Garden, and from the Garden they return and descend to Eden, as it is written: "walking in the Garden in the wind of day". And in the midst of the Garden they join together and blow from one side to the other and are perfumed with the spices of the Garden even from its remotest parts, until they separate from each other, and, filled with the scent of the pure spices, they bring the odour from the remotest parts of Eden and the spices of the Garden to the righteous and godly who in the time to come shall inherit the Garden of Eden and the Tree of Life, as it is written: "Awake, O north wind; and come thou south; blow upon my garden, that the spices thereof may flow out. Let my beloved come into his garden and eat his precious fruits".

The angel Metatron standing with Rabbi Ishmael, revealing the secrets of creation, with cosmic stars, planets, and divine symbols surrounding them.

CHAPTER 24

The different chariots of the Holy One, blessed be He

R. Ishmael said: Metatron, the Angel, the Prince of the Presence, the glory of all heaven, said to me:

Numerous chariots has the Holy One, blessed be He:

He has the "Chariots of (the) Kerubim", as it is written: "And he rode upon a cherub and did fly".

He has the "Chariots of Wind", as it is written: "and he flew swiftly upon the wings of the wind ".

He has the "Chariots of (the) Swift Cloud", as it is written: "Behold, the Lord rideth upon a swift cloud".

He has "the Chariots of Clouds", as it is written: "Lo, I come unto thee in a cloud".

He has the "Chariots of the Altar", as it is written:"I saw the Lord standing upon the Altar".

He has the "Chariots of Ribbotaim", as it is written: "The chariots of God are Ribbotaim; thousands of angels ".

He has the "Chariots of the Tent", as it is written: "And the Lord appeared in the Tent in a pillar of cloud ".

He has the "Chariots of the Tabernacle", as it is written: "And the Lord spake unto him out of the tabernacle".

He has the "Chariots of the Mercy-Seat", as it is written: "then he heard the Voice speaking unto him from upon the mercy-seat".

He has the "Chariots of Sapphire Stone", as it is written: "and there was under his feet as it were a paved work of sapphire stone".

He has the "Chariots of Eagles ", as it is written: "I bare you on eagles' wings". Eagles literally are not meant here but "they that fly swiftly as eagles".

He has the "chariots of Shout", as it is written: "God is gone up with a shout".

He has the "Chariots of Araboth", as it is written: "Extol Him that rideth upon the

Araboth".

He has the "Chariots of Thick Clouds", as it is written: "who maketh the thick

clouds His chariot".

He has the "Chariots of the Chayyoth", as it is written: "and the Chayyoth ran and returned". They run by permission and return by permission, for Shekina is above their heads.

He has the "Chariots of Wheels (Galgallim)", as it is written: "And he said: Go in between the whirling wheels". Lie has the "Chariots of a Swift Kerub", as it is written: "riding on a swift cherub".

And at the time when He rides on a swift kerub, as he sets one of His feet upon him, before he sets the other foot upon his back, he looks through eighteen thousand worlds at one glance. And he discerns and sees into them all and knows what is in all of them and then he sets down the other foot upon him, according as it is written: "Round about eighteen thousand". Whence do we know that He looks through every one of them every day? It is written: "He looked down from heaven upon the children of men to see if there were any that did understand, that did seek after God".

He has the "Chariots of the 'Ophannim", as it is written: "and the 'Ophannim were full of eyes round about".

He has the "Chariots of His Holy Throne", as it is written:" God sitteth upon his holy throne ".

He has the "chariots of the Throne of Yah", as it is written: "Because a hand is lifted up upon the Throne of Jah".

He has the "Chariots of the Throne of Judgement", as it is written: "but the Lord of hosts shall be exalted in judgment".

He has the "Chariots of the Throne of Glory ", as it is written: "The Throne of Glory, set on high from the beginning, is the place of our sanctuary".

He has the "Chariots of the High and Exalted Throne", as it is written: "I saw the Lord sitting upon the high and exalted throne".

CHAPTER 25

'Ophphanniel, the prince of the 'Ophannim.

Description of the 'Ophannim

R. Ishmael said: Metatron, the Angel, the Prince of the Presence, said to me:

Above these there is one great prince, revered, high, lordly, fearful, ancient and strong. 'OPHPHANNIEL H is his name.

He has sixteen faces, four faces on each side, (also) hundred wings on each side. And he has 8466 eyes, corresponding to the days of the year. [2190 -and some say 2116- on each side.] [2191 /2196 and sixteen on each side.]

And those two eyes of his face, in each one of them lightnings are flashing, and from each one of them firebrands are burning ; and no creature is able to behold them : for anyone who looks at them is burnt instantly.

His height is (as) the distance of 2500 years' journey. No eye can behold and no mouth can tell the mighty power of his strength save the King of kings, the Holy One, blessed be He, alone.

Why is he called 'OPHPHANNIEL ?

Because he is appointed over the 'Ophannim and the 'Ophannimare given in his charge. He stands every day and attends and beautifies them. And he exalts and orders their apartment and polishes their standing-place and makes bright their dwellings, makes their corners even and cleanses their seats. And he waits upon them early and late, by day and by night, to increase their beauty, to make great their dignity and to make them "diligent in praise of their Creator.

And all the 'Ophannim are full of eyes, and they are all full of brightness; seventy two sapphire stones are fixed on their garments on their right side and seventy two sapphire stones are fixed on their garments on their left side.

And four carbuncle stones are fixed on the crown of every single one, the splendour of which proceeds in the four directions of 'Araboth even as the splendour of the globe of the sun proceeds in all the directions of the universe. And why is it called Carbuncle (Bareqet)? Because its splendour is like the appearance of a lightning (Baraq). And tents of splendour, tents of brilliance, tents of brightness as of sapphire and carbuncle inclose them because of the shining appearance of their eyes.

CHAPTER 26

SERAPHIEL, the Prince of the Seraphim.

Description of the Seraphim

R. Ishmael said: Metatron, the Angel, the Prince of the Presence, said to me :

Above these there is one prince, wonderful, noble, great, honourable, mighty, terrible, a chief and leader 1 and a swift scribe, glorified, honoured and beloved.

He is altogether filled with splendour, full of praise and shining; and he is wholly full of brilliance, of light and of beauty; and the whole of him is filled with goodliness and greatness.

His countenance is altogether like (that of) angels, but his body is like an eagle's body.

His splendour is like unto lightnings, his appearance like fire brands, his beauty like unto sparks, his honour like fiery coals, his majesty like chashmals, his radiance like the light of the planet Venus.

The image of him is like unto the Greater Light. His height is as the seven heavens. The light from his eyebrows is like the sevenfold light.

The sapphire stone upon his head is as great as the whole universe and like unto the splendour of the very heavens in radiance.

His body is full of eyes like the stars of the sky, innumerable and unsearchable. Every eye is like the planet Venus. Yet, there are some of them like the Lesser Light and some of them like unto the Greater

Light. From his ankles to his knees (they are) like unto stars of lightning, from his knees to his thighs like unto the planet Venus, from his thighs to his loins like unto the moon, from his loins to his neck like the sun, from his neck to his skull like unto the Light Imperishable.

The crown on his head is like unto the splendour of the Throne of Glory. The measure of the crown is the distance of 502 years' journey. There is no kind of splendour, no kind of brilliance, no kind of radiance, no kind of light in the universe but is fixed on that crown.

The name of that prince is SERAPHIEL H". And the crown on his head, its name is "the Prince of Peace". And why is he called by the name of SERAPHIEL '? Because he is appointed over the Seraphim. And the flaming Seraphim are given in his charge. And he presides over them by day and by night and teaches them song, praise, proclamation of beauty, might and majesty; that they may proclaim the beauty of their King in all manner of Praise and Sanctification (Qedushsha).

How many are the Seraphim? Four, corresponding to the four winds of the world. And how many wings have they each one of them? Six, corresponding to the six days of Creation. And how many faces have they? Each one of them four faces.

The measure of the Seraphim and the height of each one of them correspond to the height of the seven heavens. The size of each wing is like the measure of all Raqia' . The size of each face is like that of the face of the East.

And each one of them gives forth light like unto the splendour of the Throne of Glory: so that not even the Holy Chayyoth, the honoured 'Ophannim, nor the majestic KeruUm are able to behold it. For everyone who beholds it, his eyes are darkened because of its great splendour.

Why are they called Seraphim? Because they burn (saraph) the writing tables of Satan : Every day Satan is sitting, together with SAMMAEL, the Prince of Rome, and with DUBBIEL, the Prince of Persia, and they write the iniquities of Israel on writing tables which they hand over to the Seraphim, in order that they may present them before the Holy One, blessed be He, so that He may destroy Israel from the world.

But the Seraphim know from the secrets of the Holy One, blessed be He, that he desires not, that this people Israel should perish. What do the Seraphim? Every day do they receive (accept) them from the hand of Satan and bum them in the burning fire over against the high and exalted Throne in order that they may not come before the Holy One, blessed be He, at the time when he is sitting upon the Throne of Judgement, judging the whole world in truth.

CHAPTER 27

RADWERIEL, the keeper of the Book of Records

R. Ishmael said: Metatron, the Angel of H', the Prince of the Presence, said to me:

Above the Seraphim there is one prince, exalted above all the princes, wondrous more than all the servants. His name is RADWERIEL H' who is appointed over the treasuries of the books.

He fetches forth the Case of Writings (with) the Book of Records in it, and brings it before the Holy One, blessed be He. And he breaks the seals of the case, opens it, takes out the books and delivers them before the Holy One, blessed be He. And the Holy One, blessed be He, receives them of his hand and gives them in his sight to the Scribes, that they may read them in the Great Beth Din (The court of justice) in the height of 'Araboth Raqia', before the heavenly household.

And why is he called RADWERIEL? Because out of every word that goes forth from his mouth an angel is created: and he stands in the songs (in the singing company) of the ministering angels and utters a song before the Holy One, blessed be He when the time draws nigh for the recitation of the (Thrice) Holy.

CHAPTER 28

The 'Irin and Qaddishin

R. Ishmael said: Metatron, the Angel, the Prince of the Presence, said to me:

Above all these there are four great princes, Irin and Qaddishin by name; high, honoured, revered, beloved, wonderful and glorious ones, greater than all the children of heaven. There is none like unto them among all the celestial princes and none their equal among all the Servants. For each one of them is equal to all the rest together.

And their dwelling is over against the Throne of Glory, and their standing place over against the Holy One, blessed be He, so that the brilliance of their dwelling is a reflection of the brilliance of the Throne of Glory. And the splendour of their countenance is a reflection of the splendour of Shekina.

And they are glorified by the glory of 4the Divine Majesty (Gebura) and praised by (through) the praise of Shekina.

And not only that, but the Holy One, blessed be He, does nothing in his world without first consulting them, but after that he doeth it. As it is written: "The sentence is by the decree of the Irin and the demand by the word of the Qaddishin."

The Urin are two and the Qaddishin are two. And how are they standing before the Holy One, blessed be He? It is to be understood, that one 'Ir is standing on one side and the other 'Ir on the other side, and one Qaddish is standing on one side and the other on the other side.

And ever do they exalt the humble, and they abase to the ground those that are proud, and they exalt to the height those that are humble.

And every day, as the Holy One, blessed be He, is sitting upon the Throne of Judgement and judges the whole world, and the Books of the Living and the Books of the Dead are opened before Him, then all the children of heaven are standing before him in fear, dread, awe and trembling. At that time, (when) the Holy One, blessed be He, is sitting upon the Throne of Judgement to execute judgement, his garment is white as snow, the hair on his head as pure wool and the whole of his cloak is like the shining light. And he is covered with righteousness all over as with a coat of mail.

And those Irm and Qaddishin are standing before him like court officers before the judge. And they raise and argue every case and close the case that comes before the Holy One, blessed be He, in judgement, according as it is written: "The sentence is by the decree of the Irm and the demand by the word of the Qaddishin"

Some of them argue and others pass the sentence in the Great Beth Din in 'Araboth. Some of them make the requests from before the Divine Majesty and some close the cases before the Most High. Others finish by going down and (confirming) executing the sentences on earth below. According as it is written: " Behold an Ir and a Qaddishcame down from heaven and cried aloud and said thus. Hew down the tree, and cut off his branches, shake off his leaves, and scatter his fruit: let the beasts get away from under it, and the fowls from his branches ".

Why are they called 'Irin and Qaddishint By reason that they sanctify the body and the spirit with lashes of fire on the third day of the judgement, as it is written: "After two days will he revive us: on the third he will raise us up, and we shall live before him."

CHAPTER 29

Description of a class of angels

R. Ishmael said: Metatron, the Angel, the Prince of the Presence, said to me:

Each one of them has seventy names corresponding to the seventy tongues of the world. And all of them are (based) upon the name of the Holy One, blessed be He. And every several name is written with a flaming style upon the Fearful Crown (Keiher Nora) which is on the head of the high and exalted King.

And from each one of them there go forth sparks and lightnings. And each one of them is beset with horns of splendour round about. From each one lights are shining forth, and each one is surrounded by tents of brilliance so that not even the Seraphim and the Chayyoth who are greater than all the children of heaven are able to behold them.

CHAPTER 30

The 72 princes of Kingdoms and the Prince of the World

officiating at the Great Sanhedrin in heaven

R. Ishmael said: Metatron, the Angel, the Prince of the Presence, said to me:

Whenever the Great Beth Din is seated in the Araboth Raqia' on high there is no opening of the mouth for anyone in the world save those great princes who are called H' by the name of the Holy One, blessed be He.

How many are those princes? Seventy-two princes of the kingdoms of the world besides the Prince of the World who speaks (pleads) in favour of the world before the Holy One, blessed be He, every day, at the hour when the book is opened in which are recorded all the doings of the world, according as it is written: "The judgement was set and the books were opened."

CHAPTER 31

(The attributes of) Justice, Mercy and Truth

by the Throne of Judgement

R. Ishmael said: Metatron, the Angel, the Prince of the Presence, said to me:

At the time when the Holy One, blessed be He, is sitting on the Throne, of Judgement, (then) Justice is standing on His right and Mercy on His left and Truth before His face.

And when man enters before Him to judgement, (then) there comes forth from the splendour of the Mercy towards him as (it were) a staff and stands in front of him. Forthwith man falls upon his face, (and) all the angels of destruction fear and tremble before him, according as it is written: "And with mercy shall the throne be established, and he shall sit upon it in truth."

CHAPTER 32

The execution of judgement on the wicked. God's sword

R. Ishmael said: Metatron, the Angel, the Prince of the Presence, said to me:

When the Holy One, blessed be He, opens the Book half of which is fire and half flame, (then) they go out from before Him in every moment to execute the judgement on the wicked by His sword (that is) drawn forth out of its sheath and the splendour of which shines like a lightning and pervades the world from one end to the other, as it is written: "For by fire will the Lord plead (and by his sword with all flesh)."

And all the inhabitants of the world (lit. those who come into the world) fear and tremble before Him, when they behold His sharpened sword like unto a lightning from one end of the world to the other, and sparks and flashes of the size of the stars of Raqia' going out from it; according as it is written:" If I whet the lightning of my sword".

CHAPTER 33

The angels of Mercy, of Peace and of Destruction by the Throne of Judgement.

The scribes, The angels by the Throne of Glory and the fiery rivers under it.

R. Ishmael said: Metatron, the Angel, the Prince of the Presence, said to me:

At the time that the Holy One, blessed be He, is sitting on the Throne of Judgement, (then) the angels of Mercy are standing on His right, the angels of Peace are standing on His left and the angels of Destruction are standing in front of Him.

And one scribe is standing beneath Him, and another scribe above Him.

And the glorious Seraphim surround the Throne on its four sides with walls of lightnings, and the 'Ophannim. surround them with fire-brands round about the Throne of Glory. And clouds of fire and clouds of flames compass them to the right and to the left; and the Holy Chayyoth carry the Throne of Glory from below: each one with three fingers. The measure of the fingers of each one is 800,000 and 700 times hundred, (and) 66,000 parasangs.

And underneath the feet of the Chayyoth seven fiery rivers are running and flowing. And the breadth of each river is 365 thousand parasangs and its depth is 248 thousand myriads of parasangs. Its length is unsearchable and immeasurable.

And each river turns round in a bow in the four directions of 'Araboth Raqict , and (from there) it falls down to Ma'on and is stayed, and from Mai on to Zebul, from Zebul to Shechaqim, from Shechaqim to Raqia' , from Raqia' to Shamayim and from Shamayim upon the heads of the wicked who are in Gehenna, as it is written: "Behold a whirlwind of the Lord, even his fury, is gone, yea, a whirling tempest; it shall burst upon the head of the wicked".

CHAPTER 34

The different concentric circles round the Chayyoth, consisting offire, water, hailstones etc. and of the angels uttering the Qedushsha responsorium

R. Ishmael said: Metatron; the Angel, the Prince of the Presence, said to me :

The hoofs of the Chayyoth are surrounded by seven clouds of burning coals. The clouds of burning coals are surrounded on the outside by seven walls of flame(s). The seven walls of flame(s) are surrounded on the outside by seven walls of hailstones. The hailstones are surrounded on the outside by xstones of hail (stone of Barad). The stones of hail are surrounded on the outside by stones of "the wings of the tempest ". The stones of "the wings of the tempest" are surrounded on the outside by flames of fire. The flames of fire are surrounded by the chambers of the whirlwind. The chambers of the whirlwind are surrounded on the outside by the fire and the water.

Round about the fire and the water are those who utter the "Holy". Round about those who utter the "Holy" are those who utter the "Blessed"'. Round about those who utter the "Blessed" are the bright clouds. The bright clouds are surrounded on the outside by coals of burning jumper ; and on the outside surrounding the coals of burning juniper there are thousand camps of fire and ten thousand hosts of flame(s). And between every several camp and every several host there is a cloud, so that they may not be burnt by the fire.

CHAPTER 35

The camps of angels in 'Araboth Raqia:

angels, performing the Qedushsha

R. Ishmael said: Metatron, the Angel, the Prince of the Presence, said to me:

506 thousand myriads of camps has the Holy One, blessed be He, in the height of Araboth Raqia. And each camp is (composed of) 496 thousand angels.

And every single angel, the height of his stature is as the great sea; and the appearance of their countenance as the appearance of the lightning, and their eyes as lamps of fire, and their arms and their feet like in colour to polished brass and the roaring voice of their words like the voice of a multitude.

And they are all standing before the Throne of Glory in four rows. And the princes of the army are standing at the head of each row.

And some of them utter the "Holy" and others utter the "Blessed", some of them run as messengers, others are standing in attendance, according as it is written: "Thousand thousands ministered unto him, and ten thousand times ten thousand stood before him: the judgment was set and the books were opened ".

And in the hour, when the time draws nigh for to say the "Holy", (then) first there goes forth a whirlwind from before the Holy One, blessed be He, and bursts upon the camp of Shekina and there arises a great commotion among them, as it is written: "Behold, the whirlwind of the Lord goeth forth with fury, a continuing commotion".

At that moment 4thousand thousands of them are changed into sparks, thousand thousands of them into firebrands, thousand thousands into flashes, thousand thousands into flames, thousand thousands into males, thousand thousands into females, thousand thousands into winds, thousand thousands into burning fires, thousand thousands into flames, thousand thousands into sparks, thousand thousands into chashmals of light; until they take upon themselves the yoke of the kingdom of heaven, the high and lifted up, of the Creator of them all with fear, dread, awe and trembling, with commotion, anguish, terror and trepidation. Then they are changed again into their former shape to have the fear of their King before them alway, as they have set their hearts on saying the Song continually, as it is written: "And one cried unto another and said (Holy, Holy, Holy, etc.)".

CHAPTER 36

The angels bathe in the fiery river

before reciting the 'Song'

R. Ishmael said: Metatron, the Angel, the Prince of the Presence, said to me ;

At the time when the ministering angels desire to say (the) Song, (then) Nehar di-Nur (the fiery stream) rises with many thousand thousands and myriads of myriads" (of angels) of power and strength of fire and it runs and passes under the Throne of Glory, between the camps of the ministering angels and the troops of Araboth.

And all the ministering angels first go down into Nehar di-Nur, and they dip themselves in the fire and dip their tongue and their mouth seven times ; and after that they go up and put on the garment of 'Machaqe Samal' and cover themselves with cloaks of chashmal and stand in four rows over against the Throne of Glory, in all the heavens.

CHAPTER 37

The four camps of Shekina and their surroundings

R. Ishmael said: Metatron, the Angel, the Prince of the Presence, said to me:

In the seven Halls there are standing four chariots of Shekina, and before each one are standing the four camps of Shekina. Between each camp a river of fire is continually flowing.

Between each river there are bright clouds surrounding them], and between each cloud there are put up pillars of brimstone. Between one pillar and another there are standing flaming wheels, surrounding them. And between one wheel and another there are flames of fire round about.

Between one flame and another there are treasuries of lightnings; behind the treasuries of lightnings are the wings of the stormwind. Behind the wings of the storm-wind are the chambers of the tempest; behind the chambers of the tempest there are winds, voices, thunders, sparks [upon] sparks and earthquakes [upon] earthquakes.

CHAPTER 38

The fear that befalls all the heavens at the sound of the

'Holy? esp. the heavenly bodies. These appeased by the

Prince of the World

R. Ishmael said: Metatron, the Angel, the Prince of the Presence, said to me:

At the time, when the ministering angels utter (the Thrice) Holy, then all the pillars of the heavens and their sockets do tremble, and the gates of the Halls of Araboth Raqia' are shaken and the foundations of Shechaqim and the Universe (Tebel) are moved, and the orders of Ma'on and the chambers of Makon quiver, and all the orders of Raqia and the constellations and the planets are dismayed, and the globes of the sun and the moon haste away and flee out of their courses and run 12,000 parasangs and seek to throw themselves down from heaven, by reason of the roaring voice of their chant, and the noise of their praise and the sparks and lightnings that go forth from their faces; as it is written: "The voice of thy thunder was in the heaven (the lightnings lightened the world, the earth trembled and shook) ".

Until the prince of the world calls them, saying: "Be ye quiet in your place ! Fear not because of the ministering angels who sing the Song before the Holy One, blessed be He". As it is written: "When the morning stars sang together and all the children of heaven shouted for joy".

CHAPTER 39

The explicit names fly off from the Throne and all the

various angelic hosts prostrate themselves before it at

the time of the Qedushsha

R. Ishmael said: Metatron, the Angel, the Prince of the Presence, said to me :

When the ministering angels utter the "Holy" then all the explicit names that are graven with a flaming style on the Throne of Glory fly off like eagles, with sixteen wings. And they surround and compass the Holy One, blessed be He, on the four sides of the place of His Shekinal.

And the angels of the host, and the flaming Servants, and the mighty 'Ophannim, and the Kerubim of the Shekina, and the Holy Chayyoth, and the Seraphim, and the 'Er'ellim, and the Taphsarim and the troops of consuming fire, and the fiery armies, and the flaming hosts, and the holy princes, adorned with crowns, clad in kingly majesty, wrapped in glory, girt with loftiness, 4 fall upon their faces three times, saying: "Blessed be the name of His glorious kingdom for ever and ever".

CHAPTER 40

The ministering angels rewarded with crowns, when uttering the" Holy '
' in its right order, andpunished by consumingfire if not.

New ones created in the stead of the consumed angels

R. Ishmael said: Metatron, the Angel, the Prince of the Presence, said
to me:

When the ministering angels say "Holy" before the Holy One, blessed be
He, in the proper way, then the servants of His Throne, the attendants
of His Glory, go forth with great mirth from under the Throne of Glory.

And they all carry in their hands, each one of them thousand and ten
thousand times ten thousand crowns of stars, similar in appearance to
the planet Venus, and put them on the ministering angels and the great
princes who utter the "Holy". Three crowns they put on each one of
them: one crown because they say "Holy", another crown, because they
say "Holy, Holy", and a third crown because they say "Holy, Holy, Holy,
is the Lord of Hosts".

And in the moment that they do not utter the "Holy" in the right order,
a consuming fire goes forth from the little finger of the Holy One,
blessed be He, and falls down in the midst of their ranksand is divided
into 496 thousand parts corresponding to the four camps of the ministering angels, and consumes them in one moment, as it is written: "A fire
goeth before him and burneth up his adversaries round about".

After that the Holy One, blessed be He, opens His mouth and speaks
one word and creates others in their stead, new ones like them. And each
one stands before His Throne of Glory, uttering the "Holy", as it is written: "They are new every morning; great is thy faithfulness".

CHAPTER 41

Metatron shows R. Ishmael the letters engraved on

the Throne of Glory by which letters everything in

heaven and earth has been created

R. Ishmael said: Metatron, the Angel, the Prince of the Presence, said to me:

Come and behold the letters by which the heaven and theearth were created, the letters by which were created the mountains and hills, the letters by which were created the seas and rivers, the letters by which were created the trees and herbs, the letters by which were created the planets and the constellations, the letters by which were created the globe of the moon and the globe of the sun, Orion, the Pleiades and all the different luminaries of Raqia'.

The letters by which were created the Throne of Glory and the Wheels of the Merkaba, the letters by which were created the necessities of the worlds, the letters by which were created wisdom, understanding, knowledge, prudence, meekness and righteousness by which the whole world is sustained.

And I walked by his side and he took me by his hand and raised me upon his wings and showed me those letters, all of them, that are graven with a flaming style on the Throne of Glory: and sparks go forth from them and cover all the chambers of 'Araboth.

CHAPTER 42

Instances of polar opposites kept in balance by several

Divine Names and other similar wonders

R. Ishmael said: Metatron, the Angel, the Prince of the Presence, said to me:

Come and I will show thee, where the waters are suspended in the highest, where fire is burning in the midst of hail, where lightnings lighten out of the midst of snowy mountains, where thunders are roaring in the celestial heights, where a flame is burning in the midst of the burning fire and where voices make themselves heard in the midst of thunder and earthquake.

Then I went by his side and he took me by his hand and hfted me up on his wings and showed me all those things. I beheld the waters suspended on high in Araboth Raqia' by (force of) the name YAH 'EHYE ASHER 'EHYE (Jah, I am that I am).

And their fruits going down from heaven and watering the face of the world, as it is written: "(He watereth the mountains from his chambers :) the earth is satisfied with the fruit of thy work".

And I saw fire and snow and hailstone that were mingled together within each other and yet were undamaged, by (force of) the name 'ESH 'OKELA (consuming fire), as it is written: "For the Lord, thy God, is a consuming fire".

And I saw lightnings that were hghtening out of mountains of snow and yet were not damaged (quenched), by (force of) the name YAH SUR 'OLAMIM (Jah, the everlasting rock), as it is written: "For in Jah, YHWH, the everlasting rock".

And I saw thunders and voices that were roaring in the midst of fiery flames and were not damaged (silenced), by (force of) the name 'EL-SHADDAI RABBA (the Great God Almighty) as it is written: "I am God Almighty".

And I beheld a flame (and) a glow (glowing flames) that were flaming and glowing in the midst of burning fire, and yet were not damaged (devoured), by (force of) the name YAD 'AL KES YAH (the hand upon the Throne of the Lord) as it is written: " And he said: for the hand is upon the Throne of the Lord ".

And I beheld rivers of fire in the midst of rivers of water and they were not damaged (quenched) by (force of) the name 'OSE SHALOM (Maker of Peace) as it is written: "He maketh peace in his high places". For he makes peace between the fire and the water, between the hail and the fire, between the wind and the cloud, between the earthquake and the sparks.

CHAPTER 43

Metatron shows R. Ishmael the abode of the unborn spirits

and of the spirits of the righteous dead

R. Ishmael said: Metatron said to me:

Come and I will show thee Iwhere arel the spirits of the righteous that
have been created and have returned, and the spirits of the righteous
that have not yet been created.

And he lifted me up to his side, took me by his hand and hfted me up
near the Throne of Glory by the place of the Shekina ; and he revealed
the Throne of Glory to me, and he showed me the spirits that have been
created and had returned : and they were flying above the Throne of
Glory before the Holy One, blessed be He.

After that I went to interpret the following verse of Scripture and I
found in what is written: "for the spirit clothed itself before me, and the
souls I have made" that ("for the spirit was clothed before me") means
the spirits that have been created in the chamber of creation of the
righteous and that have returned before the Holy One, blessed be He;
(and the words:) "and the souls I have made" refer to the spirits 4 of the
righteous that have not yet been created in the chamber (GUPH).

CHAPTER 44

Metatron shows R. Ishmael the abode of the wicked

and the intermediate in Sheol.

The Patriarchs pray for the deliverance of Israel

R. Ishmael said: Metatron, x the Angel, the Prince of the Presence, said
to me:

Come and I will show thee the spirits of the wicked and the spirits of
the intermediate where they are standing, and the spirits of the intermediate, whither they go down, 3and the spirits of the wicked, where they
go down.

And he said to me: The spirits of the wicked go down to She'ol by the hands of two angels of destruction: ZAAPHIEL and SIMKIEL are their names.

SIMKIEL is appointed over the intermediate to support them and purify them because of the great mercy of the Prince of the Place (Maqom). ZAAPHIEL is appointed over the spirits of the wicked in order to cast them down from the presence of the Holy One, blessed be He, and from the splendour of the Shekina to She'ol, to be punished in the fire of Gehenna with staves of burning coal.

And I went by his side, and he took me by his hand and showed me all of them with his fingers.

And I beheld the appearance of their faces (and, lo, it was) as the appearance of children of men, and their bodies like eagles. And not only that but (furthermore) the colour of the countenance of the intermediate was like pale grey on account of their deeds, for there are stains upon them until they have become cleaned from their iniquity in the fire.

And the colour of the wicked was like the bottom of a pot on account of the wickedness of their doings.

And I saw the spirits of the Patriarchs Abraham Isaac and Jacob and the rest of the righteous whom they have brought up out of their graves and who have ascended to the Heaven (Raqirf). And they were praying before the Holy One, blessed be He, saying intheir prayer: "Lord of the Universe! How long wilt thou sit upon (thy) Throne like a mourner in the days of his mourning with thy right hand behind thee and not deliver thy children and reveal thy Kingdom in the world? And for how long wilt thou have no pity upon thy children who are made slaves among the nations of the world?

Nor upon thy right hand that is behind thee wherewith thou didst stretch out the heavens and the earth and the heavens of heavens? When wilt thou have compassion?"

Then the Holy One, blessed be He, answered every one of them, saying: "Since these wicked do sin so and so, and transgress with such and such transgressions against me, how could I deliver my great Right Hand in the downfall by their hands (caused by them).

In that moment Metatron called me and spake to me: "My servant! Take the books, and read their evil doings!" Forthwith I took the books and read their doings and there were to be found 36 transgressions (written down) with regard to each wicked one and besides, that they have transgressed all the letters in the Tora, as it is written (Dan. ix. u) : "Yea, all Israel have transgressed thy Law". It is not written 'al torateka but 'et (JIN) torateka, for they have transgressed from 'Aleph to Taw, 40 statutes have they transgressed for each letter.

Forthwith Abraham, Isaac and Jacob wept. Then said to them the Holy One, blessed be He: "Abraham, my beloved, Isaac, my Elect one, Jacob, my firstborn! How can I now deliver them from among the nations of the world?" And forthwith MIKAEL, the Prince of Israel, cried and wept with a loud voice and said: "Why standest thou afar off, O Lord?".

A depiction of the angel Metatron being humbled by God, his wings and light dimming as other angels surround him with a mix of jealousy and awe, all under the powerful presence of God's divine light.

CHAPTER 45

Metatron shows R. Ishmael past and future events

recorded on the Curtain of the Throne

R. Ishmael said: Metatron said to me:

Come, and I will show thee the Curtain of MAQOM (the Divine Majesty) which is spread before the Holy One, blessed be He, (and) whereon are graven all the generations of the world and all their doings, both what they have done and what they will do until the end of all generations.

And I went, and he showed it to me pointing it out with his fingers Mike a father who teaches his children the letters of Tora. And I saw each generation, the rulers of each generation, and the heads of each generation, the shepherds of each generation, the oppressors (drivers) of each generation, the keepers of each generation, the scourgers of each generation, the overseers of each generation, the judges of each generation, the court officers of each generation, the teachers of each generation, the supporters of each generation, the chiefs of each generation, the presidents of academies of each generation, the magistrates of each generation, the princes of each generation, the counsellors of each generation, the nobles of each generation, and the men of might of each generation, the elders of each generation, and the guides of each generation.

And I saw Adam, his generation, their doings and their thoughts, Noah and his generation, their

doings and their thoughts, and the generation of the flood, their doings and their thoughts, Shem and his generation, their doings and their thoughts, Nimrod and the generation of the confusion of tongues, and his generation, their doings and their thoughts, Abraham and his generation, their doings and their thoughts, Isaac and his generation, their doings and their thoughts, Ishmael and his generation, their doings and their thoughts, Jacob and his generation, their doings and their thoughts, Joseph and his generation, their doings and their thoughts, the tribes and their generation, their doings and their thoughts, Amram and his generation, their doings and their thoughts, Moses and his generation, their doings and their thoughts, Aaron and Mirjam their works and their doings, the princes and the elders, their works and doings, Joshua and his generation, their works and doings, the judges and their generation, their works and doings, Eli and his generation, their works and doings, "Phinehas, their works and doings, Elkanah and his generation, their works and their doings, Samuel and his generation, their works and doings, the kings of Judah with their generations, their works and their doings, the kings of Israel and their generations, their works and their doings, the princes of Israel, their works and their doings; the princes of the nations of the world, their works and their doings, the heads of the councils of Israel, their works and their doings ; the heads of (the councils in) the nations of the world, their generations, their works and their doings; the rulers of Israel and their generation, their works and their doings ; the nobles of Israel and their generation, their works and their doings ; the nobles of the nations of the world and their generation(s), their works and their doings; the men of reputation in Israel, their generation, their works and their doings ; the judges of Israel, their generation, their works and their doings ; the judges of the nations of the world and their generation, their works and their doings ; the teachers of children in Israel, their generations, their works and their doings ; the teachers of children in the nations of the world, their generations, their works and their doings; the counsellors (interpreters) of Israel, their generation, their works and their doings ; the counsellors (interpreters) of the nations of the world, their generation, their works and their doings ; all the prophets of Israel, their generation, their works and their doings ; all the prophets of the nations of the world, their generation, their works and their doings; and all the fights and wars that the nations 16 of the world wrought against the people of Israel in the time of their kingdom. And I saw Messiah, son of Joseph, and his generation "and their" works and their doings that they will do against the nations of the world. And I saw Messiah, son of David, and his generation, and all the fights and wars, and their works and their doings that they will do with Israel both for good and evil. And I saw all the fights and wars that Gog and Magog will fight in the days of Messiah, and all that the Holy One, blessed be He, will do with them in the time to come.

And all the rest of all the leaders of the generations and all the works of the generations both in Israel and in the nations of the world, both what is done and what will be done hereafter to all generations until the end of time, (all) were graven on the Curtain of MAQOM. And I saw all these things with my eyes; and after I had seen it, I opened my mouth in praise of MAQOM (the Divine Majesty): "For the King's word hath power (and who may say unto him: What doest thou?) Whoso keepeth the commandments shall know no evil thing". And I said: "O Lord, how manifold are thy works!".

CHAPTER 46

The place of the stars shown to R. Ishmael

R. Ishmael said : Metatron said to me :

(Come and I will show thee) the space of the stars a that are standing in Raqia' night by night in fear of the Almighty (MAQOM) and (I will show thee) where they go and where they stand.

I walked by his side, and he took me by his hand and pointed out all to me with his fingers. And they were standing on sparks of flames round the Merkaba of the Almighty (MAQOM). What did Metatron do? At that moment he clapped his hands and chased them off from their place. Forthwith they flew off on flaming wings, rose and fled from the four sides of the Throne of the Merkaba, and (as they flew) he told me the names of every single one. As it is written:" He telleth the number of the stars; he giveth them all their names", teaching, that the Holy One, blessed be He, has given a name to each one of them.

And they all enter in counted order under the guidance of (lit. through, by the hands of) RAHATIEL to Raqia' ha-sh SHamayim to serve the world. And they go out in counted order to praise the Holy One, blessed be He, with songs and hymns, according as it is written: "The heavens declare the glory of God".

But in the time to come the Holy One, blessed be He, will create them anew, as it is written: "They are new every morning". And they open their mouth and utter a song. Which is the song that they utter?: "When I consider thy heavens".

CHAPTER 47

Metatron shows R. Ishmael the spirits

of the punished angels

R. Ishmael said; Metatron said to me;

Come and I will show thee the souls of the angels and the spirits of the ministering servants whose bodies have been burnt in the fire of MAQOM (the Almighty) that goes forth from his little finger. And they have been made into fiery coals in the midst of the fiery river (Nehar di-Nur). But their spirits and their souls are standing behind the Shekina.

Whenever the ministering angels utter a song at a wrong timeor as not appointed to be sung they are burnt and consumed by the fire of their Creator and by a flame from their Maker, in the places (chambers) of the whirlwind, for it blows upon them and drives them into the Nehar di-Nur; and there they are made into numerous mountains of burning coal. But their spirit and their soul return to their Creator, and all are standing behind their Master.

And I went by his side and he took me by his hand; and he showed me all the souls of the angels and the spirits of the ministering servants who were standing behind the Shekina upon wings of the whirlwind and walls of fire surrounding them.

At that moment Metatron opened to me the gates of the walls within which they were standing behind the Shekina, And I lifted up my eyes and saw them, and behold, the likeness of every one was as (that of) angels and their wings hke birds' (wings), made out of flames, the work of burning fire. In that moment I opened my mouth in praise of MAQOM and said: "How great are thy works, O Lord ".

CHAPTER 48A

Metatron shows R. Ishmael the Right Hand of the

Most High, now inactive behind Him, but in the

future destined to work the deliverance of Israel

R. Ishmael said ; Metatron said to me;

Come, and I will show thee the Right Hand of MAQOM, laid behind (Him) because of the destruction of the Holy Temple ; from which all kinds of splendour and light shine forth and by which the 955 heavens were created ; and whom not even the Seraphim and the 'Ophannim are permitted (to behold), until the day of salvation shall arrive.

And I went by his side and he took me by his hand and showed me (the Right Hand of MAQOM), with all manner of praise, rejoicing and song: and no mouth can tell its praise, and no eye can behold it, because of its greatness, dignity, majesty, glory and beauty.

And not only that, but all the souls of the righteous who are counted worthy to behold the joy of Jerusalem, they are standing by it, praising and praying before it three times every day, saying: "Awake, awake, put on strength, arm of the Lord" according as it is written: "He caused his glorious arm to go at the right hand of Moses".

In that moment the Right Hand of MAQOM was weeping. And there went forth from its five fingers five rivers of tears and fell down into the great sea and shook the whole world, according as it is written: "The earth is utterly broken, the earth is clean dissolved, the earth is moved exceedingly, the earth shall stagger like a drunken man and shall be moved to and fro like a hut", five times corresponding to the fingers of his Great Right Hand.

But when the Holy One, blessed be He, sees, that there is no righteous man in the generation, and no pious man (Chasid] on earth, and no justice in the hands of men; and (that there is) no man like unto Moses, and no intercessor as Samuel who could pray before MAQOM for the salvation and for the deliverance, and for His Kingdom, that it be revealed in the whole world; and for His great Right Hand that He put it before Himself again to work great salvation by it for Israel, then forth-with will the Holy One, blessed be He, remember His own justice, favour, mercy and grace: and He will dehver His great Arm by himself, and His righteousness will support Him. According as it is written: "And he saw, that there was no man" (that is:) like unto Moses who prayed countless times for Israel in the desert and averted the (Divine) decrees from them" and he wondered, that there was no intercessor" like unto Samuel who intreated the Holy One, blessed be He, and called unto Him and he answered him and fulfilled his desire, even if it was not fit (in accordance with the Divine plan), according as it is written: "Is it not wheat-harvest to-day? I will call unto the Lord".

And not only that, but He joined fellowship with Moses in every place, as it is written: "Moses and Aaron among His priests." And again it is written: "Though Moses and Samuel stood before me": "Mine own arm brought salvation unto me".

Said the Holy One, blessed be He in that hour: " How long shall I wait for the children of men to work salvation according to their right-eousness for my arm? For my own sake and for the sake of my merit and righteousness will I deliver my arm and by it redeem my children from among the nations of the world. As it is written: "For my own sake will I do it. For how should my name be profaned".

In that moment will the Holy One, blessed be He, reveal His Great Arm and show it to the nations of the world: for its length is as the length of the world and its breadth is as the width of the world. And the appear-ance of its splendour is like unto the splendour of the sunshine in its might, in the summer solstice.

Forthwith Israel will be saved from among the nations of the world. And Messiah will appear unto them and He will bring them up to Jerusalem with great joy. And not only that but Israel will come from the four quarters of the World and eat with Messiah. But the nations of the world shall not eat with them, as it is written: "The Lord hath made bare his holy arm in the eyes of all the nations ; and all the ends of the earth shall see the salva-tion of our God". And again: "The Lord alone did lead him, and there was no strange god with him". "And the Lord shall be king over all the earth".

CHAPTER 48B

The Divine Names that go forth from the Throne of Glory,

crowned and escorted by numerous angelic hosts through the

heavens and back again to the Throne the angels sing the

'Holy' and the 'Blessed'

These are the seventy-two names written on the heart of the Holy One, blessed be He:

SS, SeDeQ {righteousness), SaHPeL SUR, SBI, SaDdlQ{righteous}, STh, SHN, SeBa'oTh {Lord ofHostsKShaDdaY {God Almighty}, 'eLoHIM {God},YHWH, SH, DGUL, W'DOM, SSS", 'YW, 'F, 'HW, HB, YaH, HW, WWW, SSS, PPP, NN, HH, HaY {living}, HaY, ROKeB 'aRa-BOTh {riding upon the 'Araboth'} YH, HH, WH, MMM, NNN, HWW, YH, YHH, HPhS, H'S, ı, W, S", Z', "', QQQ {Holy, Holy, Holy}, QShR, BW, ZK, GINUR, GINURYa', Y', YOD, 'aLePh, H'N, P'P, R'W, YYWy YYW, BBS, DDD, TTT, KKK, KLL, SYS, 'XT', BShKMLW {blessed be the Name of His glorious kingdom for ever and ever}, completed for MeLeK HalOLaM {the King of the Universe}, JBRH LB' {the beginning of Wisdom for the children of men}, BNLK W" Y {blessed be He who gives strength to the weary and increaseth strength to them that have no might.}that go forth (adorned) with numerous crowns of fire with numerous crowns of flame, with numerous crowns of chashmal, with numerous crowns of lightning from before the Throne of Glory.

And with them (there are) thousand hundreds of power (i.e. powerful angels) who escort them like a king with trembling and dread, with awe and shivering, with honour and majesty and fear, with terror, with greatness and dignity, with glory and strength, with understanding and knowledge and with a pillar of fire and a pillar of flame and lightning and their light is as lightnings of light and with the likeness of the chashmal.

And they give glory unto them and they answer and cry before them: Holy, Holy, Holy.

And they roll (convoy) them through every heaven as mighty and honoured princes. And when they bring them all back to the place of the Throne of Glory, then all the Chayyoth by the Merkaba open their mouth in praise of His glorious name, saying: "Blessed be the name of His glorious kingdom for ever and ever".

CHAPTER 48C

An Enoch-Metatron piece

ALT 1

"I seized him, and I took him and I appointed him" that is Enoch, the son of Jared, whose name is Metatron and I took him from among the children of men and made him a Throne over against my Throne. Which is the size of that Throne? Seventy thousand parasangs (all) of fire.

I committed unto him 70 angels corresponding to the nations (of the world) and I gave into his charge all the household above and below.

And I committed to him Wisdom and Intelligence more than (to) all the angels. And I called his name "the LESSER YAH", whose name is by Gematria 71. And I arranged for him all the works of Creation. And I made his power to transcend (lit. I made for him power more than) all the ministering angels.

ALT 2

He committed unto Metatron that is Enoch, the son of Jared all treasuries. And I appointed him over all the stores that I have in every heaven. And I committed into his hands the keys of each heavenly store.

I made (of) him the prince over all the princes, and I made (of) him a minister of my Throne of Glory, to provide for and arrange the Holy Chayyoth, to wreathe crowns for them (to crown them with crowns), to clothe them with honour and majesty to prepare for them a seat when he is sitting on his throne to magnify his glory in the height.

The height of his stature among all those (that are) of high stature (is) seventy thousand parasangs. And I made his glory great as the majesty of my glory. and the brilliance of his eyes as the splendour of the Throne of Glory. His garment honour and majesty, his royal crown 500 by 500 parasangs.

ALT 3

Alephl I made him strong, I took him, I appointed him: (namely) Metatron, my servant who is one (unique) among all the children of heaven. I made him strong in the generation of the first Adam. But when I beheld the men of the generation of the flood, that they were corrupt, then I went and removed my Shekina from among them. And I lifted it up on high with the sound of a trumpet and with a shout, as it is written: "God is gone up with a shout, the Lord with the sound of a trumpet".

"And I took him": (that is) Enoch, the son of Jared, from among them. And I lifted him up with the sound of a trumpet and with a tera'a (shout) to the high heavens, to be my witness together with the Chayyoth by the Merkaba in the world to come.

I appointed him over all the treasuries and stores that I have in every heaven. And I committed into his hand the keys of every several one.

I made (of) him the prince over all the princes and a minister of the Throne of Glory (and) the Halls of 'Araboth: to open their doors to me, and (of) the Throne of Glory, to exalt an arrange it; (and I appointed him over) the Holy Chayyot to wreathe crowns upon their heads; the majestic 'Ophannim, to crown them with strength and glory; the; honoured Kerubim, to clothe: them in majesty; over the radiant sparks, to make them to shine with splendour and brilliance; over the flaming Seraphim, to cover them with highness; the Chashmallim of light, to make them radiant with Light and to prepare the seat for me every morning as I sit upon the Throne of Glory. And to extol and magnify my glory inthe height of my power; (and I have committed unto him) the secrets of above and the secrets of below (heavenly secrets and earthly secrets).

I made him higher than all. The height of his stature, in the midst of all (who are) high of stature (I made) seventy thousand parasangs. I made his Throne great by the majesty of my Throne. And I increased its glory by the honour of my glory.

I transformed his flesh into torches of fire, and all the bones of his body into fiery coals; and I made the appearance of his eyes as the lightning, and the light of his eyebrows as the imperishable light. I made his face bright as the splendour of the sun, and his eyes as the splendour of the Throne of Glory.

I made honour and majesty his clothing, beauty and highness his covering cloak and a royal crown of 500 by (times) 500 parasangs (his) diadem. And I put upon him of my honour, my majesty and the splendour, of my glory that is upon my Throne of Glory. I called him the LESSER YHWH, the Prince of the Presence, the Knower of Secrets: for every secret did I reveal to him as a father and all mysteries declared I unto him in uprightness.

I set up his throne at the door of my Hall that he may sit and judge the heavenly household on high. And I placed every prince before him, to receive authority from him, to perform his will.

Seventy names did I take from (my) names and called him by them to enhance his glory.

Seventy princes gave I into his hand, to command unto them my precepts and my words in every language:

to abase by his word the proud to the ground, and to exalt by the utterance of his lips the humble to the height ; to smite kings by his speech, to turn kings away from their paths, to set up(the) rulers over their dominion as it is written: "and he changeth the times and the seasons, and to give wisdom unto all the setwise of the world and understanding (and) knowledge to all who understand knowledge, as it is griten: " and knowledge to them that know understanding", to reveal to them the secrets of my words and to teach the decree of my righteous judgement, as it is written: "so shall my word be that goeth forth out of my mouth; it shall not return unto me void but shall accomplish (that which I please)". 'E'eseh' (I shall accomplish) is not written here, but "asdh' (he shall accomplish), meaning, that whatever word and whatever utterance goes forth from before the Holy One, blessed be He, Metatron stands and carries it out. And he establishes the decrees of the Holy One, blessed be He.

CHAPTER 48D

The names of Metatron. The treasuries of Wisdom opened to
Moses on mount Sinai. The angels protest against Metatron for
revealing the secrets to Moses and are answered and rebuked by
God. The chain of tradition and the power of the transmitted
mysteries to heal diseases

Seventy names has Metatron which the Holy One, blessed be He, took
from his own name and

put upon him. And these they are:

YeHOEL, YaH, YeHOEL, YOPHIEL and Yophphiel, and APHPHIEL
and MaRGeZIEL, GIPpUYEL, Pa'aZIEL, 'A'aH, PeRIEL, TaTRIEL,
TaBKIEL,'W, YHWH, DH, WHYH, 'eBeD, DiBbURIEL, 'aPh'aPIEL,
SPPIEL, PaSPaSIEL, SeNeGRON, MeTaTRON, SOGDIN, ADRIGON,
ASUM, SaQPaM, SaQTaM, MIGON MITTON, MOTTRON,
ROSPHIM, QINOTh, ChaTaTYaH, DeGaZYaH, PSPYaH, BSKNYH,
MZRG, BaRaD.., MKRKK, MSPRD, ChShG, ChShB, MNRTTT,
BSYRYM, MITMON, TITMON, PiSQON, SaPhSaPhYaH, ZRCh,
ZRChYaH, B', BeYaH, HBH BeYaH, PeLeT, PLTYaH, RaBRaBYaH,
ChaS, ChaSYaH, TaPhTaPhYaH, TaMTaMYaH, SeHaSYaH, IRURYaH,
'aL'aLYaH, BaZRIDYaH, SaTSaTKYaH, SaSDYaH, RaZRaZYAH,
BaZRaZYaH, 'aRIMYaH, SBHYaH, SBIBKHYH, SiMKaM, YaHSeYaH,
SSBIBYaH, SaBKaSBeYaH, QeLILQaLYaH, fKIHHH, HHYH, WH,
WHYH, ZaKklKYaH, TUTRISYaH, SURYaH, ZeH, PeNIRHYaH,
ZIZ'H, GaL RaZaYYa, MaMLIKYaH, TTYaH, eMeQ, QaMYaH,
MeKaPpeRYaH, PeRISHYaH, SePhaM, GBIR, GiBbORYaH, GOR,
GORYaH, ZIW, 'OKBaR, the LESSER YHWH, after the name of his
Master, (Ex. xxiii. 21) "for my name is in him", RaBIBIEL, TUMIEL,
Segansakkiel ('Sagnezagiel' / 'Neganzegael), the Prince of Wisdom.

And why is he called by the name Sagnesakiel? Because all the treasuries
of wisdom are committed in his hand.

And all of them were opened to Moses on Sinai, so that he learnt them during the forty days, while he was standing (remaining): the Torah in the seventy aspects of the seventy tongues, the Prophets in the seventy aspects of the seventy tongues, the Writings in the seventy aspects of the seventy tongues, "the Halakas in the seventy aspects of the seventy tongues, the Traditions in the seventy aspects of the seventy tongues, the Haggadas in the seventy aspects of the seventy tongues and the Toseftas in the seventy aspects of the seventy tongues'.

But as soon as the forty days were ended, he forgot all of them in one moment. Then the Holy One, blessed be He, called Yephiphyah, the Prince of the Law, and (through him) they were given to Moses as a gift. As it is written: "and the Lord gave them unto me". And after that it remained with him. And whence do we know, that it remained (in his memory)? Because it is written: " Remember ye the Law of Moses my servant which I commanded unto him in Horeb for all Israel, even my statutes and judgements". The Law of Moses': that is the Tora, the Prophets and the Writings, 'statutes': that is the Halakas and Traditions, 'judgements'; that is the Haggadas and the Toseftas. And all of them were given to Moses on high on Sinai.

These seventy names (are) a reflection of the Explicit Name(s) on the Merkaba which are graven upon the Throne of Glory. For the Holy One, blessed be He, took from His Explicit Name(s) and put upon the name of Metatron: Seventy Names of His by which the ministering angels call the King of the kings of kings, blessed be He, in the high heavens, and twenty-two letters that are on the ring upon his finger with which are sealed the destinies of the princes of kingdoms on high in greatness and power and with which are sealed the lots of the Angel of Death, and the destinies of every nation and tongue.

Said Metatron, the Angel, the Prince of the Presence; the Angel, the Prince of the Wisdom; the Angel, the Prince of the Understanding; the Angel, the Prince of the Kings; the Angel, the Prince of the Rulers; the angel, the Prince of the Glory; the angel, the Prince of the high ones, and of the princes, the exalted, great and honoured ones, in heaven and on earth:

"H, the God of Israel, is my witness in this thing, (that] when I revealed this secret to Moses, then all the hosts in every heaven on high raged against me and said to me:

Why dost thou reveal this secret to son of man, born of woman, tainted and unclean, a man of a putrefying drop, the secret by which were created heaven and earth, the sea and the dry land, the mountains and hills, the rivers and springs, Gehenna of fire and hail, the Garden of Eden and the Tree of Life; and by which were formed Adam and Eve, and the cattle, and the wild beasts, and the fowl of the air, and the fish of the sea, and Behemoth and Leviathan, and the creeping things, the worms, the dragons of the sea, and the creeping things of the deserts; and the Tora and Wisdom and Knowledge and Thought and the Gnosis of things above and the fear of heaven.

Why dost thou reveal this to flesh and blood?

I answered them: Because the Holy One, blessed be He, has given me authority. And furthermore, I have obtained permission from the high and exalted Throne, from which all the Explicit Names go forth with lightnings of fire and flaming chashmallim.

But they were not appeased, until the Holy One, blessed be He, rebuked them and drove them away with rebuke from before him, saying to them: "I delight in, and have set my love on, and have entrusted and committed unto Metatron, my Servant, alone, for he is One (unique) among all the children of heaven.

And Metatron brought them out from his house of treasuries and committed them to Moses, and Moses to Joshua, and Joshua to the elders, and the elders to the prophets and the prophets to the men of the Great Synagogue, and the men of the Great Synagogue to Ezra and Ezra the Scribe to Hillel the elder, and Hillel the elder to R. Abbahu and R. Abbahu to R. Zera, and R. Zera to the men of faith, and the men of faith (committed them) to give warning and to heal by them all diseases that rage in the world, as it is written: "If thou wilt diligently hearken to the voice of the

Lord, thy God, and wilt do that which is right in his eyes, and wilt give ear to his commandments, and keep all his statutes, I will put none of the diseases upon thee, which I have put upon the Egyptians: for I am the Lord, that healeth thee".

Ended and finished. Praise be unto the Creator of the World.

BONUS: FRAGMENT OF ASCENSION OF MOSES

R. Ishmael said:

Said to me Metatron, the Prince of the Presence and the prince over all the princes and he stands before Him who is greater than all the Elohim. And he goes in under the Throne of Glory. And he has a great tabernacle of light on high. And he brings forth the fire of deafness and puts (it) into the ears of the Holy Chayyoth, that they may not hear the voice of the Word (Dibbur) that goes forth from the mouth of the Divine Majesty.

And when Moses ascended on high, he fasted 121 fasts, till the habitations of the chashmal were opened to him; and he saw the heart within the heart of the Lion and he saw the innumerable companies of the hosts Around about him. And they desired to burn him. But Moses prayed for mercy, first for Israel and after that for himself: and He who sitteth on the Merkaba opened the windows that are above the heads of the Kerubim. And a host of 1800 advocates and the Prince of the Presence, Metatron, with them went forth to meet Moses. And they took the prayers of Israel and put them as a crown on the head of the Holy One, blessed be He.

And they said:

"Hear, O Israel; the Lord our God is one Lord"and their face shone and rejoiced over Shekinaand they said to Metatron: "What are these? And to whom do they give all this honour and glory?" And they answered: "To the Glorious Lord of Israel".

And they spake: "Hear, O Israel: the Lord, our God, is one Lord. To whom shall be given abundance of honour and majesty but to Thee YHWH, the Divine Majesty, the King, living and eternal".

In that moment spake Akatriel Yah Yehod Sebaoth and said to Metatron, the Prince of the Presence: "Let no prayer that he prayeth before me return (to him) void. Hear thou his prayer and fulfil his desire whether (it be) great or small".

Forthwith Metatron, the Prince of the Presence, said to Moses:

"Son of Amram! Fear not, for now God delights in thee. And ask thou u thy desire of the Glory and Majesty. For thy face shines from one end of the world to the other". But Moses answered him: "(I fear) lest I bring guiltiness upon myself". Metatron said to him: "Receive the letters of the oath, in (by) which there is no breaking the covenant" (which precludes any breach of the covenant).

A depiction of Moses ascending into the heavens, surrounded by radiant light and angelic beings, with the celestial realm unfolding before him.

BONUS: THE TESTAMENT OF ABRAHAM

TRANSLATION: M. R. JAMES

CHAPTER 1

It came to pass, when the days of the death of Abraham drew near, that the Lord said to Michael: Arise and go to Abraham, my servant, and say to him, Thou shalt depart from life, for lo! the days of thy temporal life are fulfilled: so that he may set his house in order before he dies.

CHAPTER 2

And Michael went and came to Abraham and found him sitting before his oxen for ploughing, and he was exceedingly old in appearance and had his son in his arms. Abraham, therefore, seeing the archangel Michael, rose from the ground and saluted him, not knowing who he was, and said to him: The Lord preserves thee. May thy journey be prosperous with thee. And Michael answered him: Thou art kind, good father. Abraham answered and said to him: Come, draw near to me, brother, and sit down a little while, that I may order a beast to be brought that we may go to my house, and thou mayest rest with me, for it is toward evening, and in the morning arise and go whithersoever thou wilt, lest some evil beast meet thee and do thee harm. And Michael inquired of Abraham, saying: Tell me thy name before I enter thy house, lest I be burdensome to thee. Abraham answered and said, My parents called me Abram, and the Lord named me Abraham, saying: Arise and depart from thy house and from thy kindred, and go into the land which I shall show unto thee. And when I went away into the land which the Lord showed me, he said to me: Thy name shall no more be called Abram, but thy name shall be Abraham. Michael answered and said to him: Pardon me, my father, experienced man of God, for I am a stranger, and I have heard of thee that thou didst go forty furlongs and didst bring a goat and slay it, entertaining angels in thy house, that they might rest there. Thus speaking together, they arose and went towards the house. And Abraham called one of his servants and said to him: Go, bring me a beast that the stranger may sit upon it, for he is wearied with his journey. And Michael said: Trouble not the youth, but let us go lightly until we reach the house, for I love thy company.

CHAPTER 3

And arising they went on, and as they drew nigh to the city, about three furlongs from it, they found a great tree having three hundred branches, like to a tamarisk tree. And they heard a voice from its branches singing, "Holy art thou because thou hast kept the purpose for which thou wast sent." And Abraham heard the voice and hid the mystery in his heart, saying within himself, What is the mystery that I have heard? As he came into the house, Abraham said to his servants, Arise, go out to the flocks, and bring three sheep, and slay them quickly, and make them ready that we may eat and drink, for this day is a feast for us. And the servants brought the sheep, and Abraham called his son Isaac, and said to him, My son Isaac, arise and put water in the vessel that we may wash the feet of this stranger. And he brought it as he was commanded, and Abraham said, I perceive, and so it shall be, that in this basin I shall never again wash the feet of any man coming to us as a guest. And Isaac, hearing his father say this, wept, and said to him, My father, what is this that thou sayest? This is my last time to wash the feet of a stranger? And Abraham, seeing his son weeping, also wept exceedingly, and Michael, seeing them weeping, wept also, and the tears of Michael fell upon the vessel and became a precious stone.

CHAPTER 4

When Sarah, being inside her house, heard their weeping, she came out and said to Abraham, Lord, why is it that ye thus weep? Abraham answered and said to her, It is no evil. Go into thy house, and do thy own work, lest we be troublesome to the man. And Sarah went away, being about to prepare the supper. And the sun came near to setting, and Michael went out of the house, and was taken up into the heavens to worship before God, for at sunset all the angels worship God, and Michael himself is the first of the angels. And they all worshipped him, and went each to his own place, but Michael spoke before the Lord and said, Lord, command me to be questioned before thy holy glory! And the Lord said to Michael, Announce whatsoever thou wilt! And the Archangel answered and said, Lord, thou didst send me to Abraham to say to him, Depart from thy body, and leave this world; the Lord calls thee; and I dare not, Lord, reveal myself to him, for he is thy friend, and a righteous man, and one that receives strangers. But I beseech thee, Lord, command the remembrance of the death of Abraham to enter into his own heart, and bid not me tell it him, for it is great abruptness to say, Leave the world, and especially to leave one's own body, for thou didst create him from the beginning to have pity on the souls of all men. Then the Lord said to Michael, Arise and go to Abraham, and lodge with him, and whatever thou seest him eat, eat thou also, and wherever he shall sleep, sleep thou there also. For I will cast the thought of the death of Abraham into the heart of Isaac his son in a dream.

CHAPTER 5

Then Michael went into the house of Abraham that evening and found them preparing supper, and they ate and drank and were merry. And Abraham said to his son Isaac, Arise, my son, and spread the man's couch that he may sleep, and set the lamp upon the stand. And Isaac did as his father commanded him, and Isaac said to his father, I too am coming to sleep beside you. Abraham answered him, Nay, my son, lest we be troublesome to this man, but go to thy own chamber and sleep. And Isaac, not wishing to disobey his father's command, went away and slept in his own chamber.

A depiction of Abraham being guided by the Archangel Michael through the heavens, witnessing souls being judged.

CHAPTER 6

And it happened about the seventh hour of the night Isaac awoke, and came to the door of his father's chamber, crying out and saying, Open, father, that I may touch thee before they take thee away from me. Abraham arose and opened to him, and Isaac entered and hung upon his father's neck weeping, and kissed him with lamentations. And Abraham wept together with his son, and Michael saw them weeping and wept likewise. And Sarah, hearing them weeping, called from her bed-chamber, saying, My Lord Abraham, why is this weeping? Has the stranger told thee of thy brother's son Lot that he is dead? Or has aught else befallen us? Michael answered and said to Sarah, Nay, Sarah, I have brought no tidings of Lot, but I knew of all your kindness of heart, that therein ye excel all men upon earth, and the Lord has remembered you. Then Sarah said to Abraham, How durst thou weep when the man of God has come in to thee, and why have thy eyes shed tears for today there is great rejoicing? Abraham said to her, How knowest thou that this is a man of God? Sarah answered and said, Because I say and declare that this is one of the three men who were entertained by us at the oak of Mamre, when one of the servants went and brought a kid, and thou didst kill it, and didst say to me, Arise, make ready that we may eat with these men in our house. Abraham answered and said, Thou hast perceived well, O woman, for I too, when I washed his feet, knew in my heart that these were the feet which I had washed at the oak of Mamre, and when I began to inquire concerning his journey, he said to me, I go to preserve Lot thy brother from the men of Sodom, and then I knew the mystery.

CHAPTER 7

And Abraham said to Michael, Tell me, man of God, and show to me why thou hast come hither. And Michael said, Thy son Isaac will show thee. And Abraham said to his son, My beloved son, tell me what thou hast seen in thy dream today, and wast frightened. Relate it to me. Isaac answered his father, I saw in my dream the sun and the moon, and there was a crown upon my head, and there came from heaven a man of great size, and shining as the light that is called the father of light. He took the sun from my head, and yet left the rays behind with me. And I wept and said, I beseech thee, my Lord, take not away the glory of my head, and the light of my house, and all my glory. And the sun and the moon and the stars lamented, saying, Take not away the glory of our power. And that shining man answered and said to me, Weep not that I take the light of thy house, for it is taken up from troubles into rest, from a low estate to a high one; they lift him up from a narrow to a wide place; they raise him from darkness to light. And I said to him, I beseech thee, Lord, take also the rays with it. He said to me, There are twelve hours of the day, and then I shall take all the rays. As the shining man said this, I saw the sun of my house ascending into heaven, but that crown I saw no more, and that sun was like thee, my father. And Michael said to Abraham, Thy son Isaac has spoken the truth, for thou shalt go and be taken up into the heavens, but thy body shall remain on earth, until seven thousand ages are fulfilled, for then all flesh shall arise. Now therefore, Abraham, set thy house in order, and thy children, for thou hast heard fully what is decreed concerning thee. Abraham answered and said to Michael, I beseech thee, Lord, if I shall depart from my body, I have desired to be taken up in my body that I may see the creatures that the Lord my God has created in heaven and on earth. Michael answered and said, This is not for me to do, but I shall go and tell the Lord of this, and if I am commanded, I shall show thee all these things.

CHAPTER 8

And Michael went up into heaven, and spoke before the Lord concerning Abraham, and the Lord answered Michael, Go and take up Abraham in the body, and show him all things, and whatsoever he shall say to thee, do to him as to my friend. So Michael went forth and took up Abraham in the body on a cloud and brought him to the river of Ocean.

CHAPTER 9

And after Abraham had seen the place of judgment, the cloud took him down upon the firmament below, and Abraham, looking down upon the earth, saw a man committing adultery with a wedded woman. And Abraham turning said to Michael, Seest thou this wickedness? but, Lord, send fire from heaven to consume them. And straightway there came down fire and consumed them, for the Lord had said to Michael, Whatsoever Abraham shall ask thee to do for him, do thou. Abraham looked again and saw other men railing at their companions, and said, Let the earth open and swallow them, and as he spoke the earth swallowed them alive. Again, the cloud led him to another place, and Abraham saw some going into a desert place to commit murder, and he said to Michael, Seest thou this wickedness? but let wild beasts come out of the desert and tear them in pieces, and that same hour wild beasts came out of the desert and devoured them. Then the Lord God spoke to Michael, saying, Turn away Abraham to his own house, and let him not go round all the creation that I have made, because he has no compassion on sinners, but I have compassion on sinners that they may turn and live and repent of their sins and be saved.

CHAPTER 10

And Abraham looked and saw two gates, the one small and the other large, and between the two gates sat a man upon a throne of great glory, and a multitude of angels round about him, and he was weeping, and again laughing, but his weeping exceeded his laughter seven-fold. And Abraham said to Michael, Who is this that sits between the two gates in great glory; sometimes he laughs, and sometimes he weeps, and his weeping exceeds his laughter seven-fold? And Michael said to Abraham, Knowest thou not who it is? And he said, No, Lord. And Michael said to Abraham, Seest thou these two gates, the small and the great? These are they which lead to life and to destruction. This man that sits between them is Adam, the first man whom the Lord created, and set him in this place to see every soul that departs from the body, seeing that all are from him. When, therefore, thou seest him weeping, know that he has seen many souls being led to destruction, but when thou seest him laughing, he has seen many souls being led into life. Seest thou how his weeping exceeds his laughter? Since he sees the greater part of the world being led away through the broad gate to destruction, therefore his weeping exceeds his laughter seven-fold.

CHAPTER 11

And Abraham said, And he that cannot enter through the narrow gate, can he not enter into life? Then Abraham wept, saying, Woe is me, what shall I do? for I am a man broad of body, and how shall I be able to enter by the narrow gate, by which a boy of fifteen years cannot enter? Michael answered and said to Abraham, Fear not, father, nor grieve, for thou shalt enter by it unhindered, and all those who are like thee. And as Abraham stood and marveled, behold an angel of the Lord driving sixty thousand souls of sinners to destruction. And Abraham said to Michael, Do all these go into destruction? And Michael said to him, Yea, but let us go and search among these souls, if there is among them even one righteous. And when they went, they found an angel holding in his hand one soul of a woman from among these sixty thousand, because he had found her sins weighing equally with all her works, and they were neither in motion nor at rest, but in a state between; but the other souls he led away to destruction. Abraham said to Michael, Lord, is this the angel that removes the souls from the body or not? Michael answered and said, This is death, and he leads them into the place of judgment, that the judge may try them.

CHAPTER 12

And Abraham said, My Lord, I beseech thee to lead me to the place of judgment so that I too may see how they are judged. Then Michael took Abraham upon a cloud, and led him into Paradise, and when he came to the place where the judge was, the angel came and gave that soul to the judge. And the soul said, Lord have mercy on me. And the judge said, How shall I have mercy upon thee, when thou hadst no mercy upon thy daughter which thou hadst, the fruit of thy womb? Wherefore didst thou slay her? It answered, Nay, Lord, slaughter has not been done by me, but my daughter has lied upon me. But the judge commanded him to come that wrote down the records, and behold cherubim carrying two books. And there was with them a man of exceeding great stature, having on his head three crowns, and the one crown was higher than the other two. These are called the crowns of witness. And the man had in his hand a golden pen, and the judge said to him, Exhibit the sin of this soul. And that man, opening one of the books of the cherubim, sought out the sin of the woman's soul and found it. And the judge said, O wretched soul, why sayest thou that thou hast not done murder? Didst thou not, after the death of thy husband, go and commit adultery with thy daughter's husband, and kill her? And he convicted her also of her other sins, whatsoever she had done from her youth. Hearing these things the woman cried out, saying, Woe is me, all the sins that I did in the world I forgot, but here they were not forgotten. Then they took her away also and gave her over to the tormentors.

CHAPTER 13

And Abraham said to Michael, Lord, who is this judge, and who is the other, who convicts the sins? And Michael said to Abraham, Seest thou the judge? This is Abel, who first testified, and God brought him hither to judge, and he that bears witness here is the teacher of heaven and earth, and the scribe of righteousness, Enoch, for the Lord sent them hither to write down the sins and righteousnesses of each one. Abraham said, And how can Enoch bear the weight of the souls, not having seen death? or how can he give sentence to all the souls? Michael said, If he gives sentence concerning the souls, it is not permitted; but Enoch himself does not give sentence, but it is the Lord who does so, and he has no more to do than only to write. For Enoch prayed to the Lord saying, I desire not, Lord, to give sentence on the souls, lest I be grievous to anyone; and the Lord said to Enoch, I shall command thee to write down the sins of the soul that makes atonement and it shall enter into life, and if the soul makes not atonement and repent, thou shalt find its sins written down and it shall be cast into punishment. And about the ninth hour Michael brought Abraham back to his house. But Sarah, his wife, not seeing what had become of Abraham, was consumed with grief, and gave up the ghost, and after the return of Abraham, he found her dead and buried her.

CHAPTER 14

But when the day of the death of Abraham drew nigh, the Lord God said to Michael, Death will not dare to go near to take away the soul of my servant because he is my friend, but go thou and adorn Death with great beauty, and send him thus to Abraham, that he may see him with his eyes. And Michael straightway, as he was commanded, adorned Death with great beauty, and sent him thus to Abraham that he might see him. And he sat down near to Abraham, and Abraham seeing Death sitting near to him was afraid with a great fear. And Death said to Abraham, Hail, holy soul! hail, friend of the Lord God! hail, consolation and enter-tainment of travelers! And Abraham said, Thou art welcome, servant of the Most High God. I beseech thee, tell me who thou art; and entering into my house, partake of food and drink, and depart from me, for since I have seen thee sitting near to me my soul has been troubled. For I am not at all worthy to come near thee, for thou art an exalted spirit and I am flesh and blood, and therefore I cannot bear thy glory, for I see that thy beauty is not of this world. And Death said to Abraham, I tell thee, in all the creation that God has made, there has not been found one like thee, for even the Lord himself by searching has not found such a one upon the whole earth. And Abraham said to Death, How durst thou lie? for I see that thy beauty is not of this world. And Death said to Abraham, Think not, Abraham, that this beauty is mine, or that I come thus to every man. Nay, but if anyone is righteous like thee, I thus take crowns and come to him, but if it is a sinner, I come in great corruption, and out of their sin I make a crown for my head, and I shake them with great fear, so that they are dismayed. Abraham therefore said to him, And whence comes thy beauty? And Death said, There is none other more full of corruption than I am. Abraham said to him, And art thou indeed he that is called Death? He answered him and said, I am the bitter name. I am weeping....

CHAPTER 15

And Abraham said to Death, Show us thy corruption. And Death made manifest his corruption; and he had two heads, the one had the face of a serpent and by it, some die at once by asps, and the other head was like a sword; by it some die by the sword as by bows. In that day the servants of Abraham died through fear of Death, and Abraham seeing them prayed to the Lord, and he raised them up. But God returned and removed the soul of Abraham as in a dream, and the archangel Michael took it up into the heavens. And Isaac buried his father beside his mother Sarah, glorifying and praising God, for to him is due glory, honor, and worship, of the Father, Son, and Holy Ghost, now and always and to all eternity. Amen.

BONUS: THE APOCALYPSE OF ABRAHAM

TRANSLATION: ANONYMOUS

CHAPTER 1

On the day I was guarding the gods of my father Terah and the gods of my brother Nahor, while I was testing to find out which god is in truth the strongest, I, Abraham, at the time when my lot came, when I was completing the services of my father Terah's sacrifice to his gods of wood, of stone, of gold, of silver, of copper, and of iron, having entered their temple for the service, I found a god named Marumath, carved from stone, fallen at the feet of the iron god Nakhin. And it came to pass, that when I saw it my heart was perplexed and I thought in my mind that I, Abraham, could not put it back in its place alone because it was heavy, being made of a big stone. But I went and told my father, and he came in with me. And when we both lifted it to put it in its place, its head fell off, even while I was holding it by its head. And it came to pass, when my father saw that the head of his god Marumath had fallen, he said to me, "Abraham!" And I said, "Here I am!" And he said to me, "Bring me the axes and chisels from the house." And I brought them to him from the house. And he cut another Marumath from another stone, without a head, and he smashed the head that had fallen off Marumath and the rest of Marumath.

CHAPTER 2

He made five other gods and he gave them to me and ordered me to sell them outside on the town road. I saddled my father's ass and loaded them on it and went out on the highway to sell them. And behold, merchants from Phandana of Syria were coming with camels, on their way to Egypt to buy kokonil from the Nile. I asked them a question and they answered me. And walking along I conversed with them. One of their camels screamed. The ass took fright and ran away and threw off the gods. Three of them were crushed and two remained intact. And it came to pass that when the Syrians saw that I had gods, they said to me, "Why did you not tell us that you had gods? We would have bought them before the ass heard the camel's voice and you would have had no loss. Give us at least the gods that remain and we will give you a suitable price." I considered it in my heart. And they paid both for the smashed gods and the gods which remained. For I had been grieving in my heart how I would bring payment to my father. I threw three broken gods into the water of the river Gur, which was in this place. And they sank into the depths of the river Gur and were no more.

CHAPTER 3

As I was still walking on the road, my heart was disturbed and my mind distracted. I said in my heart, "What is the inequality of activity which my father is doing? Is it not he rather who is god for his gods because they come into being from his sculpting, his planning, and his skill? They ought to honor my father because they are his work. What is this food of my father in his works? Behold, Marumath fell and could not stand up in his sanctuary, nor could I myself lift him until my father came and we raised him up. And even so we were not able to do it, and his head fell off of him. And he put it on another stone of another god, which he had made without a head. And... the other five gods which got smashed in falling from the ass, who could not save themselves and injure the ass because it smashed them, nor did their shards come up out of the river. And I said to my heart, "If it is so, how then can my father's god

Marumath, which has the head of another stone and which is made from another stone, save a man, or hear a man's prayer, or give him any gift?"

CHAPTER 4

And thinking thus, I came to my father's house. And I watered the ass and gave him hay. And I took out the silver and placed it in the hand of my father Terah. And when he saw it, he was glad, and he said, "You are blessed, Abraham, by the god of my gods, since you have brought me the price for the gods so that my labor was not in vain." And answering I said to him, "Listen, father Terah! The gods are blessing you, because you are a god for them, because you made them, for their blessing is their perdition and their power is vain. They did not help themselves; how then can they help you or bless me? I was good for you in this transaction, for through my good sense I brought you the silver for the smashed gods." And when he heard my speech he became furiously angry with me because I had spoken harsh words against his gods.

CHAPTER 5

But having pondered my father's anger, I went out. And afterward when I had gone out, he called me saying, "Abraham!" And I said, "Here I am!" And he said, "Up, gather wood chips, for I was making gods from fir before you came, and prepare with them food for my midday meal." And it came to pass, when I was choosing the wooden chips, I found among them a small god which would fit in my left hand. And on its forehead was written: god Barisat. And it came to pass when I put the chips on the fire in order to prepare the food for my father, and going out to inquire about the food, I put Barisat near the enkindling fire, saying to him threateningly, "Barisat, watch that the fire does not go out before I come back! If the fire goes out, blow on it so it flares up." I went out and I made my counsel. When I returned I found Barisat fallen on his back. His feet were enveloped by fire and burning fiercely. And it came to pass when I saw it, I laughed and said to myself, "Barisat, truly you know how to light a fire and cook food!" And it came to pass while saying this in my laughter, I saw that he burned up slowly from the fire and became ashes.

I carried the food to my father to eat. I gave him wine and milk, and he drank and he enjoyed himself and he blessed Marumath his god. And I said to him, "Father Terah, do not bless Marumath your god, do not praise him! Praise rather Barisat, your god, because, as though loving you, he threw himself into the fire in order to cook your food." And he said to me, "Then where is he now?" And I said, "He has burned in the fierceness of the fire and become dust." And he said, "Great is the power of Barisat! I will make another today, and tomorrow he will prepare my food."

CHAPTER 6

When I, Abraham, heard words like this from my father, I laughed in my mind, and I groaned in the bitterness and anger of my soul. I said, "How then is a figment of a body made by him an aid for my father? Or can he have subordinated his body to his soul, his soul to a spirit, and the spirit to stupidity and ignorance?" And I said, "It is only proper to endure evil that I may throw my mind to purity and I will expose my thoughts clearly to him." I answered and said, "Father Terah, whichever of these gods you extol, you err in your thought. Behold, the gods of my brother Nahor standing in the holy sanctuary are more venerable than yours. For behold, Zouchaios, my brother Nahor's god, is more venerable than your god Marumath because he is made of gold, valued by man. And if he grows old with time, he will be remolded, whereas Marumath, if he is changed or broken, will not be renewed, because he is stone. What about Ioav, the god on the other god, who stands with Zouchaios? For he is also more venerable than the god Barisat; he is carved from wood and forged from silver. Because he too is a term of comparison, being valued by man according to external experience. But Barisat, your god, when he was still not carved, rooted in the earth, being great and wondrous, with branches and flowers; and praise...But you made him with an axe, and by your skill he was made a god. And behold he has already dried up and his fatness has perished. He fell from the height to the earth, he came from greatness to smallness, and the appearance of his face wasted away. And, he himself was burned up by the fire and he became ashes and is no more. And you say, Let me make another and tomorrow he will make my food for me. But in perishing he left himself no strength for his own destruction."

CHAPTER 7

This I say: Fire is more venerable in formation, for even the unsubdued things are subdued in it, and it mocks that which perishes easily by means of its burning. But neither is it venerable, for it is subject to the waters. But rather the waters are more venerable than it, because they overcome fire and sweeten the earth with fruits. But I will not call them god either, for the waters subside under the earth and are subject to it. But I will not call it a goddess either, for it is dried by the sun and subordinated to man for his work. More venerable among the gods, I say, is the sun, for with its rays it illuminates the whole universe and the various airs. Nor will I place among the gods the one who obscures his course by means of the moon and the clouds. Nor again shall I call the moon or the stars gods, because they too at times during the night dim their light. Listen, Terah my father, I shall seek before you the God who created all the gods supposed by us to exist. For who is it, or which one is it who made the heavens crimson and the sun golden, who has given light to the moon and the stars with it, who has dried the earth in the midst of the many waters, who set you yourself among the things and who has sought me out in the perplexity of my thoughts? I, only God, will reveal himself by himself to us!"

CHAPTER 8

And it came to pass as I was thinking things like these with regard to my father Terah in the court of my house, the voice of the Mighty One came down from the heavens in a stream of fire, saying and calling, "Abraham, Abraham!" And I said, "Here I am." And he said, "You are searching for the God of gods, the Creator, in the understanding of your heart. I am he. Go out from Terah, your father, and go out of the house, that you too may not be slain in the sins of your father's house." And it came to pass as I went out—I was not yet outside the entrance of the court—that the

sound of a great thunder came and burned him and his house and everything in his house, down to the ground, forty cubits.

CHAPTER 9

Then a voice came speaking to me twice: "Abraham, Abraham!" And I
said, "Here I am." And he said, "Behold, it is I, Fear not, for I am Before-
the-World and Mighty, the God who created previously, before the light
of the age. I am the protector for you and I am your helper. Go, get me a
three-year-old heifer, a three-year-old she-goat, a three-year-old ram, a
turtledove, and a pigeon, and make me a pure sacrifice. And in this sacrifice I will place the ages. I will announce to you guarded things and you
will see great things which you have not seen, because you desired to
search for me, and I called you my beloved. But for forty days abstain
from every kind of food cooked by fire, and from drinking of wine and
from anointing yourself with oil. And then you shall set out for me the
sacrifice, which I have commanded you, in the place which I will show
you on a high mountain. And there I will show you the things which
were made by the ages and by my word, and affirmed, created, and
renewed. And I will announce to you in them what will come upon those
who have done evil and just things in the race of man."

CHAPTER 10

And it came to pass when I heard the voice pronouncing such words to
me that I looked this way and that. And behold, there was no breath of
man. And my spirit was amazed, and my soul fled from me. And I
became like a stone, and fell face down upon the earth, for there was no
longer strength in me to stand up on the earth. And while I was still face
down on the ground, I heard the voice speaking, "Go, Iaoel of the same
name, through the meditation of my ineffable name, consecrate this man
for me and strengthen him against his trembling." The angel he sent to
me in the likeness of a man came, and he took me by my right hand and
stood me on my feet. And he said to me, "Stand up, Abraham, friend of
God who has loved you, let human trembling not enfold you! For lo! I am
sent to you to strengthen you and to bless you in the name of God,

creator of heavenly and earthly things, who has loved you. Be bold and hasten to him. I am Iaoel and I was called so by him who causes those with me on the seventh expanse, on the firmament, to shake, a power through the medium of his ineffable name in me. I am the one who has been charged according to his commandment, to restrain the threats of the living creatures of the cherubim against one another, and I teach those who carry the song through the medium of man's night of the seventh hour. I am appointed to hold the Leviathans, because through me is subjugated the attack and menace of every reptile. I am ordered to loosen Hades and to destroy those who wondered at the dead. I am the one who ordered your father's house to be burned with him, for he honored the dead. I am sent to you now to bless you and the land which he whom you have called the Eternal One has prepared for you. For your sake, I have indicated the way of the land. Stand up, Abraham, go boldly, be very joyful and rejoice. And I also rejoice with you, for a venerable honor has been prepared for you by the Eternal One. Go, complete the sacrifice of the command. Behold, I am assigned to be with you and with the generation which is predestined to be born from you. And with me Michael blesses you forever. Be bold, go!"

CHAPTER 11

And I stood up and saw him who had taken my right hand and set me on my feet. The appearance of his body was like sapphire, and the aspect of his face was like chrysolite, and the hair of his head like snow. And a kidaris was on his head, its look that of a rainbow, and the clothing of his garments was purple; and a golden staff was in his right hand. And he said to me, "Abraham." And I said, "Here is your servant!" And he said, "Let my appearance not frighten you, nor my speech trouble your soul. Come with me! And I will go with you visible until the sacrifice, but after the sacrifice invisible forever. Be bold and go!"

CHAPTER 12

And we went, the two of us alone together, forty days and nights. And I ate no bread and drank no water, because my food was to see the angel who was with me, and his discourse with me was my drink. We came to God's mountain, glorious Horeb. And I said to the angel, "Singer of the Eternal One, behold I have no sacrifice with me, nor do I know a place for an altar on the mountain, so how shall I make the sacrifice?" And he said, "Look behind you." And I looked behind me. And behold all the prescribed sacrifices were following us: the calf, the she-goat, the ram, the turtledove, and the pigeon. And the angel said to me; "Abraham." And I said, "Here I am." And he said to me, "Slaughter all these and divide the animals exactly into halves. But do not cut the birds apart. And give them to the men whom I will show you standing beside you, for they are the altar on the mountain, to offer sacrifice to the Eternal One. The turtledove and the pigeon you will give to me for I will ascend on the wings of the birds to show you what is in the heavens, on the earth and in the sea, in the abyss, and in the lower depths, in the garden of Eden and in its rivers, in the fullness of the universe. And you will see its circles in all."

CHAPTER 13

And I did everything according to the angel's command. And I gave the angels who had come to us the divided parts of the animals. And the angel Iaoel took the two birds. And I waited for the evening gift. And an unclean bird flew down on the carcasses, and I drove it away. And the unclean bird spoke to me and said, "What are you doing, Abraham, on the holy heights where no one eats or drinks, nor is there upon them food for men. But these all will be consumed by fire and they will burn you up. Leave the man who is with you and flee! For if you ascend to the height, they will destroy you." And it came to pass when I saw the bird speaking I said this to the angel: "What is this, my lord?" And he said, "This is disgrace, this is Azazel!" And he said to him, "Shame on you, Azazel! For Abraham's portion is in heaven, and yours is on the earth, for you have selected here, and become enamored of the dwelling place of your blemish. Therefore the Eternal Ruler, the Mighty One, has given you a dwelling on earth. Through you the all-evil spirit is a liar, and through you are wrath and trials on the generations of men who live impiously. For the Eternal, Mighty One did not allow the bodies of the righteous to be in your hand, so through them the righteous life is affirmed and the destruction of ungodliness. Hear, counselor, be shamed by me! You have no permission to tempt all the righteous. Depart from this man! You cannot deceive him, because he is the enemy of you and of those who follow you and who love what you wish. For behold, the garment which is heaven was formerly yours has been set aside for him, and the corruption which was on him has gone over to you."

CHAPTER 14

And the angel said to me, "Abraham!" And I said, "Here I am, your servant." And he said, "Know from this that the Eternal One whom you have loved has chosen you. Be bold and do through your authority what-ever I order you against him who reviles justice. Will I not be able to revile him who has scattered about the earth the secrets of heaven and who has taken counsel against the Mighty One? Say to him, 'May you be the firebrand of the furnace of the earth! Go, Azazel, into the untrodden parts of the earth. For your heritage is over those who are with you, with the stars and with the men born by the clouds, whose portion you are, indeed they exist through your being. Enmity is for you a pious act. Therefore through your own destruction be gone from me!' And I said the words as the angel had taught me. And he said, "Abraham." And I said, "Here I am, your servant!" And the angel said to me, "Answer him not!" And he spoke to me a second time. And the angel said, "Now, whatever he says to you, answer him not, lest his will run up to you. For the Eternal, Mighty One gave him the gravity and the will. Answer him not." And I did what the angel had commanded me. And whatever he said to me about the descent, I answered him not.

A depiction of Abraham being lifted into the heavens by angels, witnessing apocalyptic visions of the cosmos.

CHAPTER 15

And it came to pass when the sun was setting, and behold a smoke like that of a furnace, and the angels who had the divided portions of the sacrifice ascended from the top of the furnace of smoke. And the angel took me with his right hand and set me on the right wing of the pigeon and he himself sat on the left wing of the turtledove, both of which were as of neither slaughtered nor divided. And he carried me up to the edge of the fiery flames. And we ascended as if carried by many winds to the heaven that is fixed on the expanses. And I saw on the air to whose height we had ascended a strong light which cannot be described. And behold, in this light, a fiery Gehenna was enkindled, and a great crowd in the likeness of men. They all were changing in aspect and shape, running and changing form and prostrating themselves and crying words I did not know.

CHAPTER 16

And I said to the angel, "Why is it you now brought me here? For now I can no longer see, because I am weakened and my spirit is departing from me." And he said to me, "Remain with me, do not fear. He whom you will see coming directly toward us in a great sound of sanctification is the Eternal One who has loved you. You will not look at him himself. But let your spirit not weaken, for I am with you, strengthening you."

CHAPTER 17

And while he was still speaking, behold the fire coming toward us round about, and a voice was in the fire like a voice of many waters, like the voice of the sea in its uproar. And the angel knelt down with me and worshipped. And I wanted to fall face down on the earth. And the place of highness on which we were standing now stopped on high, now rolled down low. And he said, "Only worship, Abraham, and recite the song which I taught you." Since there was no ground to which I could fall prostrate, I only bowed down, and I recited the song which he had taught me. And he said, "Recite without ceasing." And I recited, and he himself recited the song:

Eternal One, Mighty One, Holy El, God autocrat Self-originate, incorruptible, immaculate, Unbegotten, spotless, immortal, Self-perfected, self-devised, Without mother, without father, ungenerated, Exalted, fiery, Just, lover of men, benevolent, compassionate, bountiful, Jealous over me, Patient one, most merciful, Eli, eternal, mighty one, holy Sabaoth, Most glorious El, El, El, El, Iaoel, You are he my soul has loved, my protector. Eternal, fiery, shining, light-giving, thunder-voiced, lightning-visioned, many-eyed, receiving the petitions of those who honor you and turning away from the petitions of those who restrain you by the restraint of their provocations, redeemer of those who dwell in the midst of the wicked ones, of those who are dispersed among the just of the world, in the corruptible age. Showing forth the age of the just, You make the light shine before the morning light upon your creation from your face to spend the day on the earth, And in your heavenly dwelling place there is an inexhaustible light of an invincible dawning from the light of your face. Accept my prayer and delight in it, And accept also the sacrifice which you yourself made to yourself through me as I searched for you. Receive me favorably, Teach me, show me, and make known to your servant what you have promised me.

CHAPTER 18

And as I was still reciting the song, the mouth of the fire which was on the firmament was rising up on high. And I heard a voice like the roaring of the sea, and it did not cease from the plentitude of the fire. And as the fire rose up, soaring to the highest point, I saw under the fire a throne of fire and the many-eyed ones round about, reciting the song. And the appearance of each of them was the same, each having four faces. And this was the aspect of their faces: of a lion, of a man, of an ox, and of an eagle. Each one had four heads on its body so that the four living creatures had sixteen faces. And each one had six wings: two on the shoulders, two halfway down, and two at the loins. With the wings which were on their shoulders they covered their faces, with the wings at their loins they clothed their feet, and they would stretch the two middle wings out and fly, erect. And when they finished singing, they would look at one another and threaten one another. And it came to pass when the angel who was with me saw that they were threatening each other, he left me and went running to them. And he turned the face of each living creature from the face which was opposite it so that they could not see each other's faces threatening each other. And he taught them the song of peace which the Eternal One has in himself. And while I was still standing and watching, I saw behind the living creatures a chariot with fiery wheels. Each wheel was full of eyes round about. And above the wheels was the throne which I had seen. And it was covered with fire and the fire encircled it round about, and an indescribable light surrounded the fiery crowd. And I heard the voice of their sanctification like the voice of a single man.

CHAPTER 19

And a voice came to me out of the midst of the fire, saying, "Abraham, Abraham!" And I said, "Here I am!" And he said, "Look at the expanses which are under the firmament to which you have now been directed and see that on no single expanse is there any other but the one whom you have searched for or who has loved you." And while he was still speaking, behold, the expanses under me, the heavens, opened and I saw on the seventh firmament upon which I stood a fire spread out and a light and dew and a multitude of angels and a host of the invisible glory, and up above the living creatures I had seen; I saw no one else there. And I looked from on high, where I was standing, downward to the sixth firmament. And I saw there a multitude of spiritual angels, incorporeal, carrying out the orders of the fiery angels who were on the eighth firmament, as I was standing on its elevation. And lo, neither on this firmament was there in any shape any other host, but only the spiritual angels. And the host I saw on the seventh firmament commanded the sixth firmament and it removed itself. I saw there, on the fifth firmament, host of stars, and the orders they were commanded to carry out, and the elements of earth obeying them.

CHAPTER 20

And the Eternal, Mighty One said to me, "Abraham, Abraham!" And I said, "Here I am!" And he said, "Look from on high at the stars which are beneath you and count them for me and tell me their number!" And I said, "When can I? For I am a man." And he said to me, "As the number of the stars and their power so shall I place for your seed the nations and men, set apart for me in my lot with Azazel." And I said, "Eternal and Mighty One. Let your servant speak before you and let your fury not rage against your chosen one. Behold, before you led me up, Azazel insulted me. How then, since he is now not before you, did you establish yourself with them?"

CHAPTER 21

And he said to me, "Look now beneath your feet at the firmament and understand the creation that was depicted of old on this expanse, and the creatures which are in it and the age prepared after it." And I looked beneath the firmament at my feet and I saw the likeness of heaven and the things that were therein. And I saw there the earth and its fruit, and its moving things and its things that had souls, and its host of men and the impiety of their souls and their justification, and their pursuit of their works and the abyss and its torments, and its lower depths and the perdition in it. And I saw there the sea and its islands,

and its cattle and its fish, and Leviathan and his realm and his bed and his lairs, and the world which lay upon him, and his motions and the destruction he caused the world. I saw there the rivers and their upper reaches and their circles. And I saw there the garden of Eden and its fruits, and the source and the river flowing from it, and its trees and their flowering, making fruits, and I saw men doing justice in it, their food and their rest. And I saw there a great crowd of men and women and children, half of them on the right side of the portrayal, and half of them on the left side of the portrayal.

CHAPTER 22

And I said, "Eternal, Mighty One! What is this picture of creation?" And he said to me, "This is my will with regard to what is in the light and it was good before my face. And then, afterward, I gave them a command by my word and they came into existence. Whatever I had decreed was to exist had already been outlined in this and all the previously created things you have seen stood before me." And I said, "O sovereign, mighty and eternal! Why are the people in this picture on this side and on that?" And he said to me, "These who are on the left side are a multitude of tribes who existed previously...and after you some who have been prepared for judgment and order, others for revenge and perdition at the end of the age. Those on the right side of the picture are the people set apart for me of the people with Azazel; these are the ones I have prepared to be born of you and to be called my people."

CHAPTER 23

"Look again at the picture: Who is the one who seduced Eve, and what is the fruit of the tree? And you will know what will be and how much will be for your seed in the last days. And what you cannot understand, I will make known to you because you have been pleasing before my face and I will tell you what I have kept in my heart." And I looked at the picture, and my eyes ran to the side of the garden of Eden. And I saw there a man very great in height and terrible in breadth, incomparable in aspect, entwined with a woman who was also equal to the man in aspect and size. And they were standing under a tree of Eden, and the fruit of the tree was like the appearance of a bunch of grapes of the vine. And behind the tree was standing something like a dragon in form, but having hands and feet like a man's, on his back six wings on the right and six on the left. And he was holding the grapes of the tree and feeding them to the two I saw entwined with each other. And I said, "Who are these two entwined with each other, or who is this between them, and what is the fruit which they are eating, Mighty One, Eternal?" And he said. "This is the world of men, this is Adam and this is their thought on earth, this is Eve. And he who is between them is the impiety of their behavior unto perdition, Azazel himself." And I said. "Eternal Mighty One, why then did you adjudge him such dominion that through his works he could ruin humankind on earth?" And he said to me, "Hear, Abraham! Those who desire evil, and all whom I have hated as they commit them—over them did I give him dominion, and he was to be beloved of them." And I answered and said. "Eternal, Mighty One! Why did it please you to bring it about that evil should be desired in the heart of man, because you are angered at what was chosen by you...him who does useless things in your light?"

CHAPTER 24

And he said to me thus, "Close to the nations...for your sake and for the sake of those set apart after you, the people of your tribe, as you will see in the picture, what is burdened on them. And I will explain to you what will be, and everything that will be in the last days. Look now at everything in the picture." And I looked and saw there the creatures that had come into being before me. And I saw, as it were, Adam and Eve who was with him, and with them the crafty adversary and Cain, who had been led by the adversary to break the law, and I saw the murdered Abel and the perdition brought on him and given through the lawless one. And I saw there fornication and those who desired it, and its defilement and their zeal; and the fire of the corruption in the lower depths of the earth. And I saw there theft and those who hasten after it, and the system of their retribution, the judgment of the great court. I saw there naked men, forehead to forehead, and their shame and the harm they wrought against their friends and the retribution. And I saw there desire, and in her hand was the head of every kind of lawlessness, and her torment and her dispersal destined to destruction.

CHAPTER 25

I saw there the likeness of the idol of jealousy, like a carpenter's figure such as my father used to make, and its body was of glittering copper, and before it a man, and he was worshipping it. And there was an altar opposite it and boys being slaughtered on it in the face of the idol. And I said to him, "What is this idol, or what is the altar, or who are those being sacrificed, or who is the sacrificer, or what is the handsome temple which I see, the art and beauty of your glory that lies beneath your throne?" And he said, "Hear, Abraham! This temple which you have seen, the altar and the works of art, this is my idea of the priesthood of the name of my glory, where every petition of man will enter and dwell; the ascent of kings and prophets and whatever sacrifice I decree to be made for me among my coming people, even of your tribe. And the body you saw is my anger, because the people who will come to me out of you will make me angry. And the man you saw slaughtering is he who angers me, and the sacrifice is a killing of those who are for me a testimony of the judgment of the completion at the beginning of creation."

CHAPTER 26

And I said, "Eternal, Mighty One! Why did you establish it to be so and to call on the testimonies of this one?" And he said to me, "Hear, Abraham, and understand what I will explain to you, and answer whatever I ask you. Why did your father Terah not obey your voice and abandon the demonic worship of idols until he perished, and all his house with him?" And I said, "Eternal Mighty One, surely because it did not please him to obey me, nor did I follow his works." And he said to me, "Hear, Abraham. As the counsel of your father is in him, as your counsel is in you, so also the counsel of my will is ready. In days to come you will not know them in advance, nor the future men you will see with your own eyes that they are of your seed. Look at the picture!"

CHAPTER 27

And I looked and I saw, and behold the picture swayed. And from its left side a crowd of heathens ran out and they captured the men, women, and children who were on its right side. And some they slaughtered and others they kept with them. Behold, I saw them running to them by way of four ascents and they burned the Temple with fire, and they plundered the holy things that were in it. And I said, "Eternal One, the people you received from me are being robbed by the hordes of the heathen. They are killing some and holding others as aliens, and they burned the Temple with fire and they are stealing and destroying the beautiful things which are in it. Eternal, Mighty One! If this is so, why now have you afflicted my heart and why will it be so?" And he said to me, "Listen, Abraham, all that you have seen will happen on account of your seed who will continually provoke me because of the body which you saw and the murder in what was depicted in the Temple of jealousy, and everything you saw will be so." And I said, "Eternal, Mighty One! Let the evil works done in iniquity now pass by; but make commandments in them more than his just works. For you can do this." And he said to me, "Again the time of justice will come upon them, at first through the holiness of kings. And I will judge with justice those whom I created earlier, to rule from them in them. And from these same ones will come men who will have regard for them. As I announced to you and you saw."

CHAPTER 28

And I answered and said, "Mighty, Eternal One, you who are sanctified by your power, be merciful in my petition, since for this you informed me and showed me. Since you have brought me up on to your height, therefore inform me, your beloved, about whatever I ask: Will what I saw be their lot for long?" And he showed me a multitude of his people. And he said to me, "For this reason it is through the four ascents you say that my anger will be because of them, and in them will be retribution for their works. And in the fourth ascent is one hundred years. And one hour of the age will also be one hundred years in evil among the heathen and an hour in their mercy, even with reproaches as among the heathen."

CHAPTER 29

And I said, "Eternal, Mighty One! How long a time is an hour of the age?" And he said, "I decreed to keep twelve periods of the impious age among the heathens and among your seed, and what you have seen will be until the end of time. Count it up, and you will understand. Look down at the picture." And I looked and saw a man going out from the left, the heathen side. From the side of the heathen went out men and women and children, a great crowd, and they worshipped him. And while I was still looking, those on the right side came out, and some insulted this man, and some struck him and others worshiped him. And I saw that as they worshiped him Azazel ran and worshiped and, kissing his face, he turned and stood behind him. And I said, "Eternal, Mighty One! Who is this man insulted and beaten by the heathen, with Azazel worshiped?" And he answered and said, "Hear, Abraham, the man whom you say insulted and beaten and again worshiped is the liberation from the heathen for the people who will be born from you. In the last days, in this twelfth period of the age of my fulfillment, I will set up this man from your tribe, the one whom you have seen from my people. All will imitate him, consider him as one called by me. They are changed in their counsels. And those you saw coming out from the left side of the picture and worshipping him, this means that many of the heathen will trust in him. And those of your seed you saw on the right side, some insulting him, some beating him, and others worshiping him, many of them shall be offended because of him. It is he who will test those of your seed who have worshiped him in the fulfillment of the twelfth hour, in the curtailing of the age of impiety. Before the age of justice starts to grow, my judgment will come upon the heathen who have acted wickedly through the people of your seed who have been set apart for me. In those days I will bring upon all earthly creation ten plagues through evil and disease and the groaning of the bitterness of their souls. Such will I bring upon the generations of those who are on it, out of anger and corruption of their creations with which they provoke me. And then from your seed will be left the righteous men in their number, protected by me, who strive in the glory of my name toward the place prepared beforehand for them which you saw deserted in the picture. And they will live, being affirmed by the sacrifices and the gifts of justice and truth in the age of justice. And they will rejoice forever in me, and they will destroy those who have destroyed them, they will rebuke those who have rebuked them through their mockery, and they will spit in their faces. Those rebuked by me when they are to see me rejoicing with my people for those who rejoice and receive and truly return to me. See, Abraham, what you have seen, hear what you have heard, know what you have known. Go to your inheritance! And behold I am with you forever."

CHAPTER 30

And while he was still speaking, I found myself on the earth, and I said, "Eternal, Mighty One, I am no longer in the glory in which I was above, and all that my soul desired to understand in my heart I do not understand." And he said to me, "I will explain to you the things you desired in your heart, for you have sought to know the ten plagues which I prepared against the heathen, and I prepared them beforehand in the passing of the twelve hours on earth. Hear what I tell you, it will be thus. The first: sorrow from much need. The second: fiery conflagrations for the cities. The third: destruction by pestilence among the cattle. The fourth: famine of the world, of their generation. The fifth: among the rulers, destruction by earthquake and the sword. The sixth: increase of hail and snow. The seventh: wild beasts will be their grave. The eighth: pestilence and hunger will change their destruction. The ninth: execution by the sword and flight in distress. The tenth: thunder, voices, and destroying earthquakes."

CHAPTER 31

"And then I will sound the trumpet out of the air, and I will send my chosen one, having in him one measure of all my power, and he will summon my people, humiliated by the heathen. And I will burn with fire those who mocked them and ruled over them in this age and I will deliver those who have covered me with mockery over to the scorn of the coming age. Because I have prepared them to be food for the fire of Hades, and to be ceaseless soaring in the air of the underworld regions of the uttermost depths, to be the contents of a wormy belly. For the makers will see in them justice, the makers who have chosen my desire and manifestly kept my commandments, and they will rejoice with merrymaking over the downfall of the men who remain and who followed after the idols and after their murders. For they shall putrefy in the belly of the crafty worm Azazel, and be burned by the fire of Azazel's tongue. For I waited so they might come to me, and they did not deign to. And they glorified an alien god. And they joined one to whom they had not been allotted, and they abandoned the Lord who gave them strength."

CHAPTER 32

"Therefore, hear Abraham, and see, behold your seventh generation shall go with you. And they will go out into an alien land. And they will enslave them and oppress them as for one hour of the impious age. But of the nation whom they shall serve I am the judge." And the Lord said this too, "Have you heard, Abraham, what I told you, what your tribe will encounter in the last days?" Abraham, having heard, accepted the words of God in his heart.

BONUS: THE GOSPEL OF MARY

TRANSLATION: MARK M. MATTISON

Pages 1 through 6 are missing.

AN ETERNAL PERSPECTIVE

"Then will [matter] be [destroyed], or not?"

The Savior said, "Every nature, every form, every creature exists in and with each other, but they'll dissolve again into their own roots, because the nature of matter dissolves into its nature alone. Anyone who has ears to hear should hear!"

Peter said to him, "Since you've explained everything to us, tell us one more thing. What's the sin of the world?"

The Savior said, "Sin doesn't exist, but you're the ones who make sin when you act in accordance with the nature of adultery, which is called 'sin.' That's why the Good came among you, up to the things of every nature in order to restore it within its root."

Then he continued and said, "That's why you get sick and die, because [you love what tricks you. Anyone who] can understand should understand!

"Matter [gave birth to] a passion that has no image because it comes from what's contrary to nature. Then confusion arises in the whole body. That's why I told you to be content at heart. If you're discontented, find contentment in the presence of the various images of nature. Anyone who has ears to hear should hear!"

THE GOSPEL

When the Blessed One said these things, he greeted them all and said, "Peace be with you! Acquire my peace. Be careful not to let anyone mislead you by saying, 'Look over here!' or 'Look over there!' Because the Son of Humanity exists within you. Follow him! Those who seek him will find him.

"Go then and preach the gospel about the kingdom. Don't lay down any rules beyond what I've given you, nor make a law like the lawgiver, lest you be bound by it." When he said these things, he left.

But they grieved and wept bitterly. They said, "How can we go up to the Gentiles to preach the gospel about the kingdom of the Son of Humanity? If they didn't spare him, why would they spare us?"

A depiction of Mary Magdalene speaking to the apostles

MARY AND JESUS

Then Mary arose and greeted them all. She said to her brothers (and sisters), "Don't weep and grieve or let your hearts be divided, because his grace will be with you all and will protect you. Rather we should praise his greatness because he's prepared us and made us Humans."

When Mary said these things, she turned their hearts [toward] the Good and they [started] to debate the words of [the Savior].

Peter said to Mary, "Sister, we know the Savior loved you more than all other women. Tell us the words of the Savior that you remember – the things which you know that we don't, and which we haven't heard."

In response Mary said, "I'll tell you what's hidden from you." So she started to tell them these words: "I," she said, "I saw the Lord in a vision and I said to him, 'Lord, I saw you in a vision today.'

"In response he said to me, 'You're blessed because you didn't waver at the sight of me. For where the mind is, there is the treasure.'

"I said to him, 'Lord, now does the one who sees the vision see it /in\ the soul /or\ in the spirit?'

"In response the Savior said, 'They don't see in the soul or in the spirit, but the mind which [exists] between the two is [what] sees the vision [and] it [that ...]

Pages 11 through 14 are missing.

OVERCOMING THE POWERS

"And Desire said, 'I didn't see you going down, but now I see you're going up. So why are you lying, since you belong to me?'

"In response the soul said, 'I saw you, but you didn't see me or know me. I was to you just a garment, and you didn't recognize me.' When it said these things, it left, rejoicing greatly.

"Again, it came to the third power, which is called 'Ignorance.' [It] interrogated the soul and [said], 'Where are you going? In wickedness you're bound. Since you're bound, don't judge!'

"[And] the soul said, 'Why do you judge me, since I haven't judged? I was bound, even though I haven't bound. They didn't recognize me, but I've recognized that everything will dissolve – both the things of the [earth]and the things of [heaven].'

"When the soul had overcome the third power, it went up and saw the fourth power, which took seven forms:

The first form is Darkness;

The second, Desire;

The third, Ignorance;

The fourth, Zeal for Death;

The fifth, the Kingdom of the Flesh;

The sixth, the Foolish 'Wisdom' of Flesh;

The seventh, the 'Wisdom' of Anger.

"These are the seven powers of Wrath.

"They ask the soul, 'Where do you come from, you murderer, and where are you going, conqueror of space?'

"In response the soul said, 'What binds me has been killed, what surrounds me has been overcome, my desire is gone, and ignorance has died. In a [world] I was released from a world, [and] in a type from a type which is above, and from the chain of forgetfulness which exists only for a time. From now on I'll receive the rest of the time of the season of the age in silence.'"

When Mary said these things, she fell silent because the Savior had spoken with her up to this point.

CONFLICT OVER AUTHORITY

In response Andrew said to the brothers (and sisters), 'Say what you will about what she's said, I myself don't believe that the Savior said these things, because these teachings seem like different ideas."

In response Peter spoke out with the same concerns. He asked them concerning the Savior: "He didn't speak with a woman without our knowledge and not publicly with us, did he? Will we turn around and all listen to her? Did he prefer her to us?"

Then Mary wept and said to Peter, "My brother Peter, what are you thinking? Do you really think that I thought this up by myself in my heart, or that I'm lying about the Savior?"

In response Levi said to Peter, "Peter, you've always been angry. Now I see you debating with this woman like the adversaries. But if the Savior made her worthy, who are you then to reject her? Surely the Savior knows her very well. That's why he loved her more than us.

"Rather we should be ashamed, clothe ourselves with perfect Humanity, acquire it for ourselves as he instructed us, and preach the gospel, not laying down any other rule or other law beyond what the Savior said."

When [Levi said these things], they started to go out to teach and to preach.

FURTHER READING

To further explore the themes, narratives, and theological ideas present in the texts included in this collection, consider delving into the following related apocryphal writings. These works share connections through their focus on similar characters, events, or theological concepts.

The Book of Jubilees (The Little Genesis)

- **The Old Testament Pseudepigrapha, Volume 2** edited by James H. Charlesworth: This volume includes the *Book of Jubilees*, which expands on the narratives found in Genesis and Exodus, providing a re-interpretation that resonates with the Enochic tradition.
- **The Book of Jubilees: Rewritten Bible, Redaction, Ideology, and Theology** by Michael Segal: A comprehensive study that explores the theological and ideological underpinnings of Jubilees, emphasizing its connection to the Enochic literature.

The Apocalypse of Moses (The Life of Adam and Eve)

- **The Apocryphal Old Testament** edited by H.F.D. Sparks: Contains the *Apocalypse of Moses*, which presents an expanded narrative of the life of Adam and Eve, particularly focusing on the events after their expulsion from Eden.
- **The Life of Adam and Eve in Jewish and Christian Literature** by Gary A. Anderson: A detailed analysis of the

Apocalypse of Moses and its variations, exploring its theological significance in both Jewish and Christian traditions.

The Testaments of the Twelve Patriarchs

- **The Testaments of the Twelve Patriarchs** translated by R.H. Charles: This work, included in Charles' collection of Pseudepigrapha, offers insights into the lives and moral teachings of the twelve sons of Jacob. It is closely related to apocalyptic literature through its eschatological themes.
- **Testaments of the Twelve Patriarchs: A Commentary** by Marinus de Jonge: Provides an in-depth commentary and analysis, highlighting connections to other apocryphal and pseudepigraphal works, including the *Testament of Abraham*.

The Book of Giants

- **The Book of Giants** by W.B. Henning: This text, found among the Dead Sea Scrolls, provides further details on the fallen angels and their offspring, connecting closely to the narratives in 1 Enoch.
- **The Dead Sea Scrolls** by Geza Vermes: This collection includes fragments of the *Book of Giants*, providing context for its relationship to the Enochic literature.

The Sibylline Oracles

- **The Sibylline Oracles** translated by J.J. Collins: This apocalyptic work offers prophecies attributed to the Sibyl, a figure who also appears in Jewish and Christian traditions. It shares thematic elements with the *Apocalypse of Abraham* and other visionary literature.
- **The Sibylline Oracles of Egyptian Judaism** by John J. Collins: An exploration of the origins and development of the Sibylline Oracles, focusing on their influence on apocalyptic thought.

The Assumption of Moses

- **The Assumption of Moses** by R.H. Charles: This text offers an account of Moses' final words and his ascension, themes that resonate with the *Ascension of Moses* fragment. It is often included in collections of Old Testament Pseudepigrapha.
- **The Assumption of Moses: A Critical Edition** by Johannes Tromp: Provides a scholarly edition and commentary on the text, analyzing its historical and theological context.

The Apocalypse of Zephaniah

- **The Apocalypse of Zephaniah** translated by O.S. Wintermute, included in *The Old Testament Pseudepigrapha, Volume 1*: This lesser-known apocalyptic text presents visions of the afterlife and divine judgment, similar in theme to the *Testament of Abraham*.
- **The Apocalyptic Imagination** by John J. Collins: This book explores apocalyptic literature in general, with a focus on lesser-known texts like the *Apocalypse of Zephaniah*, emphasizing their role in the broader apocalyptic tradition.